AF379225

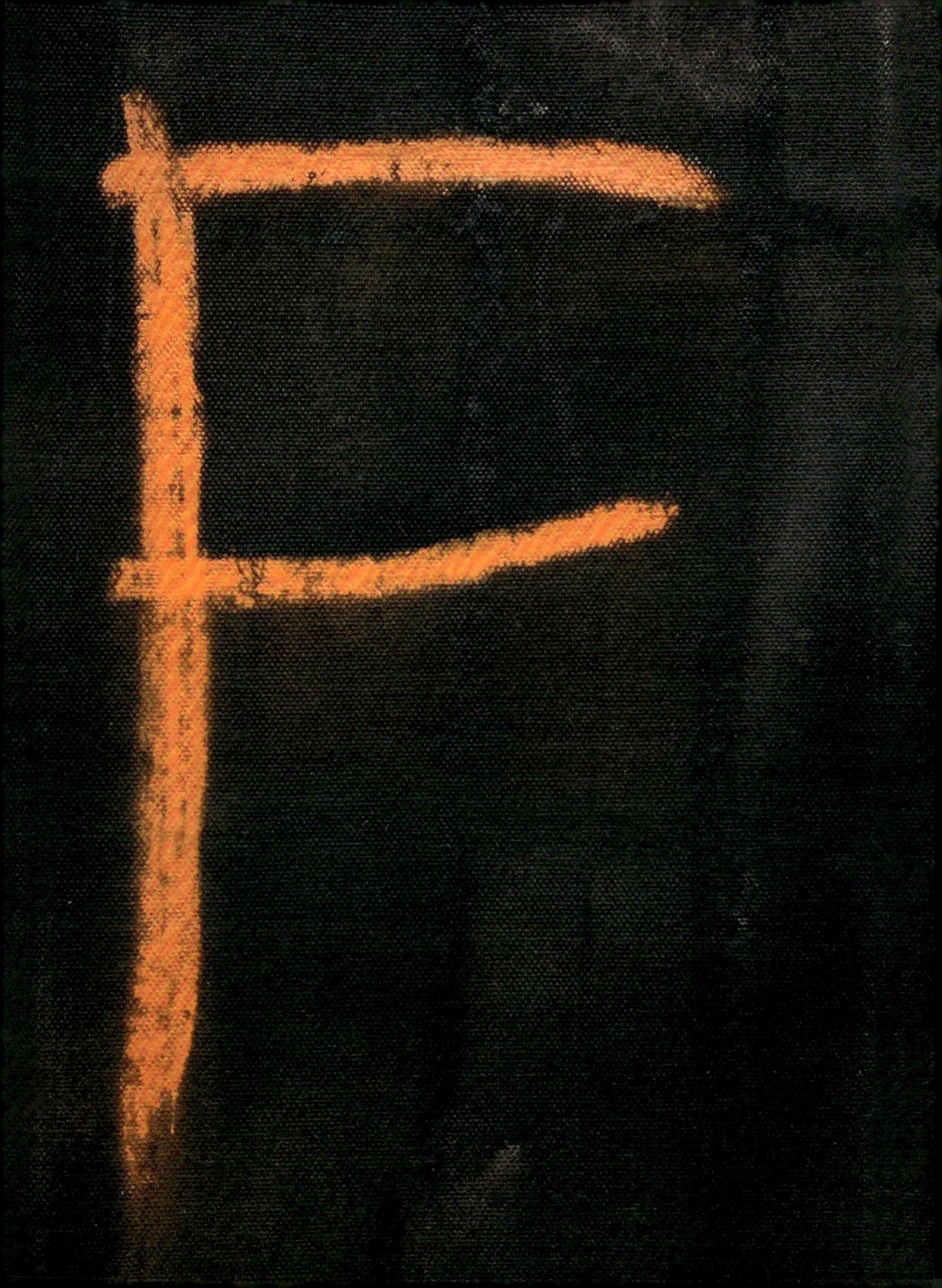

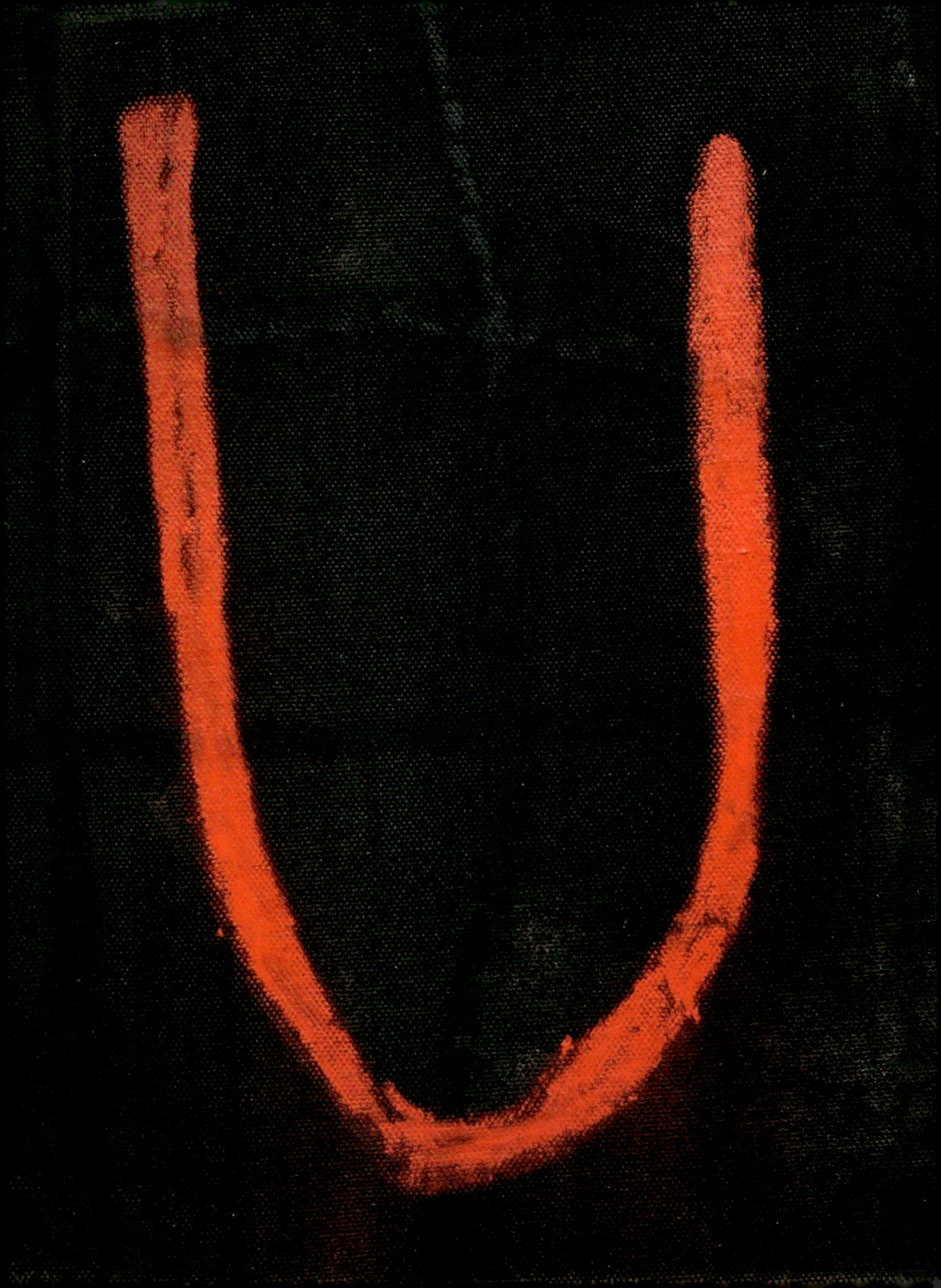

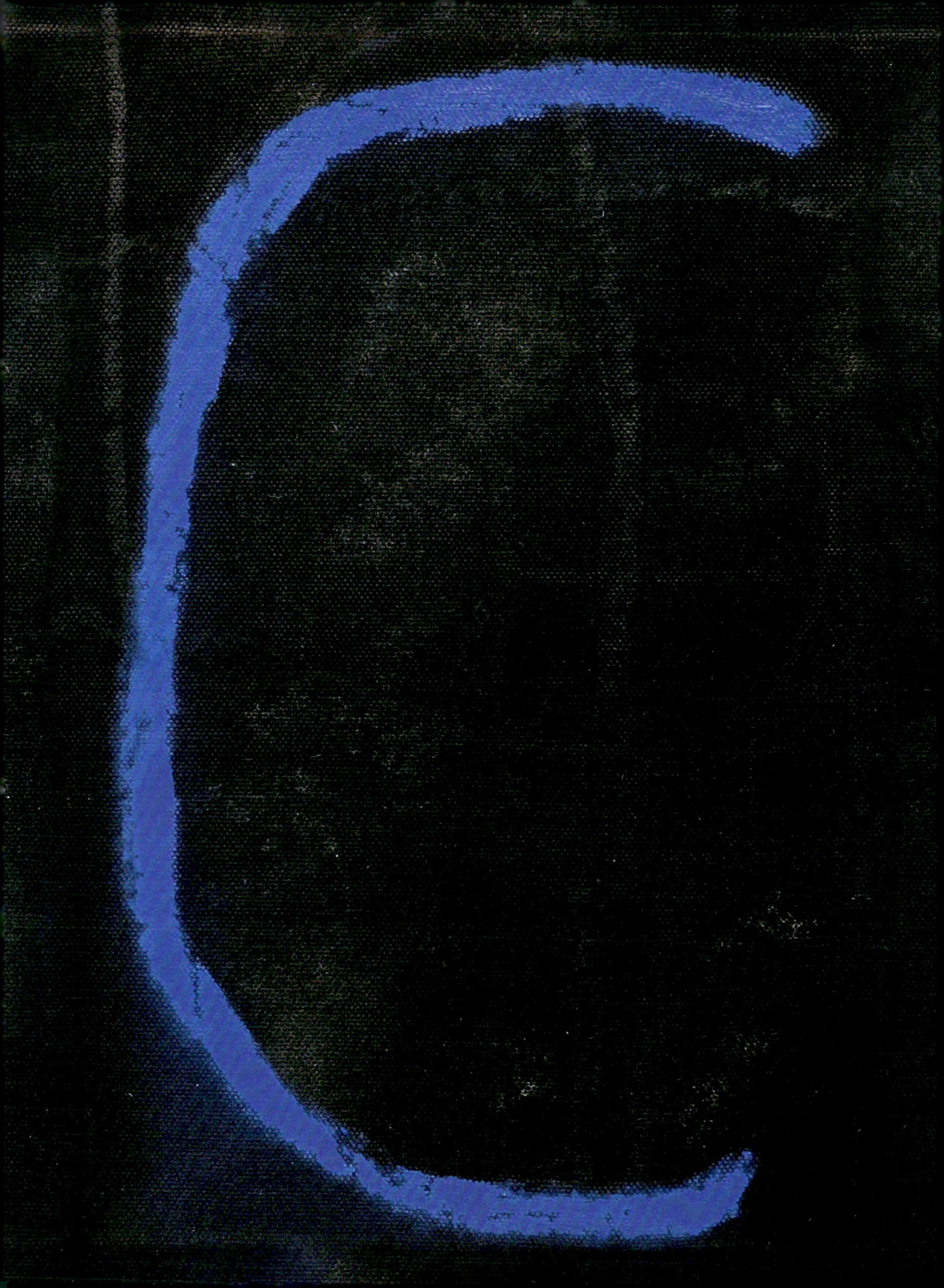

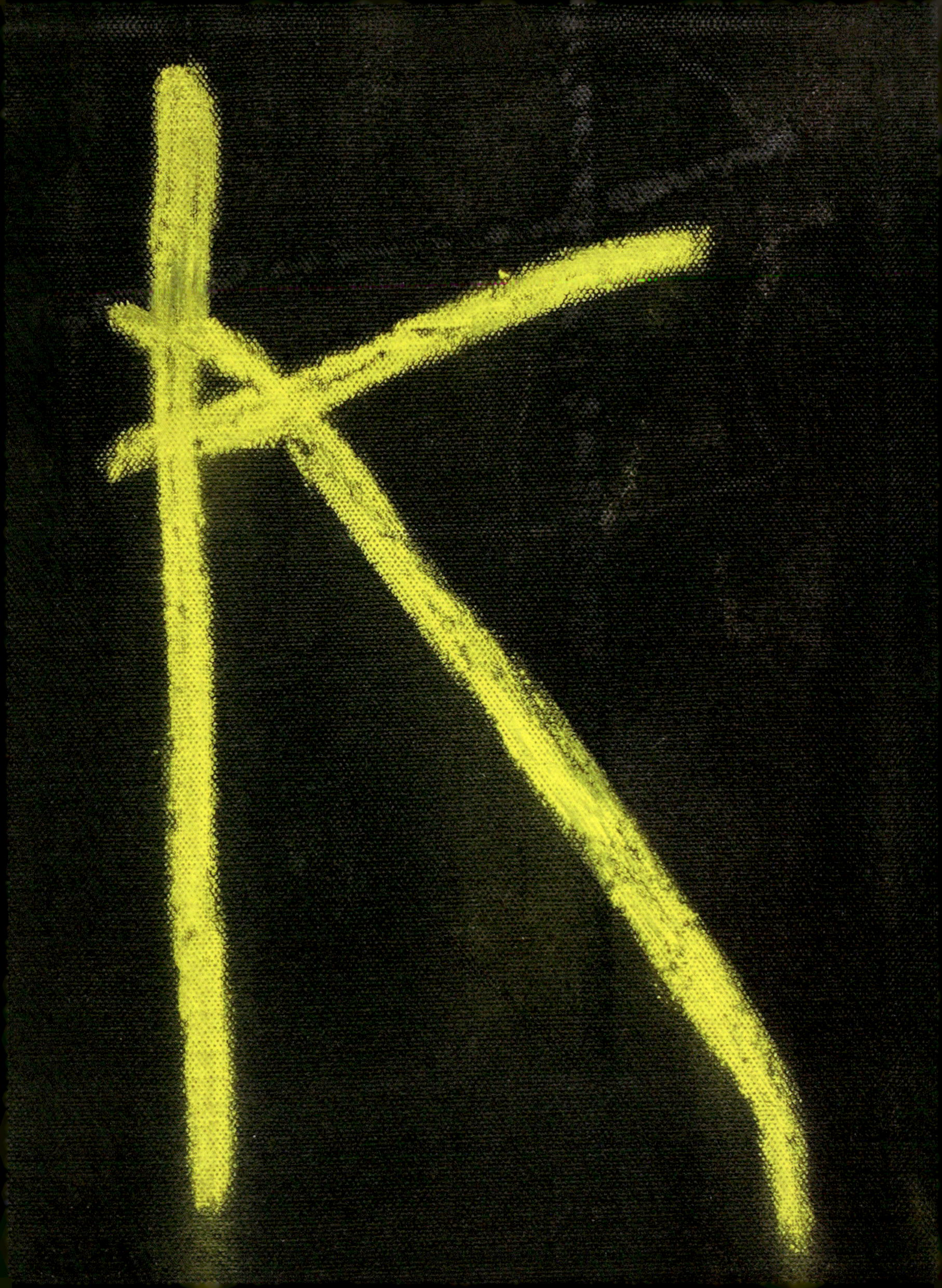

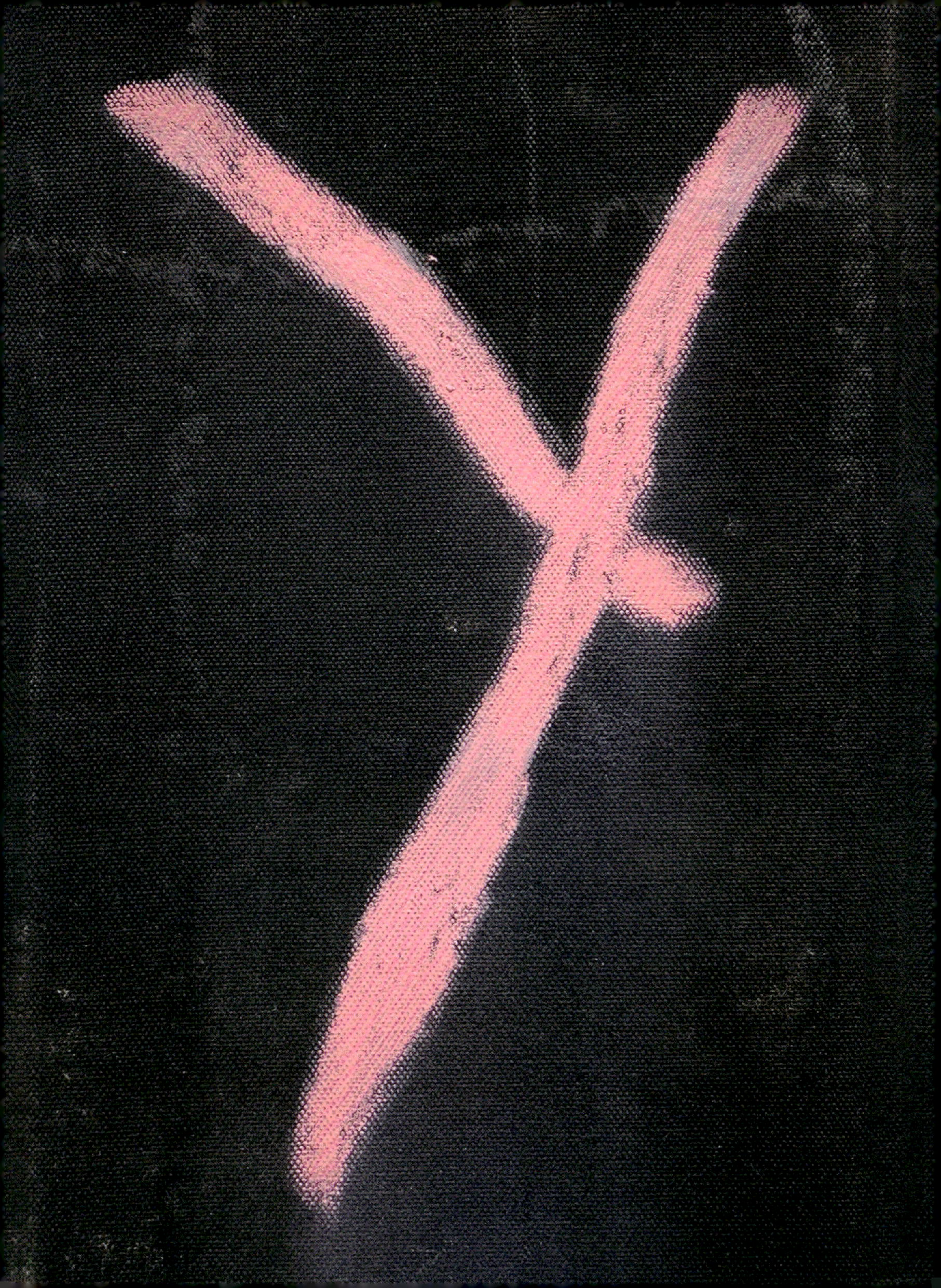

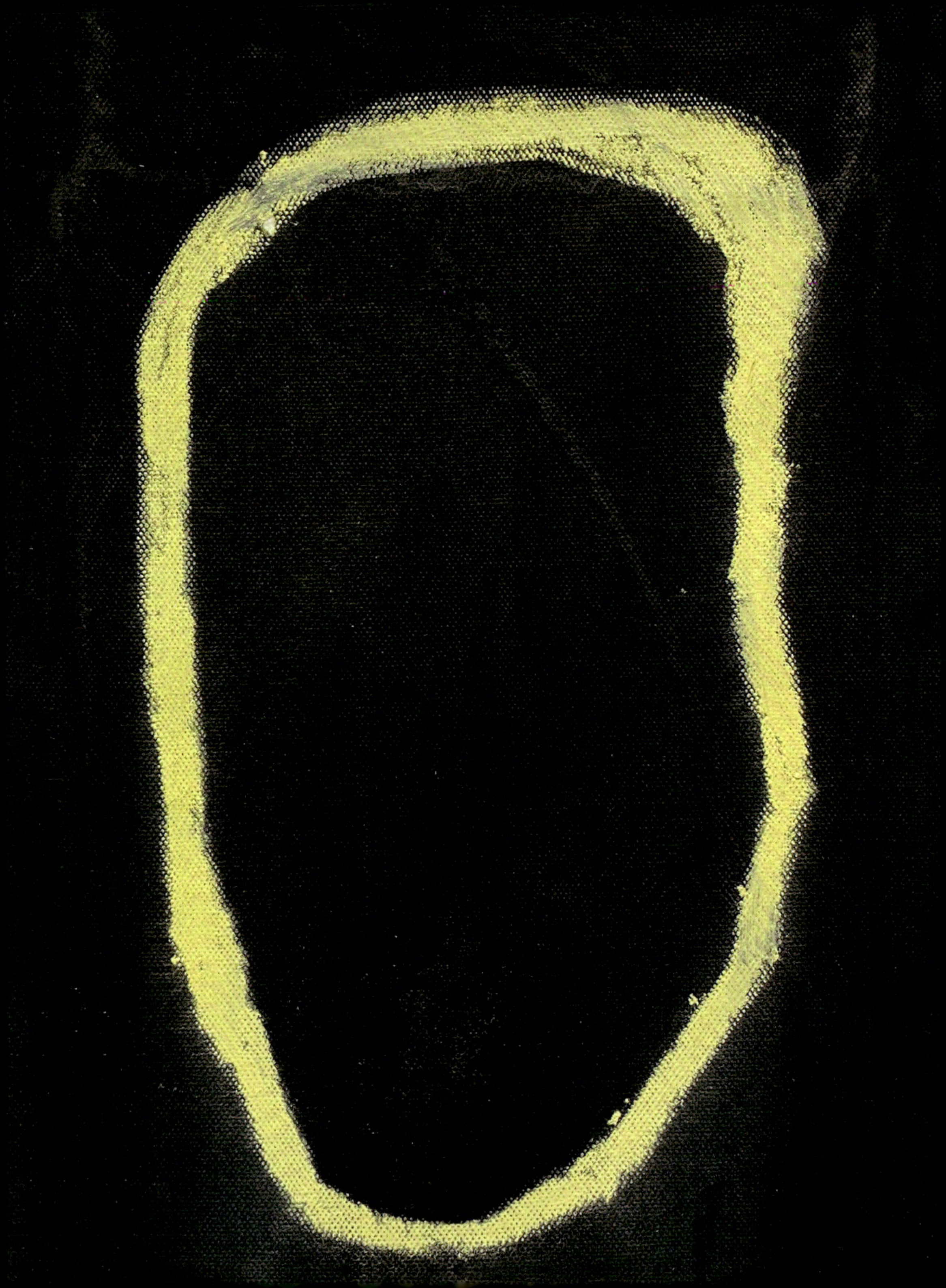

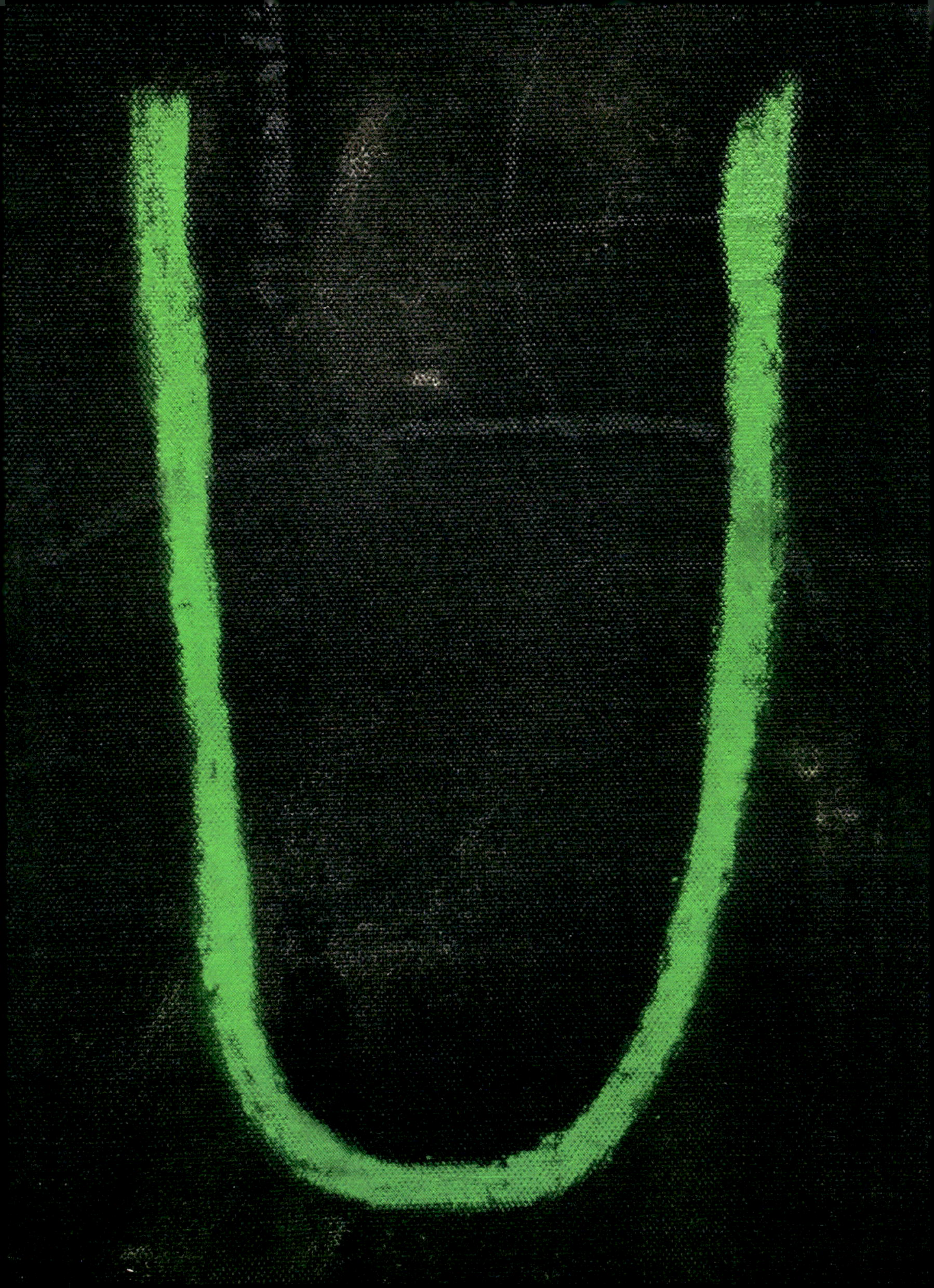

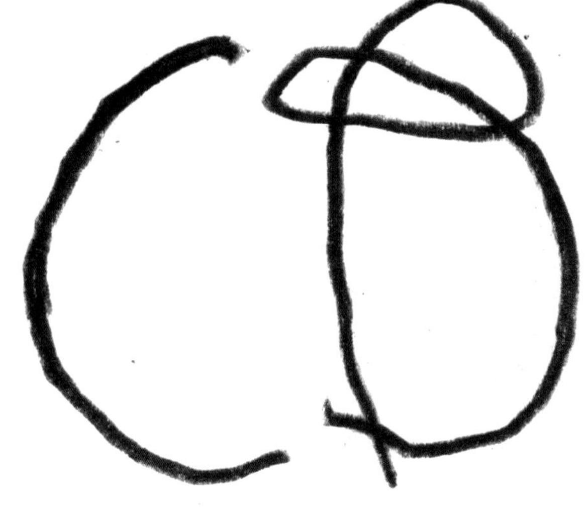

HOYO

SKIRA

Pages 1–7
Fuck You, 2020
Water-soluble oil pastels, oil sticks,
mineral water, and acrylic paint on raw
cotton canvas, 30 x 20 cm

Art Director
Marcello Francone

Design
Luigi Fiore

Editorial Coordination
Vincenza Russo

Editing
Anna Albano

Layout
Serena Parini

First published in Italy in 2021 by
Skira editore S.p.A.
Palazzo Casati Stampa
via Torino 61
20123 Milano
Italy
www.skira.net

Printed and bound in Italy. First edition

ISBN: 978-88-572-4567-6

Distributed in USA, Canada, Central
& South America by
ARTBOOK | D.A.P. 75 Broad Street Suite
630, New York, NY 10004, USA.
Distributed elsewhere in the world by
Thames and Hudson Ltd., 181A High
Holborn, London WC1V 7QX, United
Kingdom.

CONTENTS

CB Hoyo,
No Filter

Cesare Biasini Selvaggi and Jack Kyle Franklin

International porn star, international bikini model, and dyslexic poet

This is the Instagram bio of CB Hoyo. Perhaps you've heard of him? The young and unruly Cuban artist who burst onto the art scene in 2017, riding the viral wave of social media; you've likely, at the very least, seen his work pop up on your Instagram feed. Driven by natural instinct and raw talent, this self-taught artist has built a multidisciplinary practice that has made him one of the top emerging artists on the market.

Hoyo is one of those rare artists whose work resonates with a large and diverse group of individuals due to his humorous exploration of common human thoughts and behaviors. Yes. His simple and prolific commentary is mined from his own observations and concerns, capturing contemporary society's essence and challenging viewers' preconditioned perceptions of reality, all while creating a state of heightened awareness to reflect the new, bizarre normality we live in.

It is important to remember that this text is written in 2021. We live in weird times, shaped by social media personas, constant digital connection, and fake news. One of the themes Hoyo explores most is the concept of the "fake." While his original ideas were a send-up to the art world, he quickly realized the issue of *fakeness* in our contemporary moment have trickled down into all aspects of daily life. Pure originality is hard to come by, almost everything is derived from past sources, and authenticity is nearly impossible to discern. In a world where it is becoming increasingly difficult to distinguish the fake from the genuine, Hoyo's work invites others to consider these distinctions on their own.

If you live in contemporary society—meaning on the internet—then much of his work seems to require little explanation at all. Paradoxically, in order to explain this work to anyone, they must first understand the reference within the internet. It's a challenge to write about work that is so seemingly straightforward. In many ways the works are direct and self-explanatory, but that is a key to their substance. By working through these explanations of the obvious, we find a lot of complexity below the surface that explains why Hoyo's practice is so relatable.

Fakes was his first series and the one that brought him critical acclaim. He skillfully replicates master works by major art stars and then brandishes them with his own blatant remarks in a style reminiscent of late twentieth-century graffiti aesthetic. These satirical recreations of blue-chip icons highlight the paradoxes and absurdities of economic and social value systems that have come to dictate the contemporary art market as the sales platform for a medium that is supposed to be about connection and self-expression. Most notably, they are portrayed with a light-hearted playfulness that makes the work accessible to both insiders and outsiders.

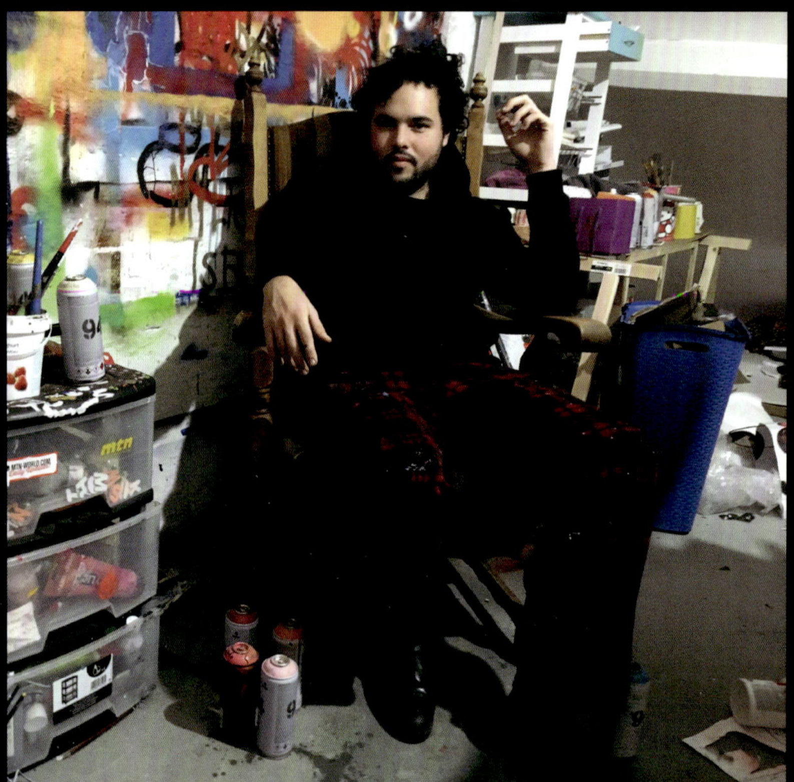

Self-portrait in
the studio, 2017

Page 16
*Somewhere
in Dominican
Republic*, 2019
Fujifilm Instax Colorfilm
Glossy, 8.6 x 10.8 cm

7/11 Bangkok, 2019
Fujifilm Instax Colorfilm
Glossy, 8.6 x 10.8 cm

Page 17
*Shopping in
Miami*, 2019
Fujifilm Instax Colorfilm
Glossy, 8.6 x 10.8 cm

Grandpa Holding Fruit,
2019
Fujifilm Instax Colorfilm
Glossy, 8.6 x 10.8 cm

Ironically, this work taunts the very market in which it circulates, calling attention to the often absurd nature of wealth, status, and cultural prestige within the art world. Naturally, collectors flock to them. In a short span of four years, Hoyo's work has increased in stature, and he's quickly amassed a large following of tastemakers, influencers, and collectors alike. His work has been exhibited on six continents and is held in numerous public and private collections.

Corny Quotes, his ongoing second series, leaves behind the imagery and focuses solely on text colorfully painted on canvas. They retain the same tongue-in-cheek commentary as *Fakes* but instead of focusing specifically on the art market, they speak to modern society as a whole. They are quick snippets of simple and direct thoughts that aren't difficult to imagine as the inner monologue of a societal collective. Hoyo gives voice to this, bridging topics that are likely thought of by many, but expressed by few. They are full of humor, irony, contradictions, and the word "fuck."

I FUCKING USE THE FUCKING WORD "FUCK" A FUCKING LOT. IF YOU FUCKING HAVE A FUCKING PROBLEM WITH IT, WELL... FUCK YOU

He has been called "provocative," and his work has an air of a punk attitude reminiscent of BORF and Baldessari. In person, however, he doesn't seem like the punk provocateur one might presume based solely on his work. To label Hoyo's remarks caustic or sarcastic undercuts what he actually stands for. He is critical, but never cynical. His tone treads a fine line. He is able to poke fun at the art market, without being too pretentious or overly preachy. He is aware of his position in the art world and the world at large and is therefore conscientious of his own contradictions. He never delivers criticism that he isn't able and willing to take on himself.

These are some of the powers of CB Hoyo's work. To bring humor to criticism and to create consciousness about all the contradictions that exist in the very act of being critical. To give voice to collective experiences, to attempt to express what everyone seems to be feeling, to say it simply, to put it out into the world, to allow others to interact with it, to connect, and hopefully feel less alone.

Beginnings, What Made CB Hoyo

CB Hoyo was born in Havana, Cuba in 1995 during the height of the Cuban economic crisis, known as the *Período especial* (Special Period in Time of Peace). This critical time period, which began in 1991 and lasted until the new millennium, was defined by a shortage of oil, diesel, and machinery. This lack of natural resources affected all aspects of Cuban life from transportation to agriculture, which led to extreme food scarcity and reductions in the state-rationed food program. In 1997, without any money, Hoyo and his mother emigrated to the Do-

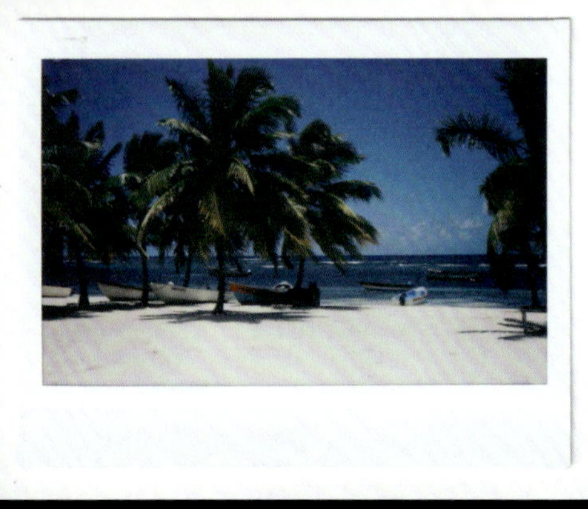 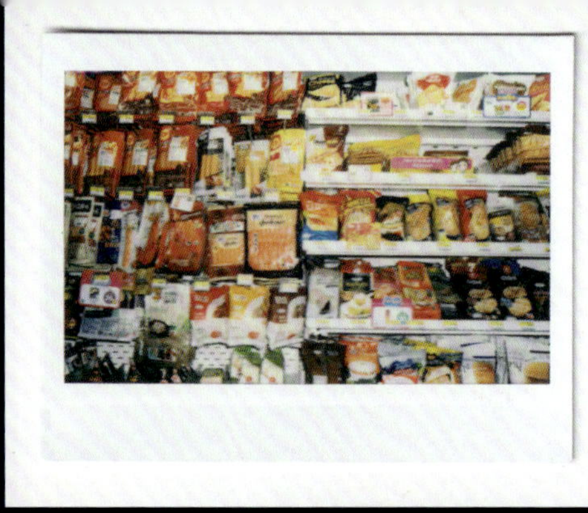

minican Republic in search of freedom and a better future. His mother left Cuba with CB in one hand, and a bag of books in the other.

Hoyo cites being raised by a single mother in a developing country as a key influence on his life perspective. Though money was scarce, she worked tirelessly to give him a good education and a full life, taking him to as many cultural events as they could manage. According to his mother, he always had a pencil or a marker in his hand; he learned to paint before he learned to walk. The education and opportunities she ensured for him and the values she instilled in him, made him stronger and helped him live his life in a positive way.

Life in the Dominican Republic was completely different from the one they left in Cuba. He attended a school where his classmates were the children of the country's elite and during the breaks between class they would recount fantastic tales of travel and experiences.

Hoyo himself did not leave the Dominican Republic until he graduated from high school at the age of 17. He wasn't sure exactly what he wanted out of life, but he did know that whatever it was, it was not in the Dominican Republic. Without a plan of what would come next, he visited some family in Europe and planned to study business administration in Holland, but while he was waiting for the academic year to begin, he took a job at a restaurant in Belgium. There, the chef encouraged him to study culinary arts, and—before

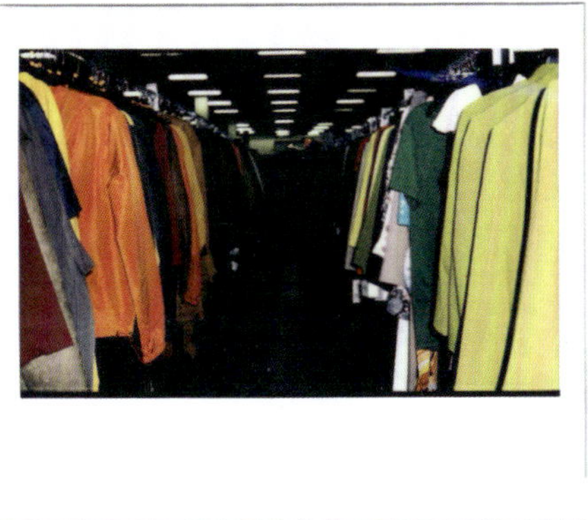 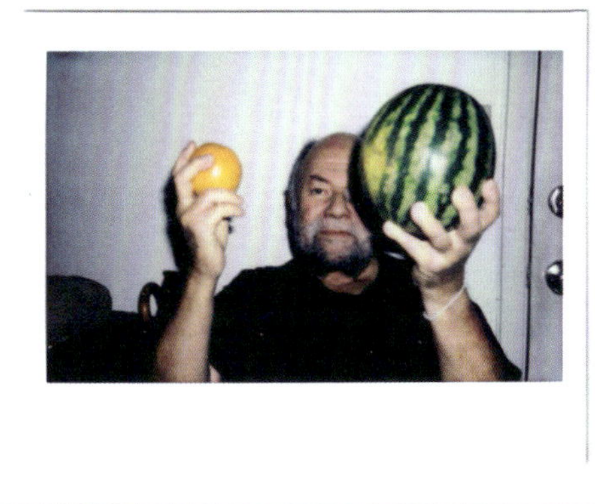

he knew it—he found himself speaking Flemish and eventually settling down in Belgium.

It was during this time that his artistic inclination was reawakened, and no matter what else he had going on, he would stay awake late into the night painting

Fake it till you make it, or whatever

Aside from a brief stint of art classes at the age of seven, Hoyo never received a formal artistic education. Like many young artists, he began by looking backwards and reproducing famous works. Copying the masters is an educational method long practiced by beginning artists as a way to improve their own painting or drawing skills by studying and recreating well-known works. This technique dates back to the sixteenth century, when masters would ask their students or apprentices to copy works in their own styles. This process of mimicry enabled students to learn various techniques while developing their own unique styles and approaches. Edgar Degas, Leonardo da Vinci, and Pablo Picasso are just a few examples of artists who learned through this technique, which is still practiced in many art schools to this day. However, reproductions of masters' works are typically regarded as studies or exercises and are not considered artworks in their own right. However, it becomes more complicated when artists copy fa

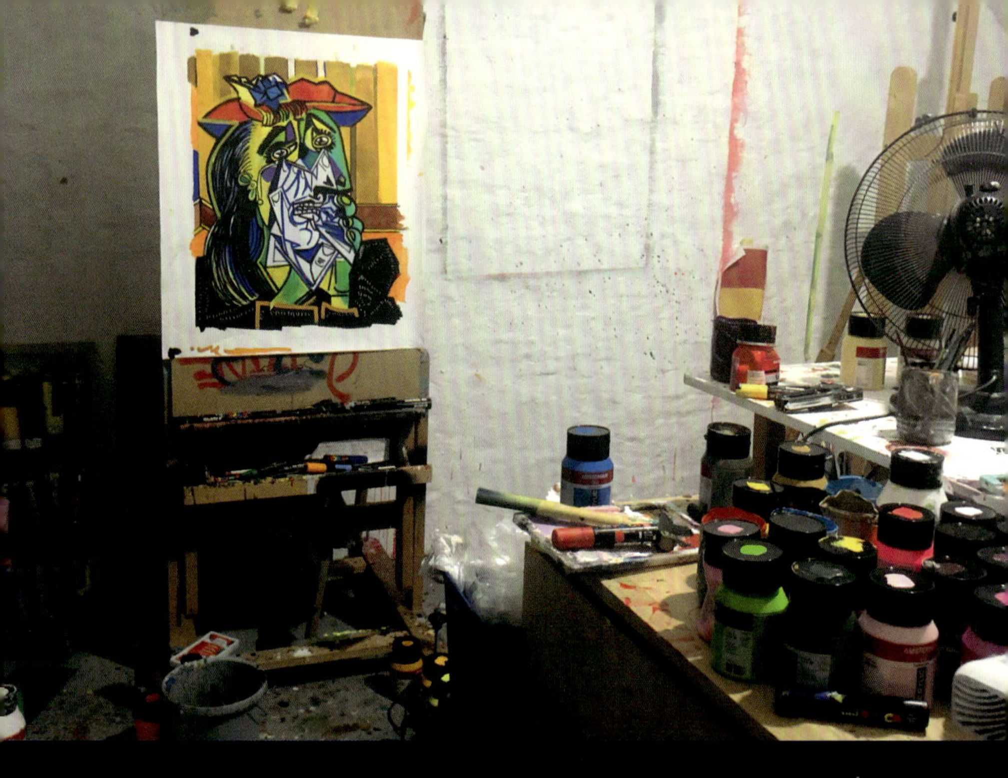

mous works for conceptual purposes. Forgery and copyright infringement laws complicate this matter even further.

Consider Sturtevant, the American conceptual artist who made her career from recreating "carefully inexact" works by her contemporaries to question authenticity and its relationship to history. Her works challenged the notion of originality in the modern age and, of course, the theme of authenticity is one that would continue to grow in contemporary discourse. Her most famous series was a reproduction of Warhol's *Flowers* which she exhibited only a few weeks after Warhol himself debuted them. Over the course of her career she mastered a handful of various and wide-ranging techniques in the fields of sculpture, painting and photography in order to produce her copies of works by prominent artists.[1]

When Hoyo was 11 years old, he had his first encounter with Picasso at the Modern Art Museum in Santo Domingo. He became obsessed with Picasso and

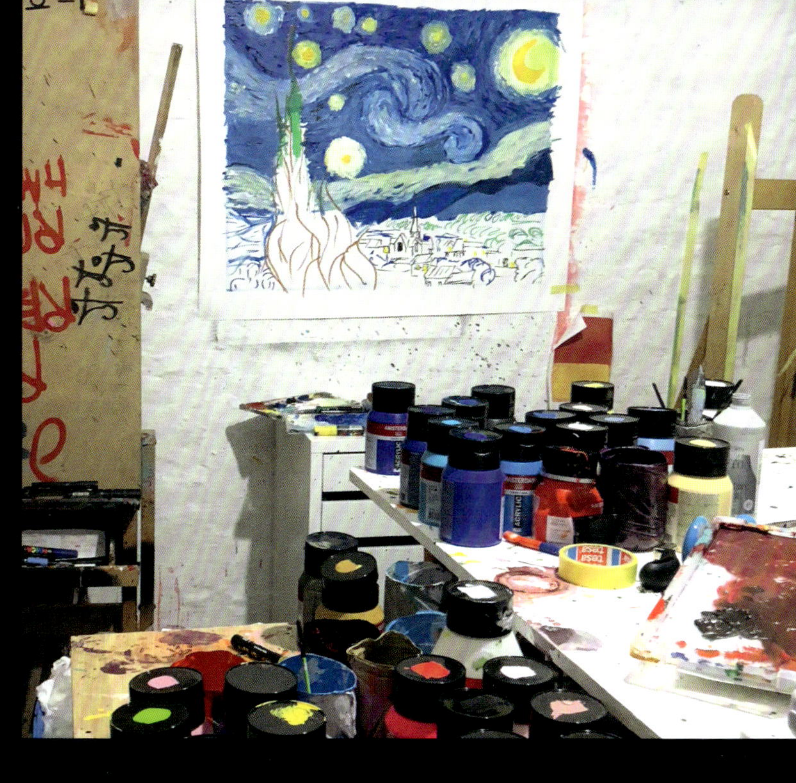

began to reproduce his paintings at home. He cites this as his first encounter with "faking" something. He learned to forge Picasso's signature, and even adapted his own to the style of Picasso's, which he still uses to this day.

His background as a self-taught artist means that the artists whose work he copied were his only teachers. All of his ideas are born of spontaneity and ex-perimentation with materials and processes based on accidents, inventions, and trial and error. This, of course, would eventually lead to his series of *Fakes*—the same series that he credits most for his artistic growth.

Fakes began in January of 2017. He was working in his studio and trying to recreate a *Mao* by Andy Warhol, without any additions or signs of ownership for the work. Instead of recreating the work using the same silkscreen process that Warhol used, Hoyo was trying to fake it with a typical inkjet printer one might find in a home office. He tried to align the black printer ink with his own painting on high

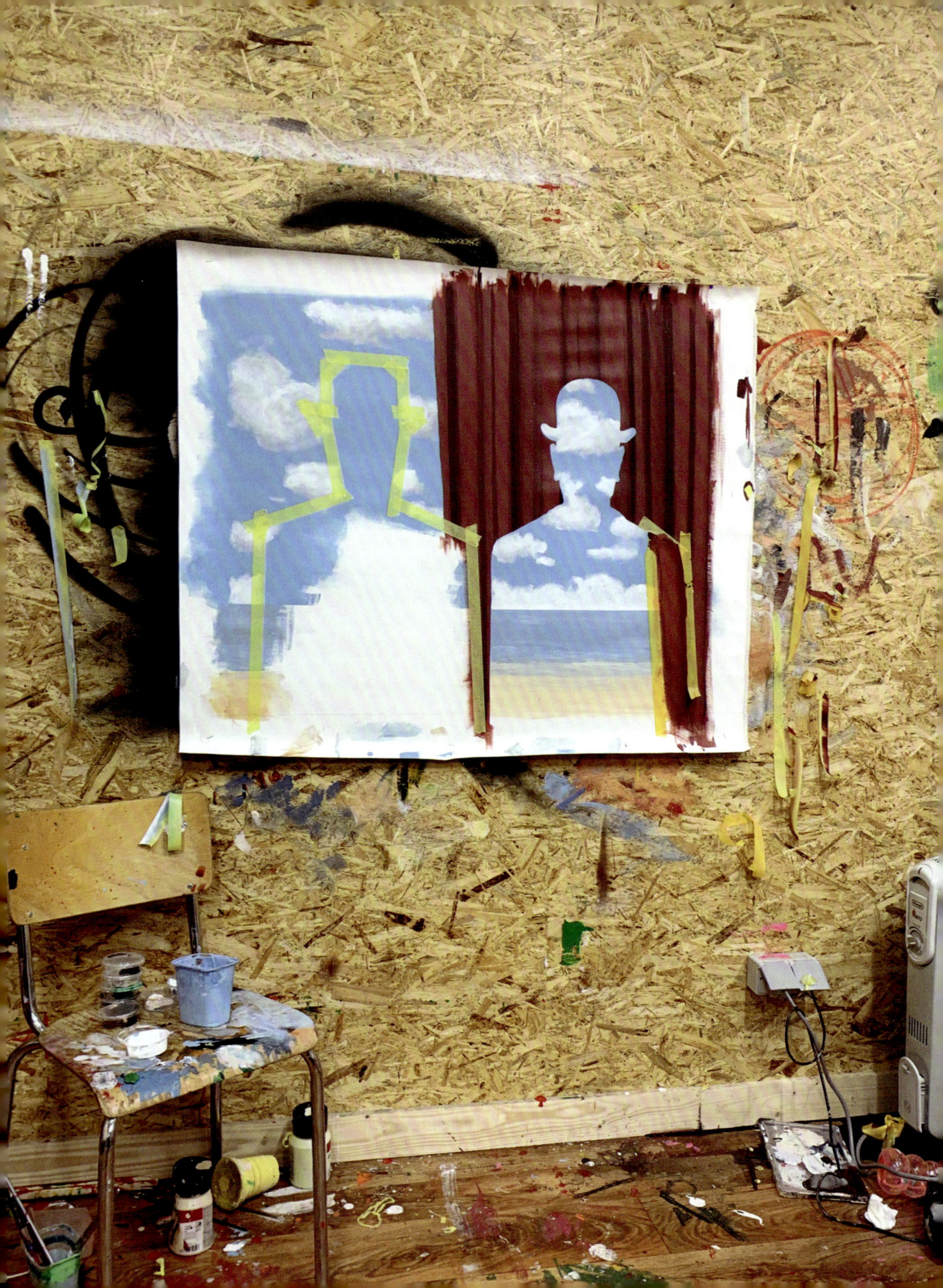

quality paper. After several hours and unsuccessful attempts at recreation, he was
frustrated but also hated to throw away an idea that he had already put so much
time and effort into; in that frustration, he decided to write on it instead. The text
was simple and direct, based on an article he had read about forgeries in the art
world and how a lot of work that is sold at auction is counterfeit. While many fake
works are passed through the art world, unperceived for *what they really are*, Hoyo
embraced the fact that his Warhol was fake and showed it for *what it really was*.

It is important to distinguish that this work is not about forgery, nor has it
ever been an attempt to forge. There was no intended trickery, deceit, or fraud
at play and the works were never intended to be passed off as originals. Forgery
was simply the catalyst for these ideas. The work is about authenticity, and pokes
fun at how the art world celebrates monetary value above all else. It was always
an attempt to playfully critique while simultaneously creating something new.

Conceptual strategies of recreating other artworks have a deep history in
contemporary art, and it is therefore equally important to distinguish works of
forgery from works of appropriation. Many artists have made their careers by creating work that interrogates the politics of appropriation and copyright laws. For
a short list, consider: Richard Prince, Banksy, John Baldessari, Claes Oldenburg,
Louise Lawler, Cindy Sherman, Kurt Schwitters, Maurizio Cattelan, Pablo Picasso,
Roy Lichtenstein, and Andy Warhol. Consider, further, that most of these artists
recreated each other's work as well. [2]

Concerns surrounding copyright infringement or the employment of appropriation as an artistic technique are not what Hoyo's works are seeking to address. He
is interested in *fakeness* as it relates to assigned social and monetary values. As he
attempts to rewrite this value system for himself, the question then becomes, can
his "fake" works achieve a "real" or "real-like" status in their own right? His *Fakes* are
not "real," but they are not "not-real" either. They exist as a third category, entirely
different in their own right. It is exactly their "unrealness" that has the power to be
subversive, controversial, and even troubling. Hoyo's work addresses these topics
with his signature humor while—like his *Fakes*—immediately calls out that his own
work might become part of the same system he is critiquing.

We can return to Sturtevant for another example from a purely financial perspective: in 2007, an original—albeit multiple editioned—print of *Crying Girl* by Roy Lichtenstein sold at auction for $78,400. Four years later, in 2011, Sturtevant's one-of-a-kind painting, though copied from *Crying Girl*, sold for $710,500. [3]

Soon, Hoyo's quest to shake up the art market may come full circle when Sotheby's or Christie's find themselves in a similar scenario. It's not impossible to imagine a comparable trajectory for a Warhol edition and a Hoyo original.

Words Matter, As Does Honesty / Take It Easy

The word *fake* is an interesting one to consider. It can be employed as an adjective, a noun, or a verb. *Fake*, as an adjective, describes a thing that is not genuine, something that is an imitation, or a counterfeit—it is usually a negation and holds a negative connotation, naming a thing as "less than" when compared to its "authentic" counterpart. As a noun, *fake* is the thing itself marked as a forgery or a sham, an embodiment of the negation of the original.

It is also important to differentiate the term *fake* from other related terms such as plagiarism, knock-off, and counterfeit. These terms are used when speaking about something that—yes—is fake, but attempts to pass itself off as authentic. Hoyo's work claims to be authentic only to itself. His Warhol is not claiming to be authentic any more than a souvenir Warhol poster one might purchase from a museum gift shop. His work is, in fact, quite the opposite. Hoyo scrawls each work's fake status across the surface like a proud scarlet letter. His *Fakes* are not a negation or a knock off, they are an entirely new thing on their own; they are honest from first sight.

We can look directly back at art history to find another example of this seemingly simple strategy.

René Magritte's 1929 painting, *The Treachery of Images*, is a depiction of a pipe. The composition features an internal caption directly painted on the surface underneath the image which states, *Ceci n'est pas une pipe* (French for "This is not a pipe."). While this seems to be a trick or a contradiction, it is actually true. Magritte described his paintings as "visible images which conceal nothing," demonstrating the troubled relationship that can occur between words, images, and reality. [4]

Magritte's work spawned an entire discourse in the fields of semantics, semiotics, and linguistics. Another example of this strategy comes from Alfred Korzybski, the Polish-American scholar who developed the field of general semantics. He sought to describe the relationship between an object and a representation of that object. His most famous remarks on this subject are "the word is not the thing" and "the map is not the territory." [5]

For Magritte's work, the pipe in the painting is not a pipe, but rather a representation of a pipe. This same logic can be applied to any painting. Take Warhol's 1967 banana for instance: the banana in the painting is not a banana, but rather a representation of a banana.

Hoyo's reproductions follow this same logic of visual and verbal representation. This is not a Warhol painting. This is a representation or painting of a Warhol painting. Hoyo took this idea one step further when he actually recreated the Warhol banana, but instead of simply writing "This is not a Warhol" he added "It's just a banana."

There is no malintent or trickery at work here. Quite the opposite in fact, both of these artists' works represent—visually and verbally—direct honesty. They are deceptive, but only in the way that they are deceptively simple. Magritte himself even said the pipe was "just a representation," adding, "If I had written on my picture 'This is a pipe,' I'd have been lying!"

Warhol's dollar sign: MAKE ME FAMOUS AND I'LL MAKE YOU RICH

After the first of his *Fakes,* the Warhol, Hoyo continued recreating works of other artists—Jean-Michel Basquiat, Mark Rothko, Pablo Picasso and Keith Haring—and writing more blatant messages on their surfaces about their status as

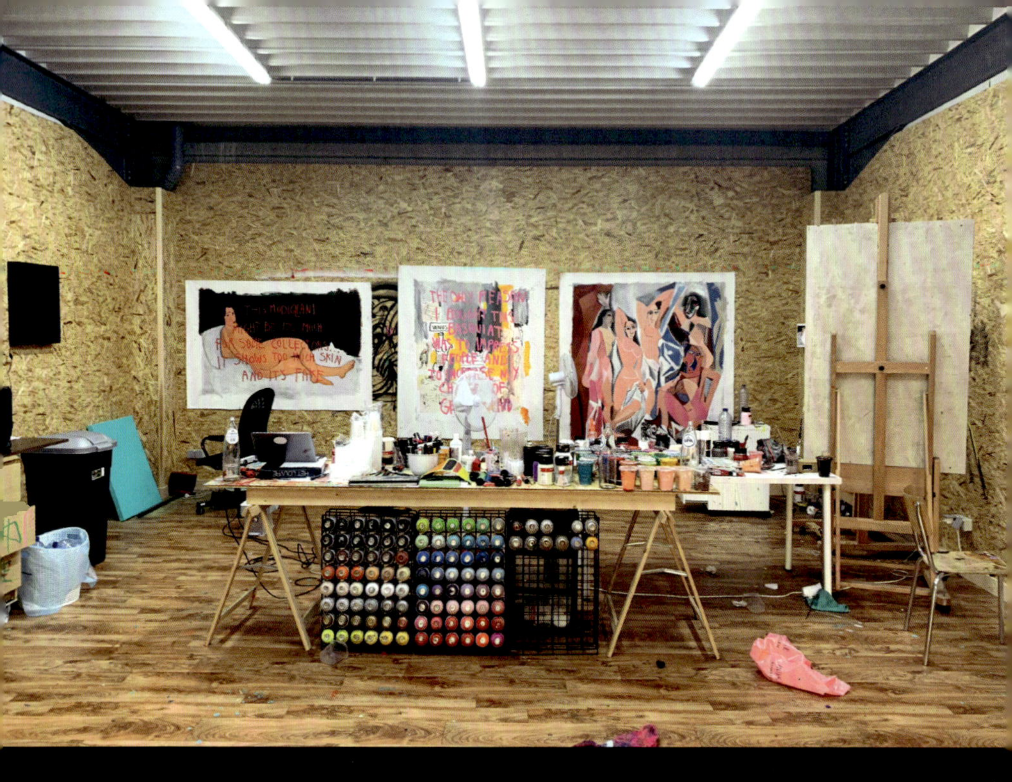

ake. By copying these works, his painting skill improved and the texts became more playful and provocative as he gradually constructed more conscious relationships between the paintings themselves and the messages of the text. He began to question authenticity and *fakeness* in a larger context—no longer solely focused on the art market—they began to better reflect the era he was living in. Fake news was only coming into our public consciousness around the same time that Hoyo started creating his *Fakes*. Now of course, here we are. His work seems to be predicated on these ideas that have quickly become part of our daily lives.

Understanding of the role that social media might play in his practice, he created an account on Instagram to begin sharing some of his work. He was still living in Europe, broke, and unhappy with his day job. In 2017, at the beginning of the New Year, he took a trip to Taiwan and, while there, decided to focus on his

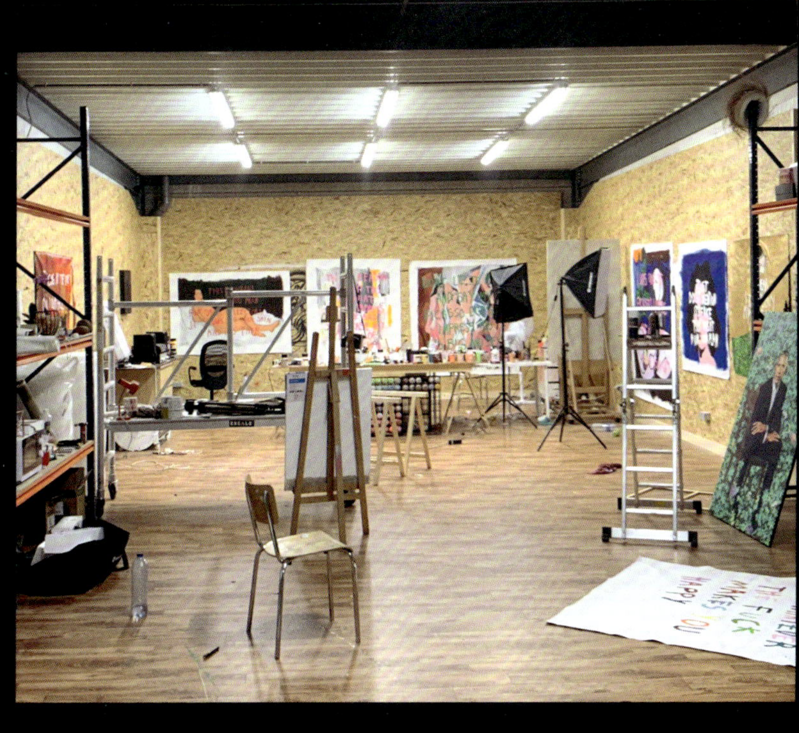

art practice full time. He visited family in Miami for two weeks and then traveled home to the Dominican Republic for a month, throughout this time sharing more and more of his work online. The London gallery, Imitate Modern, found him on Instagram and his career took off.

While working in the studio, Hoyo needs constant access to the internet because it is vital for him to be connected and see what is happening in the world. He also notes the importance of memes and considers them the best representation of our current society. Like contemporary art, they capture the time in which they are created, with humor and honesty.

The term "meme"—penned by Richard Dawkins in 1976—is a shortened version of "memetics", used to explain the phenomenon of how ideas replicate, mutate, and evolve in society.[6] It is also interesting to consider the similarities between the terms "memetics" and "mimicry" when remembering that Hoyo started his

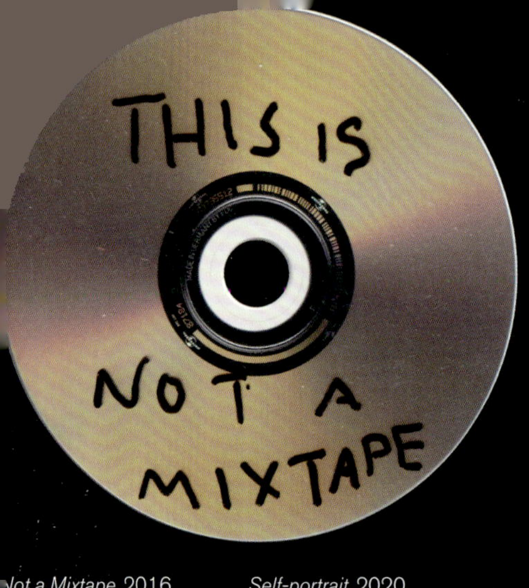

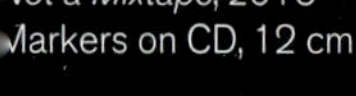

Not a Mixtape, 2016
Markers on CD, 12 cm

Self-portrait, 2020

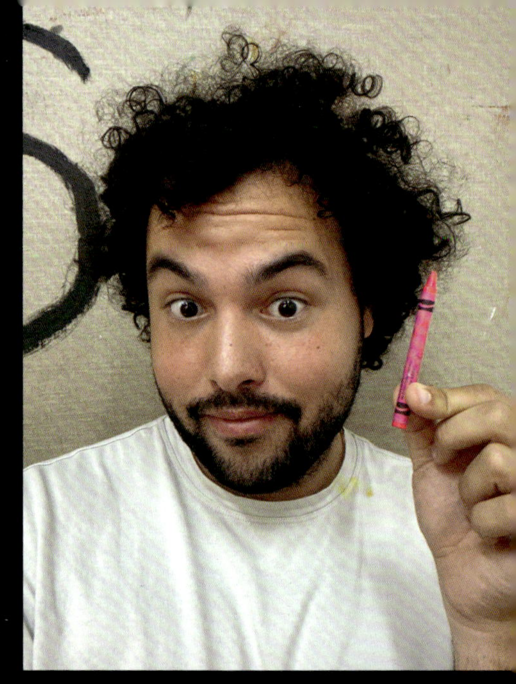

career by mimicking the masters. Memes are viral because they embody a shared experience and that is relatable with mass appeal. One could argue that Hoyo's works function as memes in their own right. His work loosely fits the definition of the Image Macro, a genre in which a popular image is overlaid with various humorous texts. But the comparison doesn't stop there. Imagery of this kind relies on social networks, without which the images and their commentary may be lost in the online oblivion.

Hoyo deeply understands this symbiotic relationship. A piece from his *Corny Quotes* series reads: IF YOU DID SOMETHING AND DIDN'T POST IT ONLINE DID YOU EVEN DO IT? The viral phenomenon of the late twentieth century allows content of popular discourse, trends, and information to spread through a large percentage of the human population in a relatively short period of time. The artistic voice has to follow the correct channels to impact society. Art captures the moment in which it is made and social media allows these captured moments to

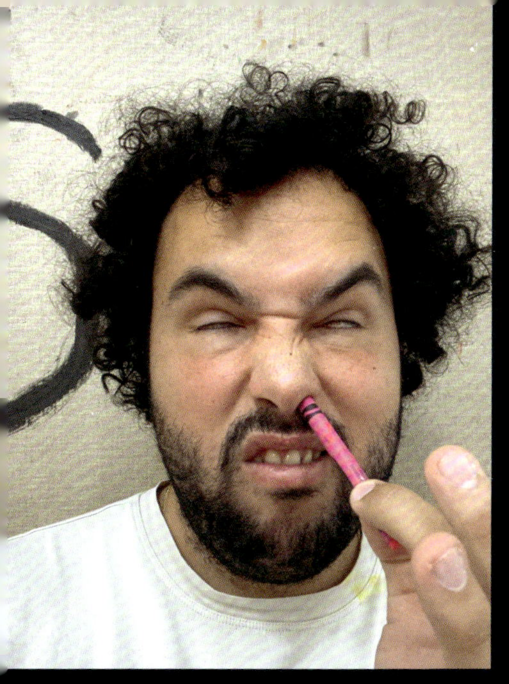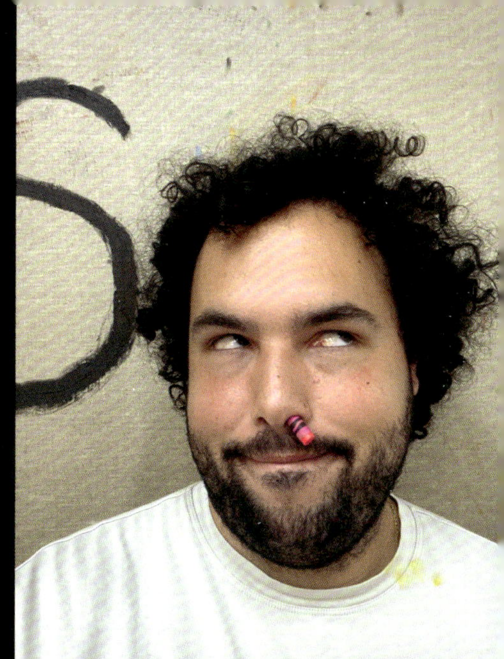

be shared immediately. It is easy to overlook the fact that a decade ago, work was often several months old before it was viewed by the general public.

While his initial success came from Instagram, he now uses the platform differently by managing multiple accounts that host various projects and engage directly with audiences. To go in-depth into a particular subject, he creates polls, poses questions to his followers, and collects their thoughts about specific topics he is interested in. These interactions with followers are a bit of a social experiment: having access to half a million people's emotions, opinions, and ideas, as well as a way to connect different individuals. Society as a whole is made up of individuals who, in many ways, are quite different yet tend to experience similar feelings and are going through the "same shit in life."

Every week he creates a poll of about 100 phrases that deal with the most disparate and discussed ideas of the moment. He is not actually asking anything specific, but instead simply posting about subjects that have come to his attention during the week with a simple "yes" or "no" response for his followers to answer. The content ranges from political happenings to pop culture to random nonsensical topics. It is a way of capturing what's happening in the world, so, naturally, contradictions are welcome. Of course, it is enticing to categorize topics and delineate positions, but this isn't always achievable and these contradictions naturally lead to confusion and frustration. Hoyo's approach offers an invitation to sit with paradoxes.

Another of his Instagram projects, *The Secret Dealer*, is his attempt to normalize topics that are often considered taboo—depression, sexual tendencies, etc. Too often, when individuals publicly express their views on these topics—especially one that is outside the status quo—they are made to feel outcast. He has likened this project to an online confessional, but instead of shame, he provides understanding. Every week he collects and shares the stories that many of us have in common, even if we might not realize it. This practice of connection offers confirmation of human nature over conformation of dogmatic ideological principles.

While there are a number of positive aspects of social media, it naturally has a negative side as well. Social media itself is inherently fake—another contradiction that Hoyo is comfortable with. Another piece from his *Corny Quotes* series reads: SOCIAL MEDIA IS NOT SOCIAL. Through this platform, we have control over our own narratives and how we are portrayed, often sharing a polished and curated version of ourselves to the world while omitting some of the less glamorous elements or aspects. This is simply human nature and cannot always be negotiated. And why should it be? We are entitled to our own privacy. We can share what we want, and decide what we want to keep for ourselves. However, it is easy for some to fall into the trap of oversharing in their never-ending quest for approval and validation. Collectively, this projection of a certain status quo is dangerous to the individual and leads to a vicious cycle where social media can be employed as a self-soothing agent and a distraction from our own reality. Yet another piece from his *Corny Quotes* series points to this contradiction without attempting to resolve it: "BUYING INSTAGRAM FOLLOWERS WON'T MAKE YOU LOOK COOL BUT AT LEAST YOU'LL FEEL LOVED."

An early concept of simulated social life was introduced in the 1962 text
The Image: A Guide to Pseudo-Events in America by the historian Daniel Boorstin. It was Boorstin's view that we seek out simulations as a means of fictional escape to cope with the mundane aspects of our daily lives. With the invention of the internet, social media, and the rise of influencer culture, this approach to consumption has grown at an exponential rate and added various levels of complication to discerning authenticity from fabrication.

Hoyo himself understands this. He knows that others are seeking realness online. He understands the nuances of digital identity and etiquette. How does he attempt to navigate these contradictions? The same way he does with everything else: by following his intuition, demonstrating honesty, accepting contradiction, and employing social media's ability to transcend and unite.

Supreme Fakes and Fake Supremes

An earlier work by Hoyo is a white envelope on which he wrote: "NOWADAYS SUCCESS IS MEASURED BY THE AMOUNT OF ONE'S INSTAGRAM FOLLOWERS AND LIKES"

Today, accumulating wealth is on par to accumulating Instagram followers. Their relationship has become symbiotic and we would be remiss to not delve into the sociological impact social media has had on the societal mindset of wealth, authenticity, exclusivity, and status symbols. Hoyo's work has always addressed these concerns. Remember, he was born during an economic crisis in Cuba, and was educated in the Dominican Republic where he experienced a great disparity in wealth compared to his upper class peers.

Another work, created in 2020, reads: "EXPENSIVE PLUS TAX PLUS CUSTOMS PLUS SHIPPING"

Earlier in his career, he painted over various paper currencies, transforming them into small works of art to explore the simple question: Will the money be worth less because there's something painted over it, or will its value increase? Money has no intrinsic value, but rather is merely a physical stand-in for the value we assign to it; in the end, it's just paper and numbers. Today, artwork is often treated as a currency, something to be bought and sold. It has become a means of investment and storing value, leveraged with the anticipation that—when sold—it will yield profitable returns.

Hoyo's series *Fakes* explores how money pours into and moves throughout the art world, revealing a market that has come to be defined for its misplaced priorities. His work is meant to draw attention to the ridiculousness of how extreme these monetary values have become in our society, not the cultural value of the original works themselves. This distinction becomes more obvious as the series evolved and expanded to include not only the monetary value of the art object, but the entire culture of consumer goods that are part of its greater orbit; the two go hand in hand. Gallery openings tend to be social events where fashion and luxury coincide with the culture of art. They are a place to see and be seen. It is nearly impossible to attend an art opening nowadays and not feel swept away in a swift visual current of luxury brands. Many designers have infiltrated the art world, consider Kanye West's Yeezy fashion show and Virgil Abloh's brand, Off-White—he even became the director of Louis Vuitton and several prominent museums hosted a retrospective of his work.

Hoyo himself has said on more than one occasion that he "likes to cover trends and hypes." This theme runs through his entire career: one of the first works from his *Fakes* series, features commentary on "FAKE LV, FAKE YEEZY'S, FAKE MURAKAMI, REAL FAKE, ORIGINAL FAKE" while a work from *Corny Quotes* in late 2020 reads "WHAT WILL WE DO ONCE THE HYPE IS OVER."

Corny Quotes, Fake World, Messy Handwriting

After he began sharing his work on Instagram, there was a blatant switch in Hoyo's work from commentary on the art market to commentary on contemporary society in general. He began by simply writing some of his thoughts on white paper in black ink. Works such as *How to get famous fast in the art world* and *How to make money*

Self-portrait, 2019
Polaroid film,
10.752 x 8.847 cm

*Fake Magritte
in the studio*, 2019
Polaroid film,
10.752 x 8.847 cm

Page 33
*Fake Modigliani
in the studio*, 2019
Fujifilm Instax Colorfilm
Glossy, 8.6 x 10.8 cm

Self-portrait, 2019
Fujifilm Instax Colorfilm
Glossy, 8.6 x 10.8 cm

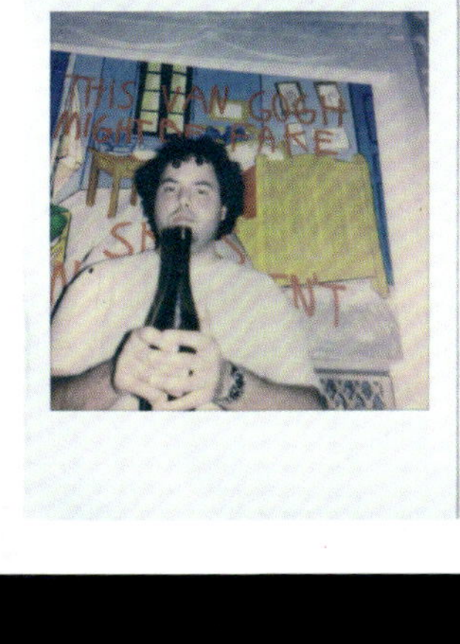

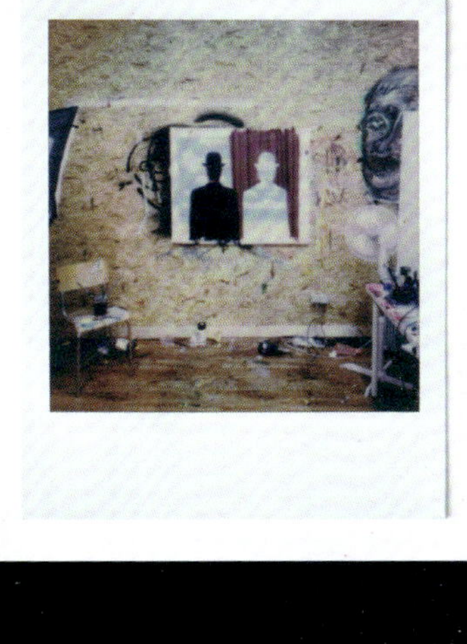

as a collector are loosely reminiscent of such works as *Tips for artists who want to sell* or *Terms Most Useful in Describing Creative Works of Art* again, recalling Baldessari.

Originally, the series was titled *Shit CB Says*, but he changed the name to *Corny Quotes* when he started using colors to write the text in August of 2019. Hoyo was in Miami visiting his grandfather, and stocking up on some personal items that he couldn't find back home in Europe. Being that it was August in the US, they were having their annual Back to School sale. Hoyo stumbled upon a 150-count box of crayons similar to the one he used during his childhood, and purchased a couple of boxes to take back to his studio, not quite knowing what he would do with them. After Miami, he flew to the Dominican Republic to visit his grandma and the two of them were going through boxes of his childhood drawings that his mother had stored away. One in particular struck his attention, featuring a phrase written on paper with each letter in a different color of crayon. As with most of his work born from experimentation and happenstance, the ideas he had been thinking about came together very quickly, and he began to recreate drawings in the style of his three-year-old self, but with content that he was observing in his current age.

As the series progressed, he added subjects, narratives, and dialogues to these works. Instead of simply writing about the art world, which is admittedly exclusive, he began to portray a more universal feeling to the world at large. In a way, it was the same thing he had always done. He was simply being honest, expressing his own feelings and thoughts that resonated with the larger society. Some examples of these works on canvas feature phrases such as:

IF YOU CAN'T CONTROL IT WHY THE FUCK ARE YOU FREAKING OUT
THE PAST IS GONE THE FUTURE IS UNCERTAIN LIVE IN THE FUCKING PRESENT
NOTHING IS PERMANENT
AM I THE ONLY ONE STARTING TO LOSE MY SHIT?
AFTER A WHILE EVERYTHING BECOMES BORING AND REPETITIVE
WHAT WILL WE DO ONCE IT'S ALL OVER
HORNY ANXIOUS SAD BORED HUNGRY DEPRESSED FRUSTRATED HAPPY CONFUSED SCARED
ARE YOU STILL WATCHING?

Regarding the style of these works, the handwriting is very much his own. It is peculiar and sloppy and incredibly raw. As a kid in school, he was chastised for his penmanship and was forced to take hours of calligraphy courses. This was to no avail, as there was no taming his wild and hieroglyphic handwriting. He also has dyslexia, which provided an additional challenge. His teachers continually mocked him and predicted that he would not find success or be taken seriously. His handwriting became a key part of his style and success; he cites this as a lesson to simply embrace the ironies of life.

This body of work marks another important departure from the *Fakes*. Hoyo was no longer making traditional pictorial based paintings. Instead, he stripped back the imagery and allowed the words to be the main focus, encouraging each

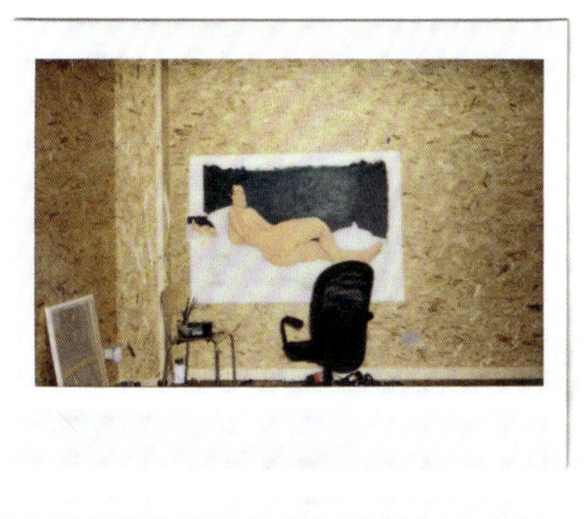 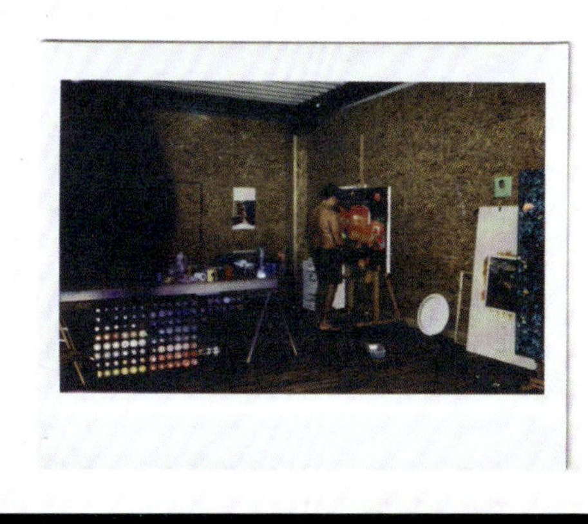

viewer to focus on the language and interpret the phrases individually. Perhaps some of Hoyo's most successful works play into these strategies, wherein text stands on its own, such as his Christopher Wools riff from the *Fakes* series. At first glance, Hoyo's piece is indistinguishable from an authentic Wools. It asks the viewer, not just to see, but to read, tapping into a deeper level of play.

Now and Next

Contemporary literally means "together with time." Contemporary is what's happening right now in this moment we are living in: climate change, COVID-19, cryptocurrency, the destabilization of the US dollar and economy, an upcoming market crash, living in the new normality, and adapting to new technologies. These are all contemporary topics. There is a close relationship between art, politics, and everything taking place today. Contemporary art captures contemporary society. Most aspects of our lives are impacted by politics, and this is reflected in creative work. While not every artist uses politics directly as the main subject of their work, it is nearly impossible for politics not to influence their work in some manner.

Hoyo has always worked with what is contemporary. For him, this simply means being a person in a shared world, seeking universality as best as one can in an increasingly unequal society.

Then, COVID-19 hit, and the entire modern world was actually dealing with the same problem. We are all missing important life moments while the world remains paused, many have lost their jobs, and others have lost their lives. Everything changes in times of crisis. Hoyo, like many in the arts sector, had projects cancelled due to the pandemic. This was of course disappointing, but also an opportunity to focus more on himself and new work. Feeling creatively stifled, he decided to end the *Fakes* series once and for all after years of struggling to keep up with the demand for them.

We have been existing in various forms of lockdown for more than a year. Now, more than ever, our lives are limited to a virtual world and are therefore more reliant on social media. People are sitting at home, bored and horny, scrolling through their smartphones, trying to seek connection, while also exhausting their ability to connect. Hoyo's work has always captured the moment we are living in, but now it is capturing the moment we are trapped in. He is now focusing on staying virtually connected to his audiences through his Instagram projects and *Corny Quotes* series.

Reading his *Corny Quotes* while in lockdown offers a reprieve from the intense struggles that the entire world is collectively experiencing. There is a strange phenomenon that occurs when reading an isolated text—each individual can begin to find relevance to whatever is happening in their life and in the greater societal context. Fortune cookies or horoscopes demonstrate this well. Hoyo's work has always strived to address universality and honesty with a bit of humor. Let's use the same examples as before, but consider them in the context of isolation and social-distancing:

IF YOU CAN'T CONTROL IT WHY THE FUCK ARE YOU
FREAKING OUT
THE PAST IS GONE THE FUTURE IS UNCERTAIN
LIVE IN THE FUCKING PRESENT
NOTHING IS PERMANENT
AM I THE ONLY ONE STARTING TO LOSE MY SHIT?

**AFTER A WHILE EVERYTHING BECOMES BORING
AND REPETITIVE**

**WHAT WILL WE DO ONCE IT'S ALL OVER
HORNY ANXIOUS SAD BORED HUNGRY
DEPRESSED
FRUSTRATED HAPPY CONFUSED SCARED
ARE YOU STILL WATCHING?**

So, what now? And what next? In this moment it is difficult, if not impossible, to imagine what the future will look like. For Hoyo, this is a non-issue:

"I live the moment. I want to say what I think, whether people like it or not. I want to make art and be happy. If I can help someone with what I do, I am satisfied. I don't particularly appreciate thinking about the future; it doesn't exist yet. Technology will take over everything, and we'll end up living more virtual lives. Climate change will hit us hard. We will be living in a matrix. I see myself making art."

Now he is on to the next, and for Hoyo, that next is now.

[1] Holland Cotter, "Taking Copycatting to a Higher Level", *The New York Times*, November 13, 2014.
[2] Hayley A. Rowe, "Appropriation in Contemporary Art," *Inquiries Journal*, June 1, 2011, http://www.inquiries-journal.com/articles/1661/appropriation-in-contemporary-art.
[3] Margalit Fox, "Elaine Sturtevant, Appropriation Artist, Is Dead at 89," *The New York Times*, May 16, 2014.
[4] Foucault, Michel, René Magritte, and J. A. Harkness, *This Is Not a Pipe* (Berkeley, CA: University of California Press, 2008).
[5] Alfred Korzybski, *Science and Sanity: an Introduction to Non-Aristotelian Systems and General Semantics* (Lancaster, PA, and New York City: The International Non-Aristotelian Library Pub. Co., 1933), pp. 747–761.
[6] Richard Dawkins, *The Selfish Gene* (Oxford: Oxford University Press, 1989).

FA

KES

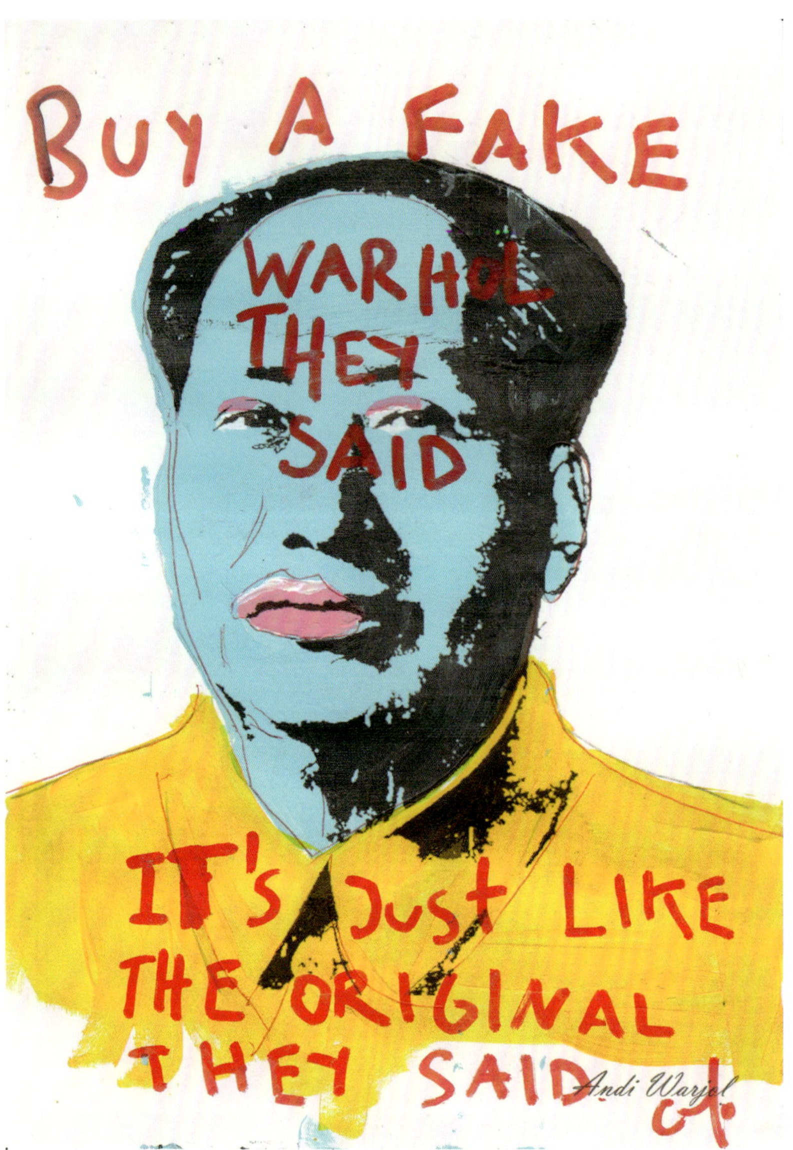

*Buy a Fake Warhol
They Said It's Just Like
the Original They Said*,
2017
Acrylic paint, ink, and
oil paint on 200g/m²
paper, 29.7 x 21 cm

*The Art Dealer Told Me
This Fake Rothko Would
Make Me Feel Rich*,
2017
Acrylic paint and oil
paint on cardboard,
31.5 x 22 cm

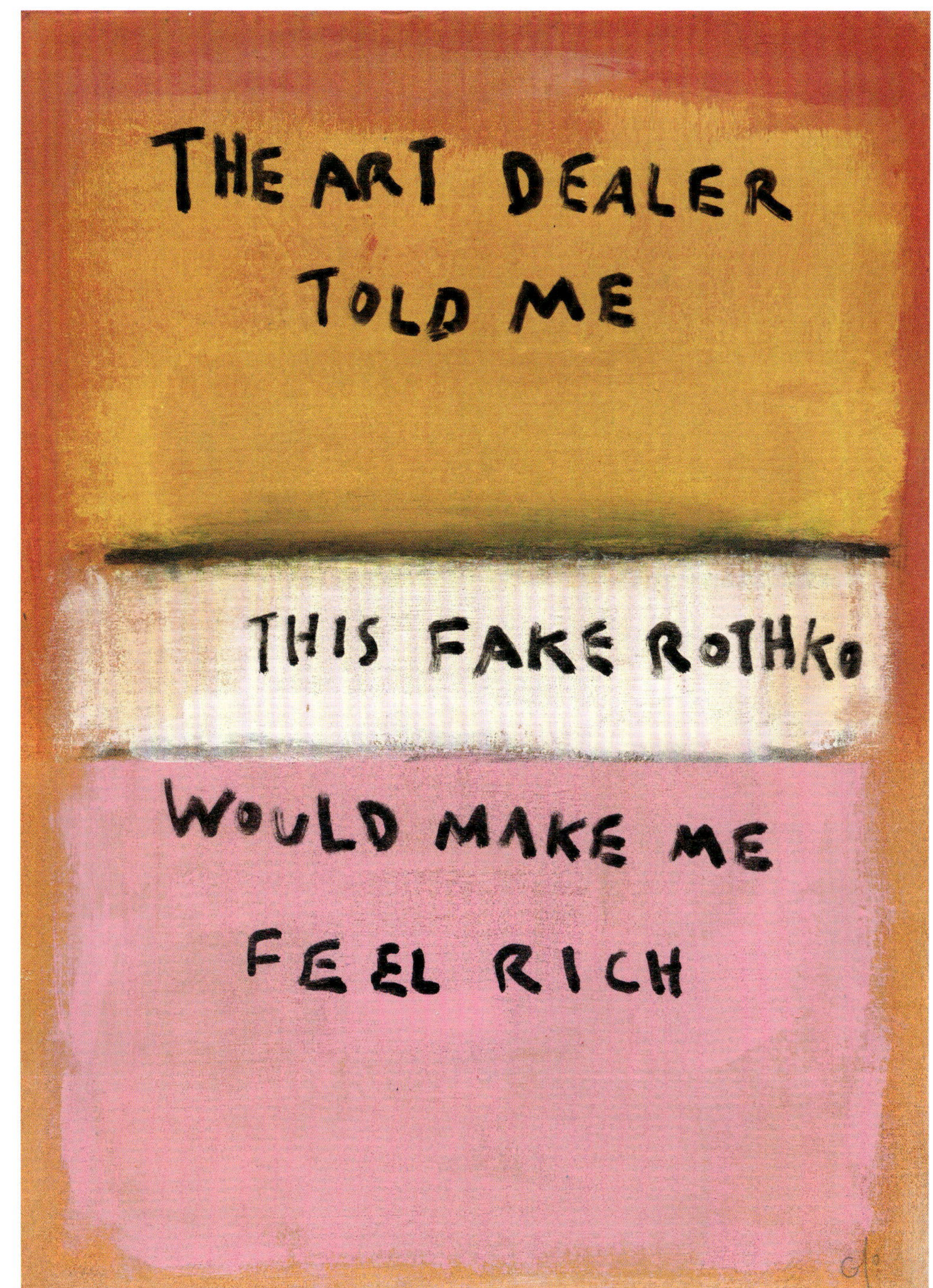

THE ART DEALER
TOLD ME
THIS FAKE ROTHKO
WOULD MAKE ME
FEEL RICH

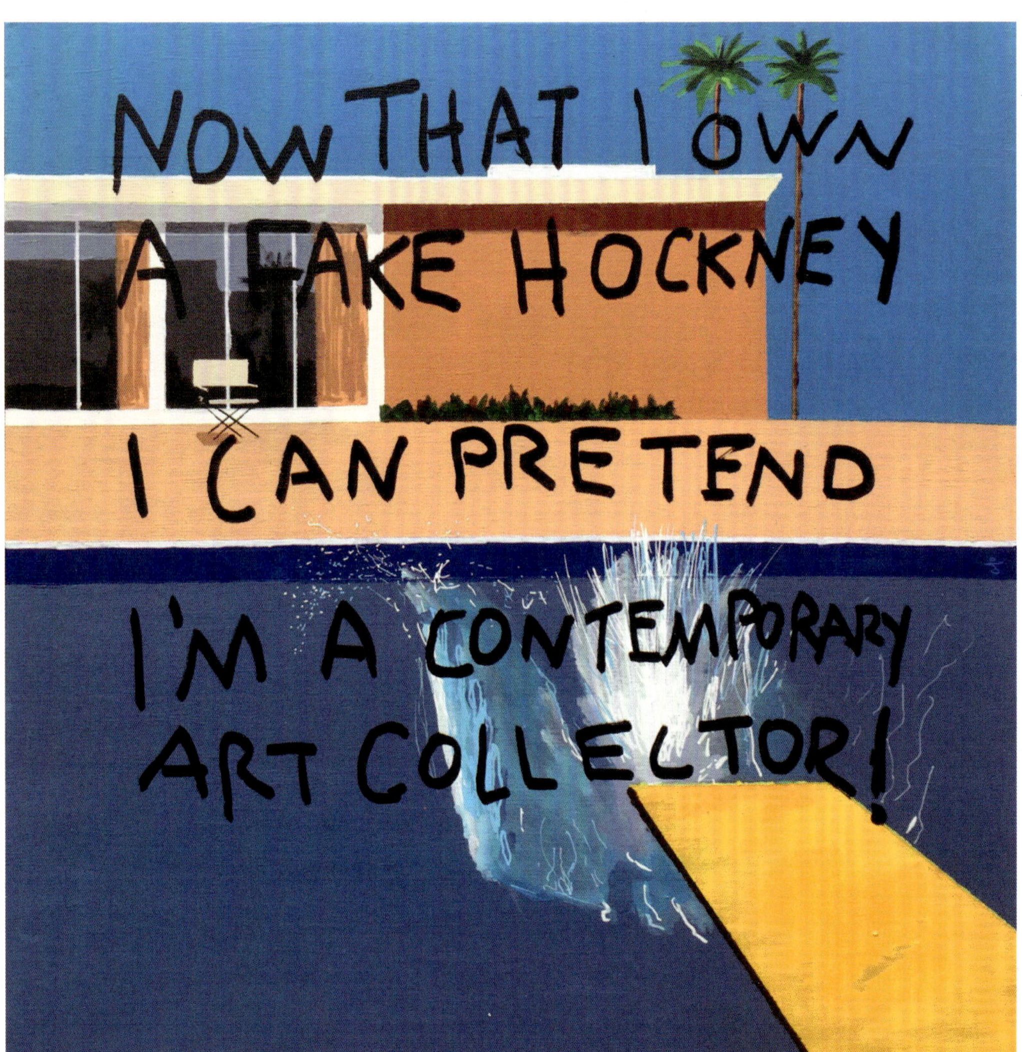

Fake Collector, 2017
Acrylic on canvas,
50 x 50 cm

Studio, *Fake Collector*
in the making, 2017

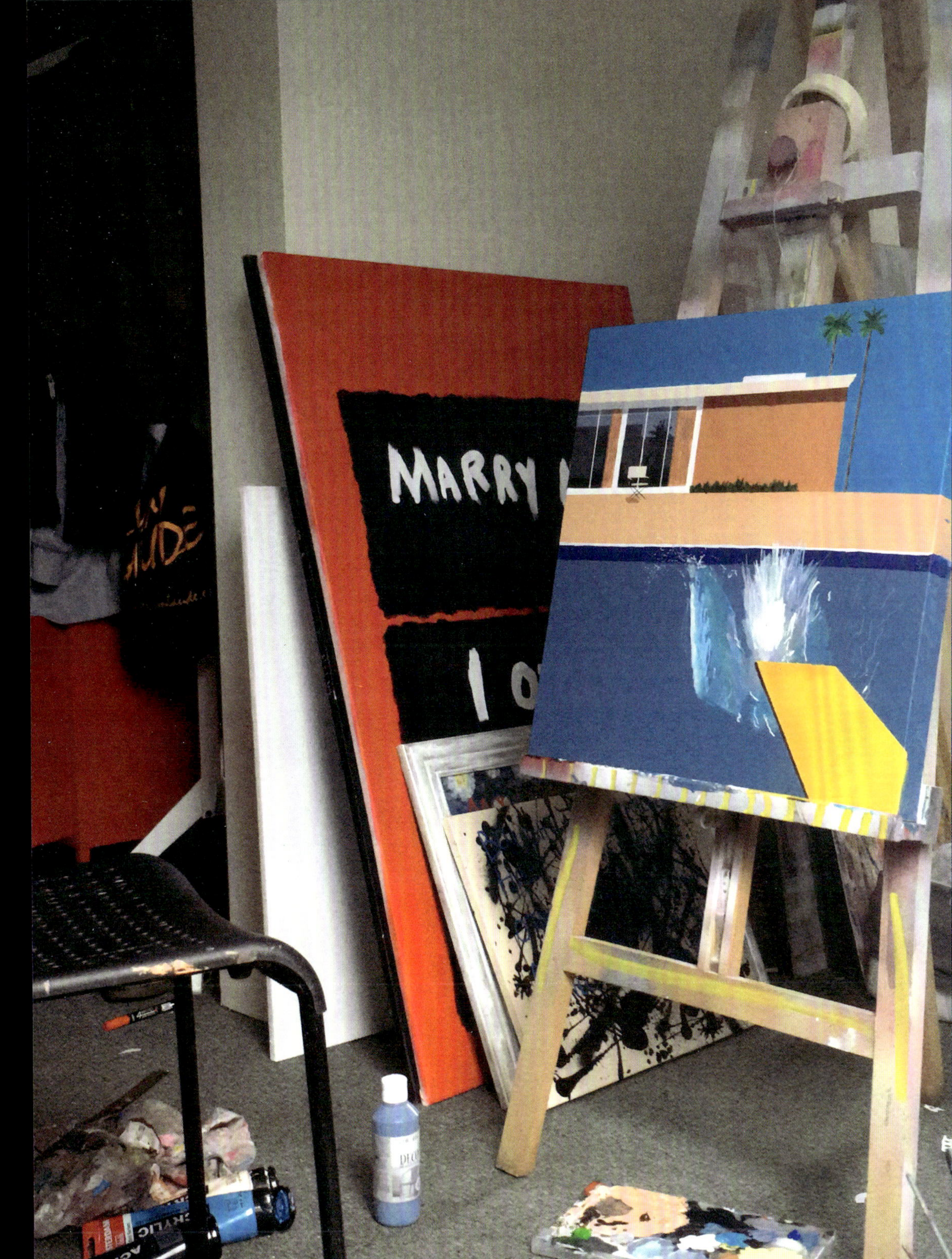

MARRY
I O

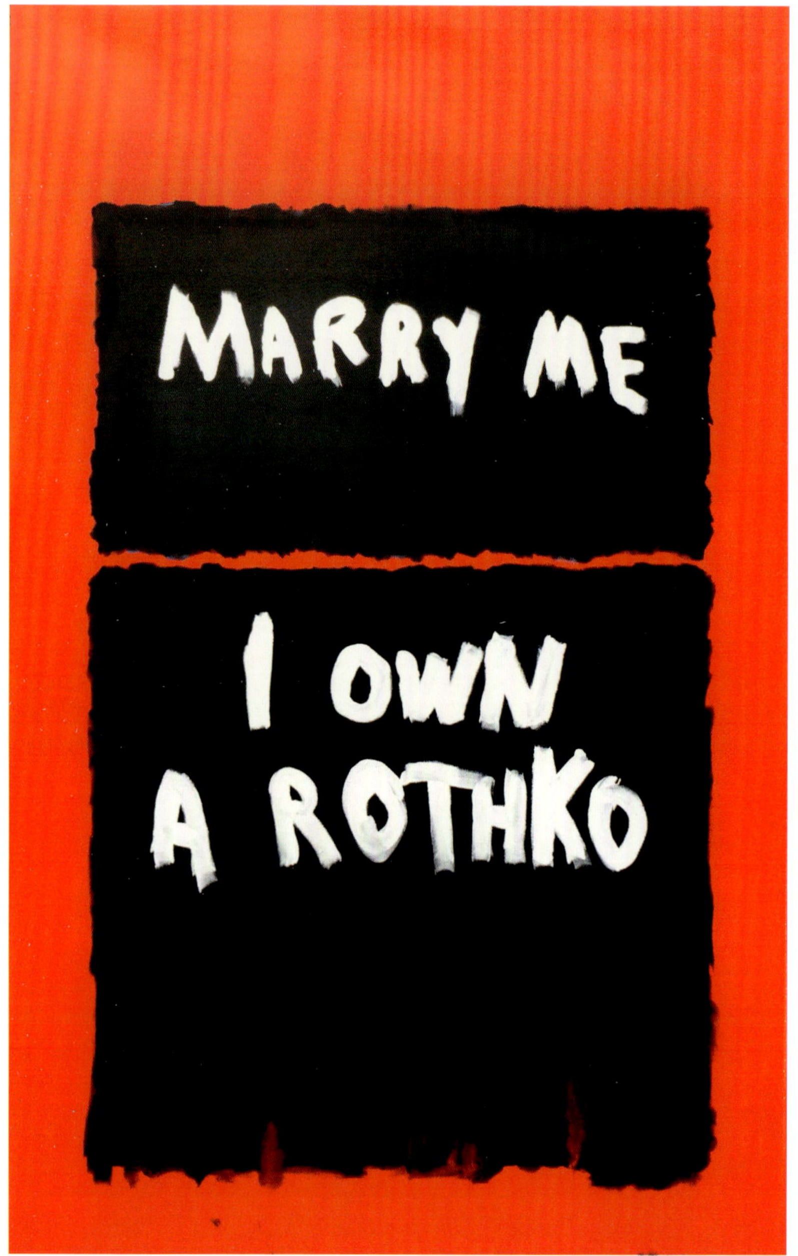

Marry Me I Own a Rothko, 2017
Acrylic and spray paint
on canvas, 115 x 75 cm

Studio shot, 2017

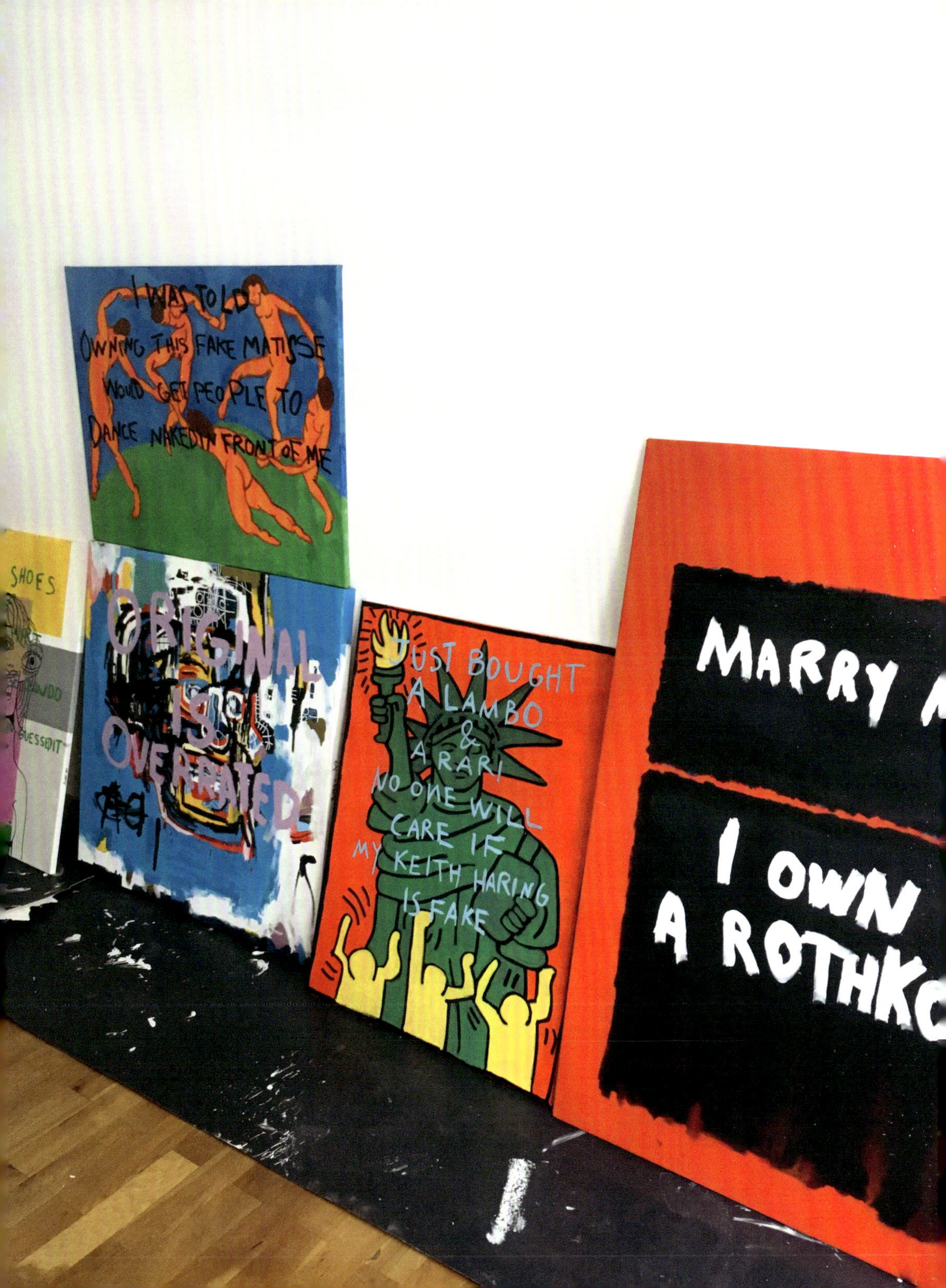

SHOES
I WAS TOLD
OWNING THIS FAKE MATISSE
WOULD GET PEOPLE TO
DANCE NAKED IN FRONT OF ME
ORIGINAL IS OVERRATED
JUST BOUGHT A LAMBO & A RARI
NO ONE WILL CARE IF MY KEITH HARING IS FAKE
MARRY A
I OWN A ROTHKO

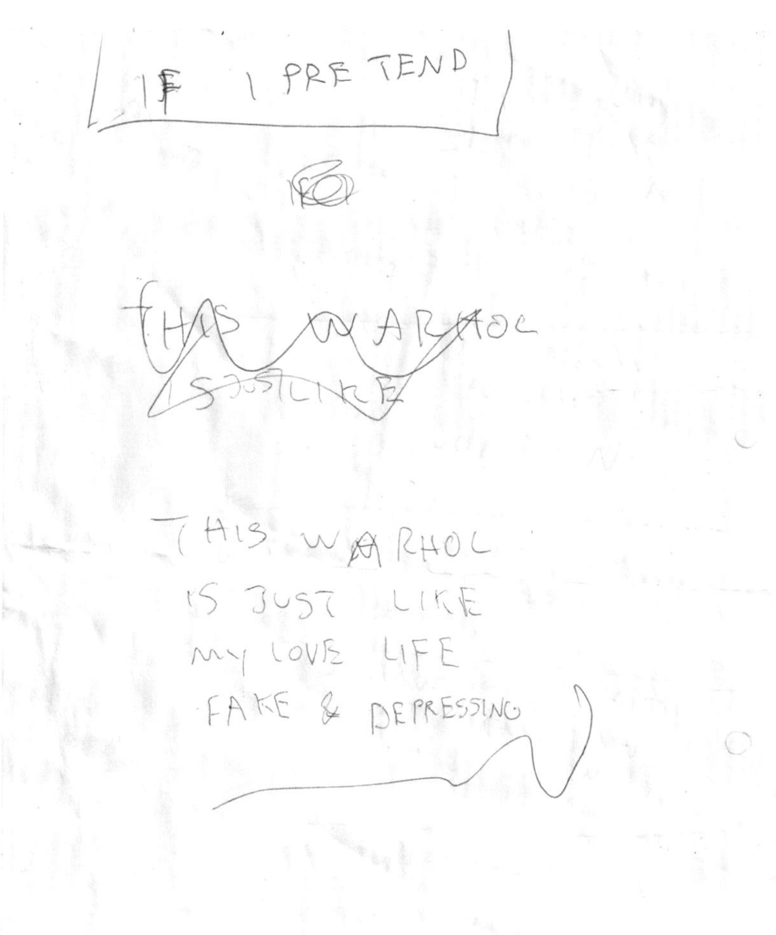

Untitled (Study), 2017
Pen on paper,
29.7 x 21 cm

*Fake and Depressing
Warhol*, 2017
Acrylic on canvas,
50 x 40 cm

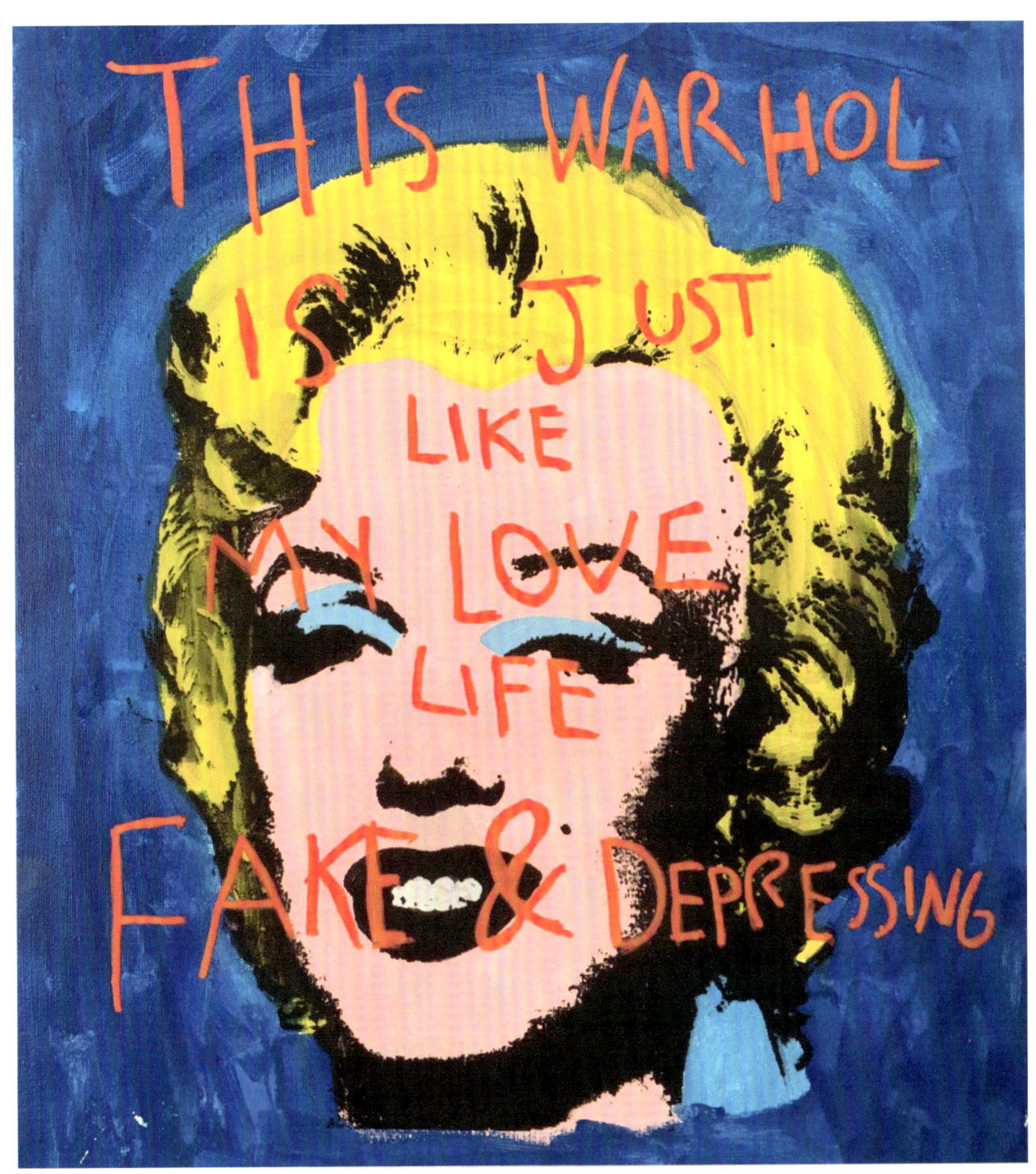

THIS WARHOL
IS   JUST
      LIKE
MY LOVE
      LIFE
FAKE & DEPRESSING

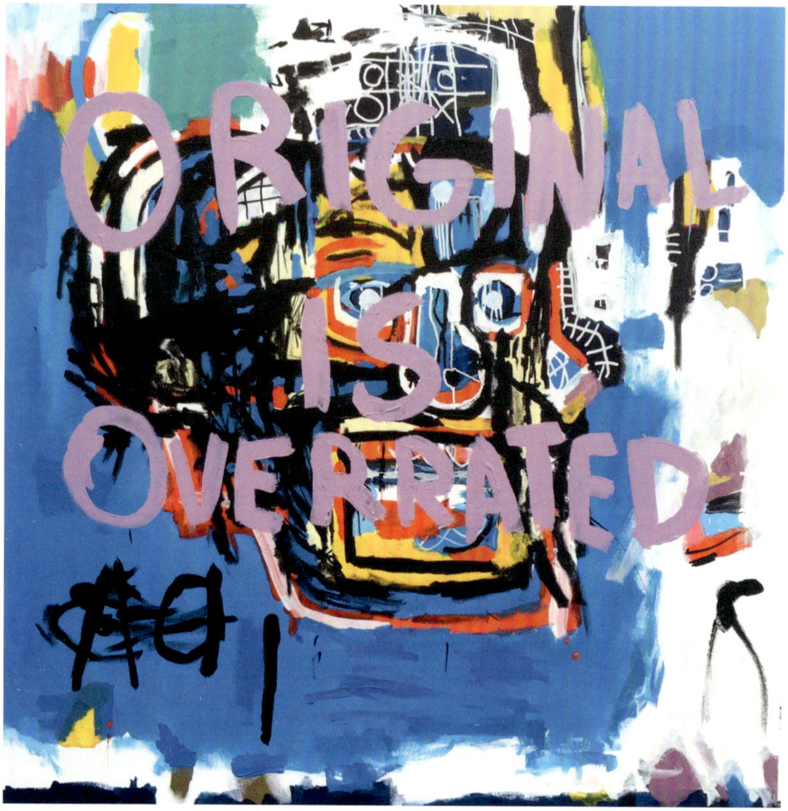

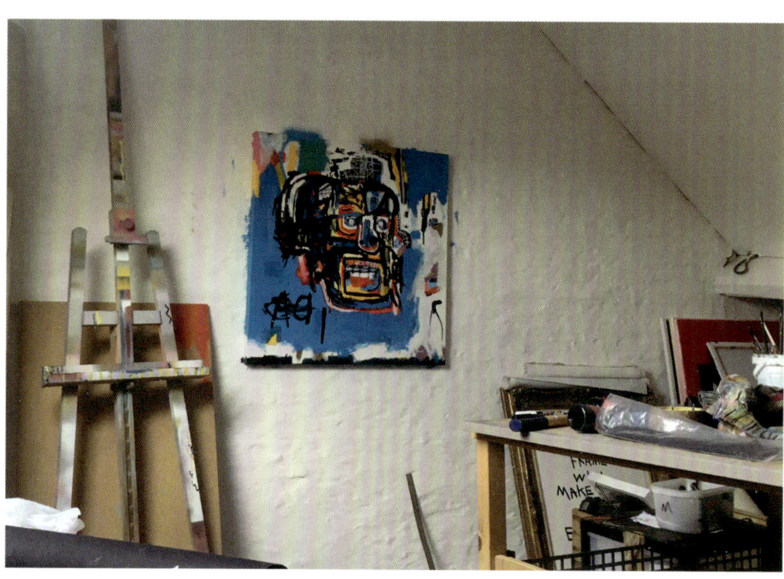

Original Is Overrated,
2017
Acrylic on canvas,
80 x 80 cm

Studio, *Original Is
Overrated* in the making,
2017

*I Was Told Owning This
Fake Matisse Would Get
People to Dance Naked
in Front of Me*, 2017
Acrylic and oil paint on
canvas, 60 x 80 cm

Studio, *I Was Told
Owning This Fake
Matisse Would Get
People to Dance Naked
in Front of Me* in the
making, 2017

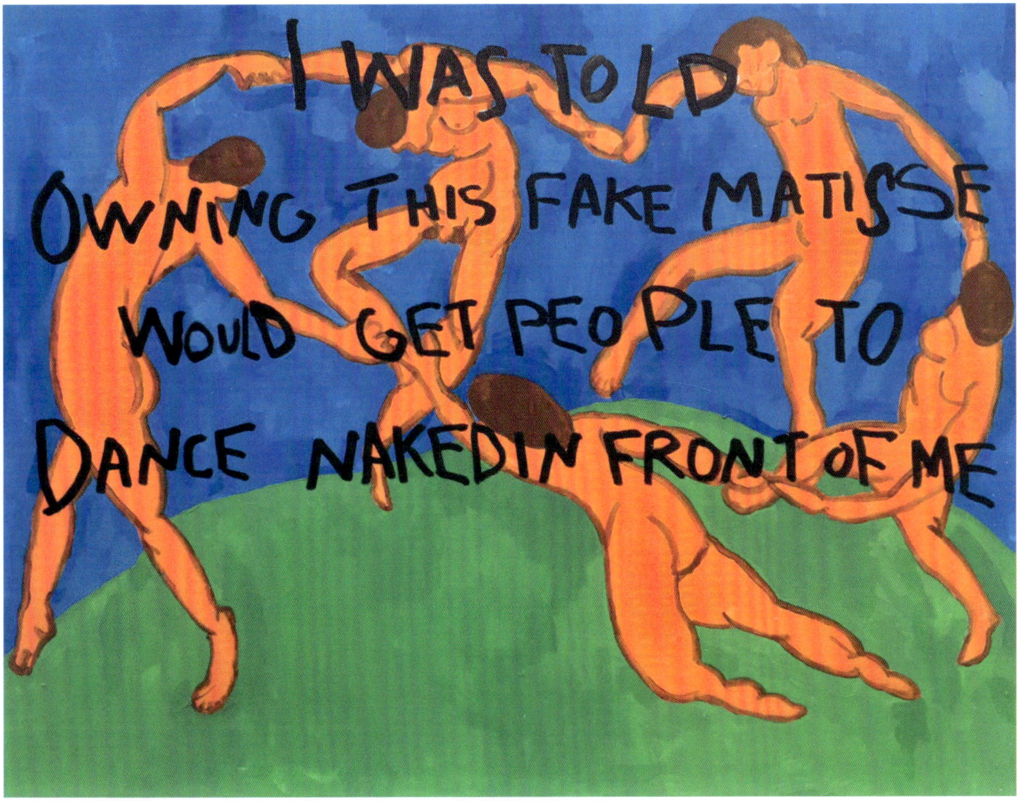

I WAS TOLD
OWNING THIS FAKE MATISSE
WOULD GET PEOPLE TO
DANCE NAKED IN FRONT OF ME

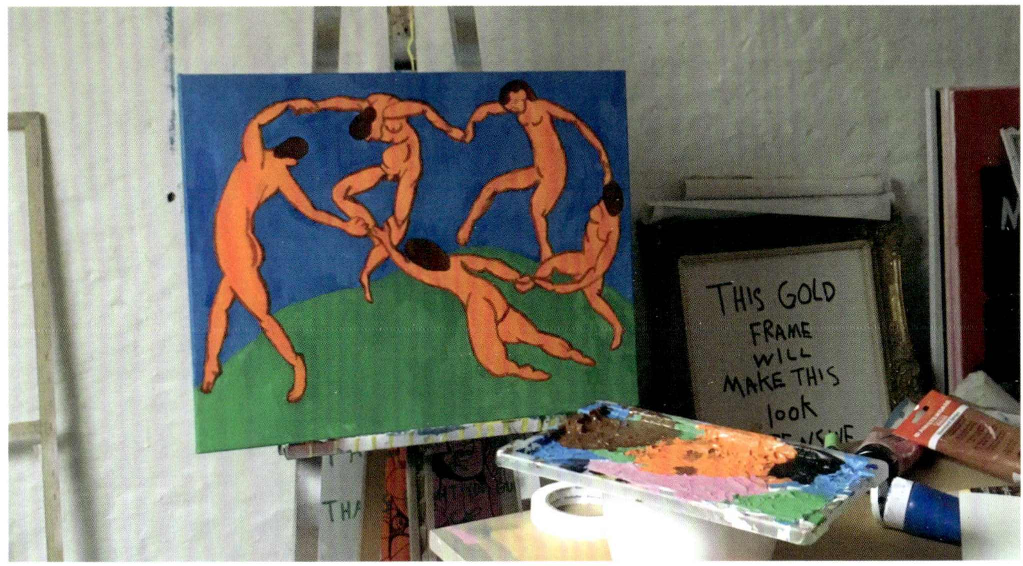

THIS GOLD
FRAME
WILL
MAKE THIS
look

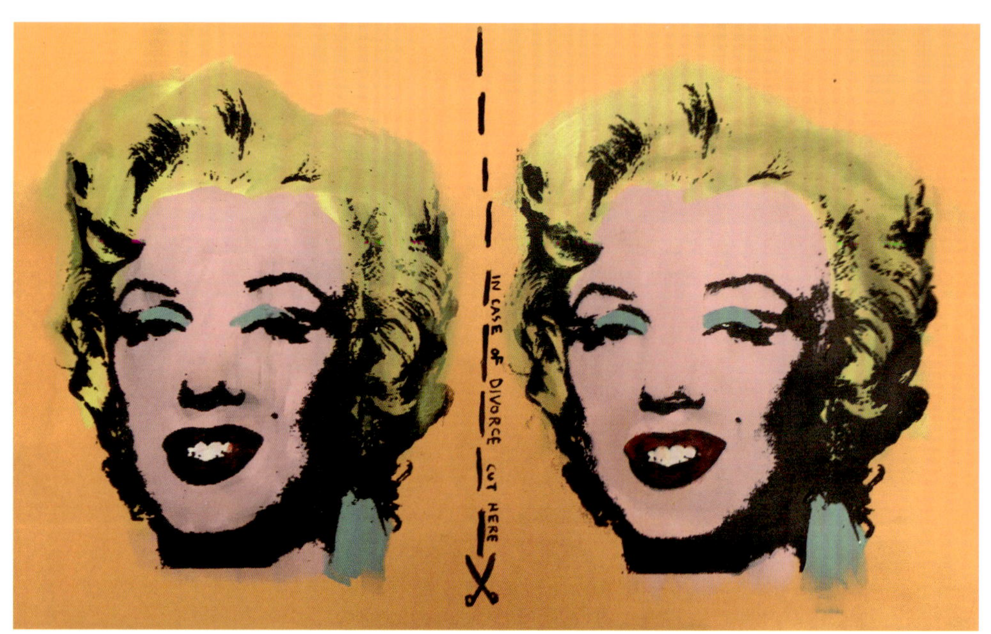

IN CASE OF DIVORCE CUT HERE

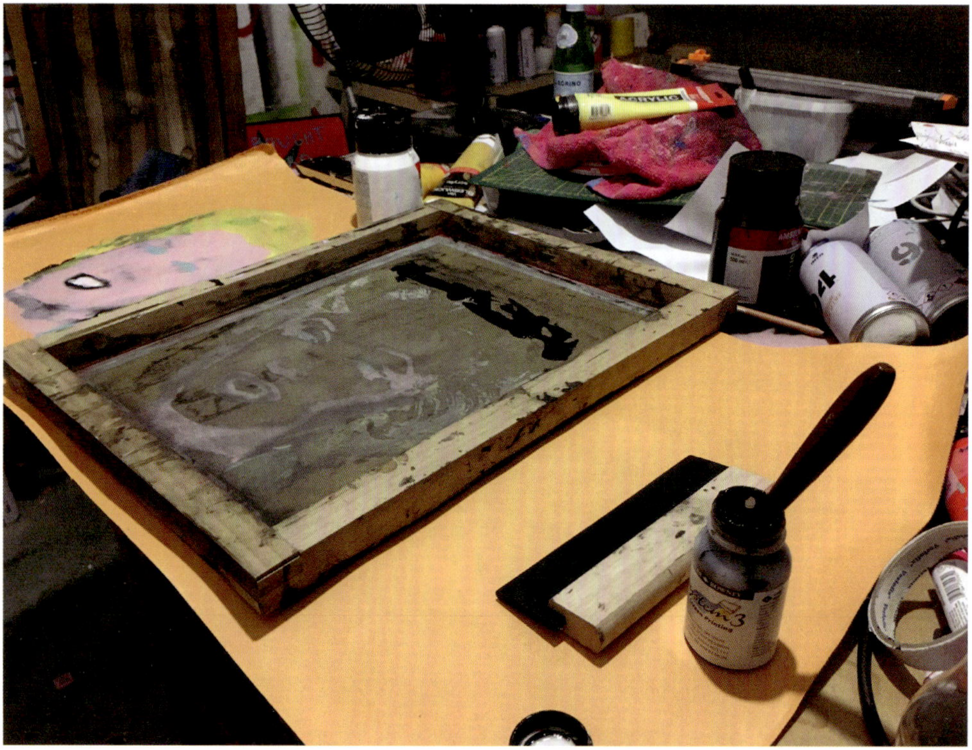

In Case of Divorce,
2017
Acrylic and spray paint
on canvas,
c. 48 x 75 cm

Studio, *In Case of
Divorce* in the making,
2017

Untitled (Study), 2017
Pen on paper,
13 x 10.5 cm

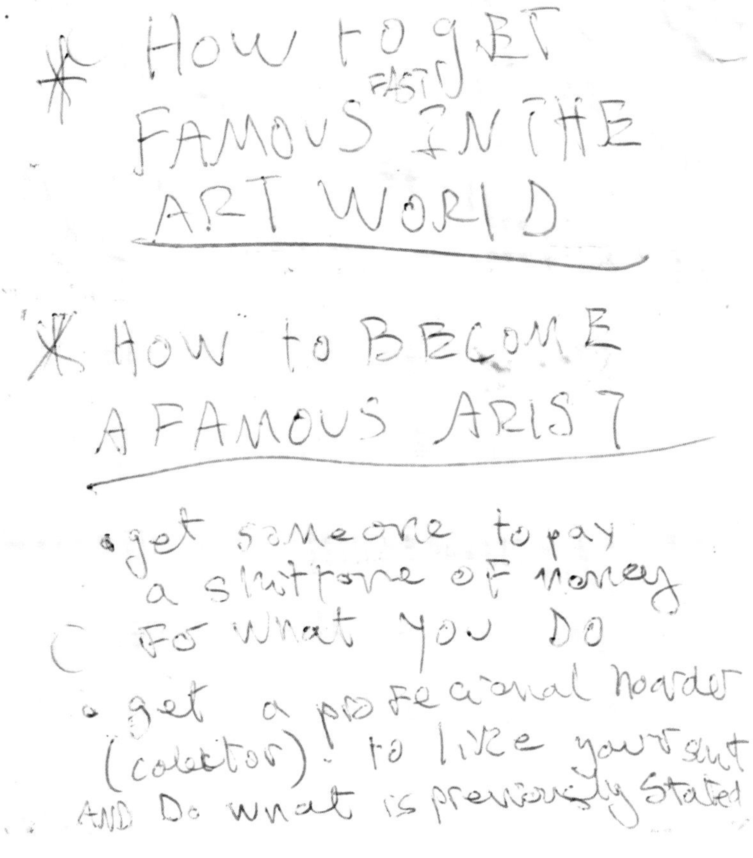

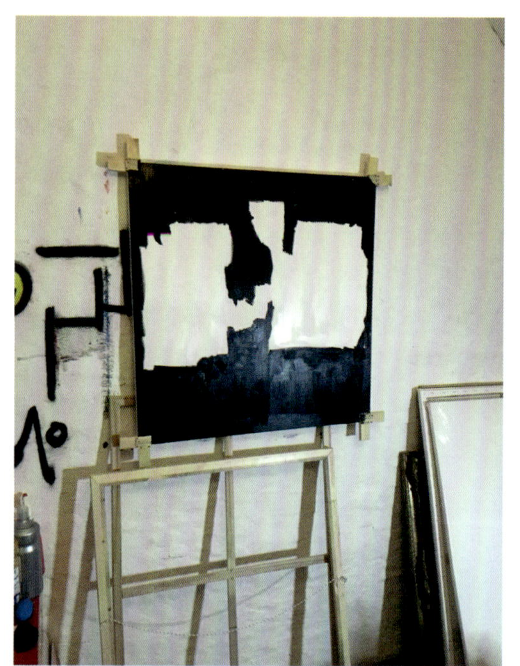

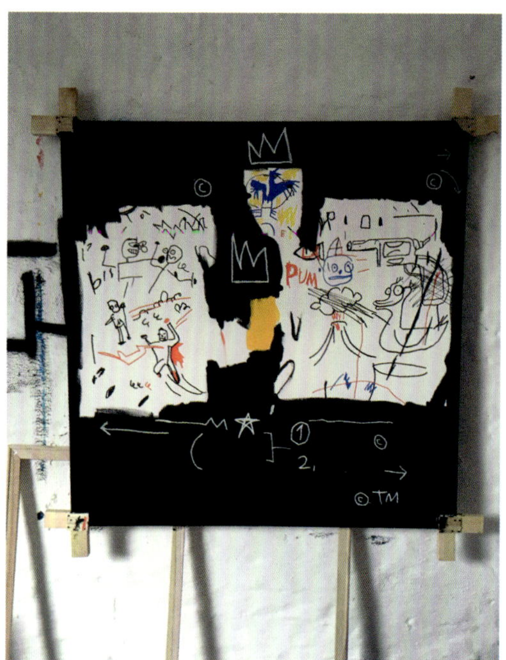

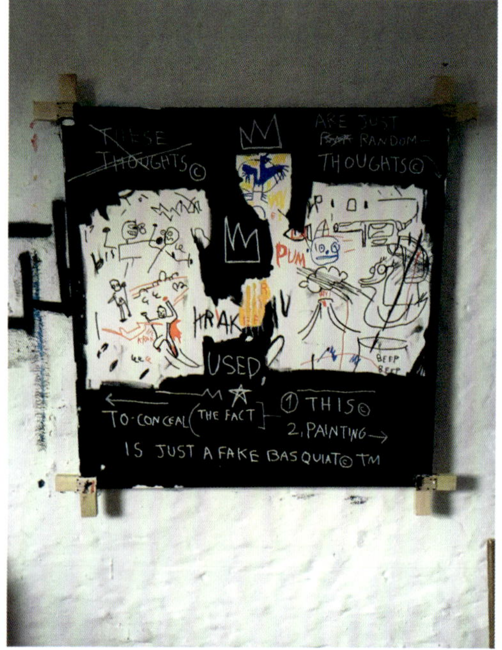

I ACTUALY PAID
MONEY FOR THIS

ALL CARDS
AND CURRENCIES
ARE ACCEPTED
JUST FUCKING PAY ME

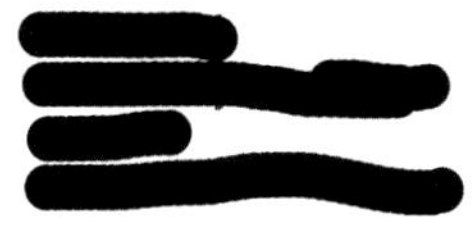
NOWADAYS SUCCESS IS MEASURED
BY THE AMOUNT OF ONE'S
INSTAGAM FOLLOWERS AND LIKES

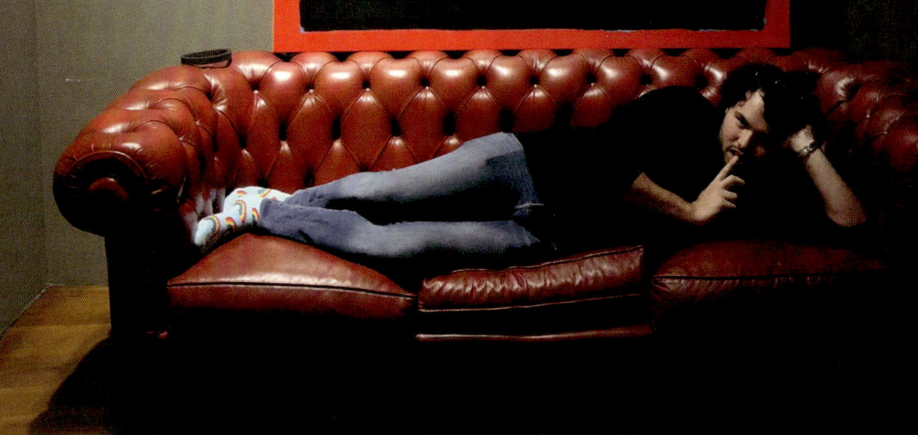

FUCK ME
I OWN A
ROTHKO

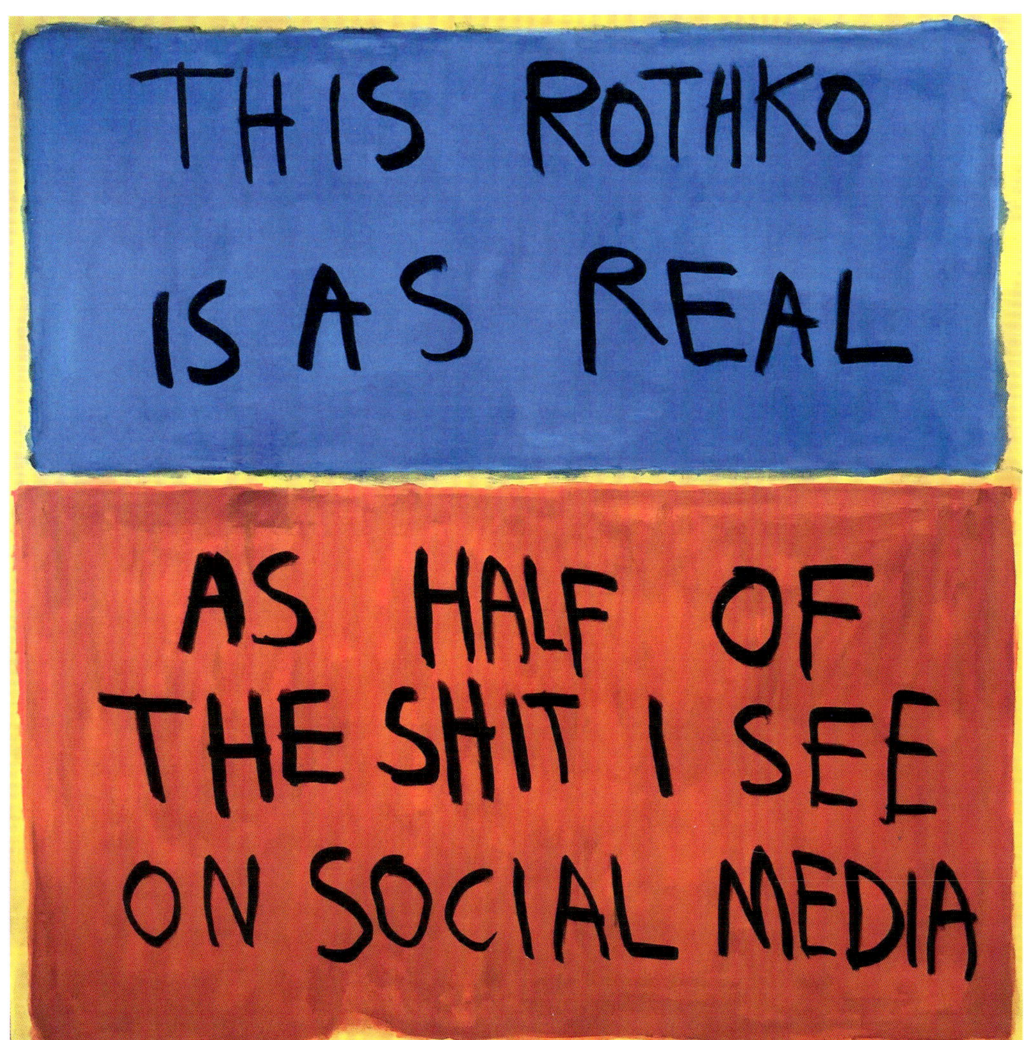

CB with *Fuck Me I Own a Rothko* in Milan, 2018

Shit on Social Media,
2018
Acrylic paint on canvas,
100 x 100 cm

Untitled (Study), 2018
Color and lead pencils
on paper,
29.7 x 21 cm

100% Real, 2018
Acrylic and spray paint
on canvas,
200 x 150 cm

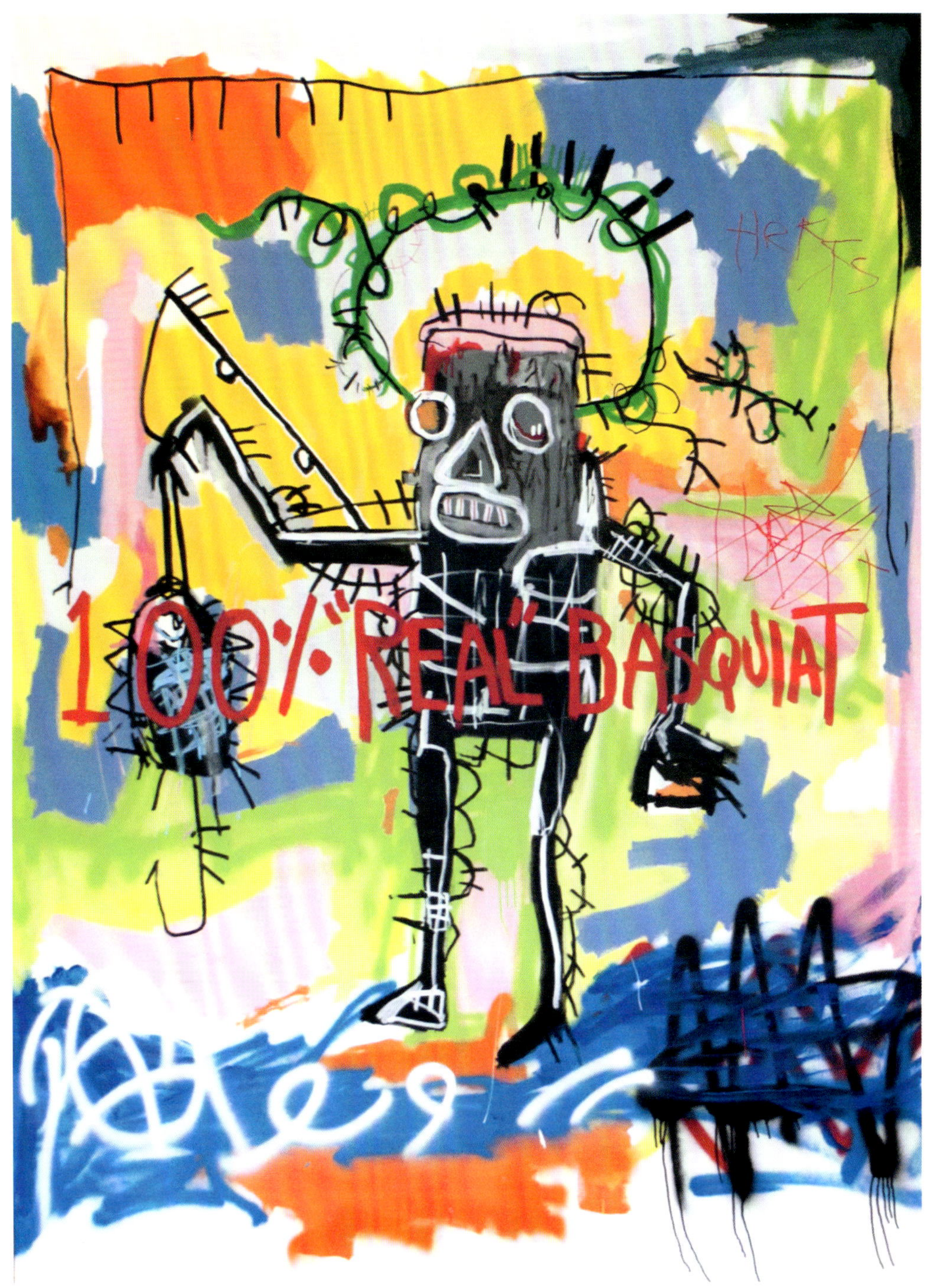

100% "REAL" BASQUIAT

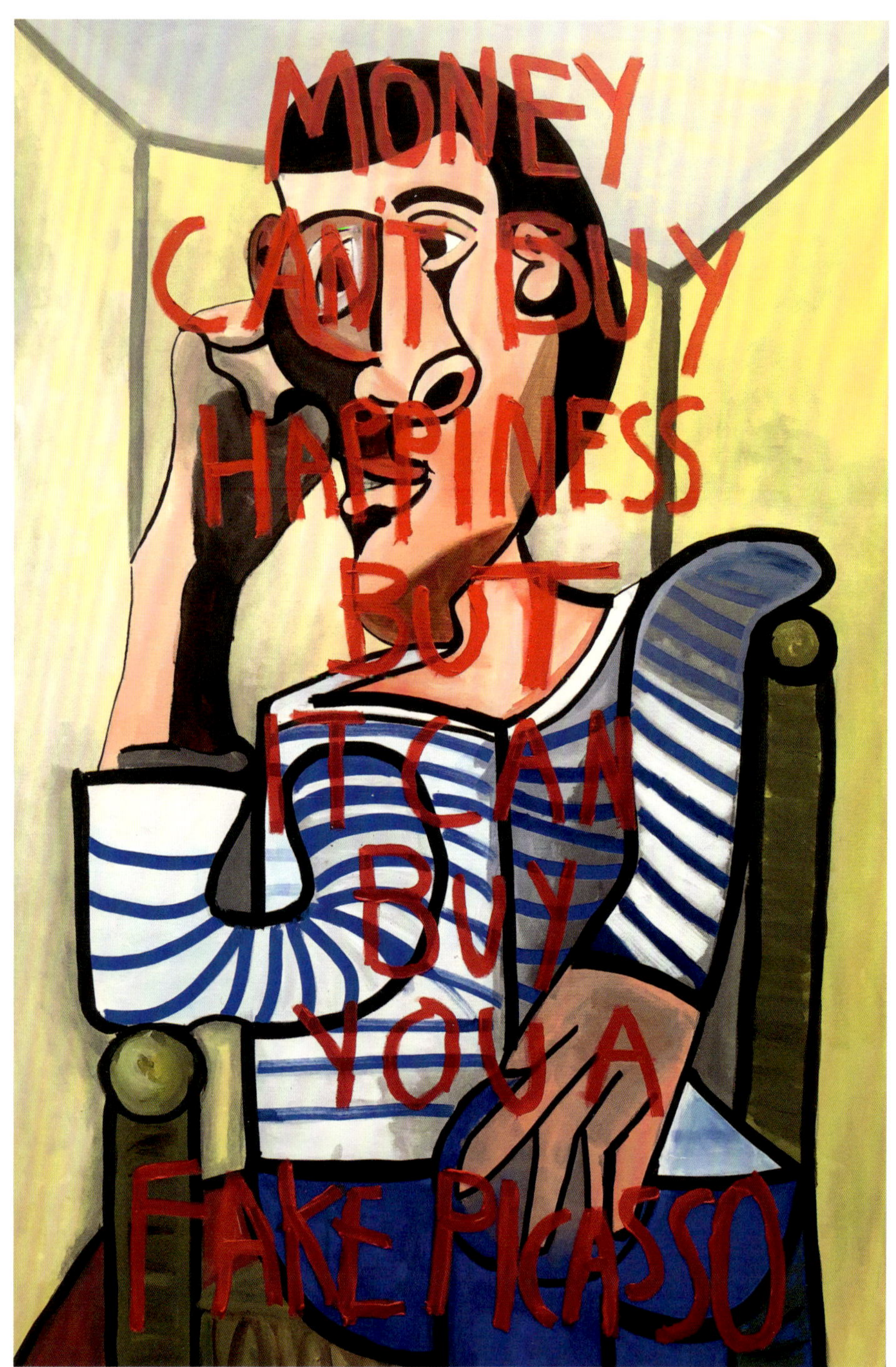

MONEY
CAN'T BUY
HAPPINESS
BUT
IT CAN
BUY
YOU A
FAKE PICASSO

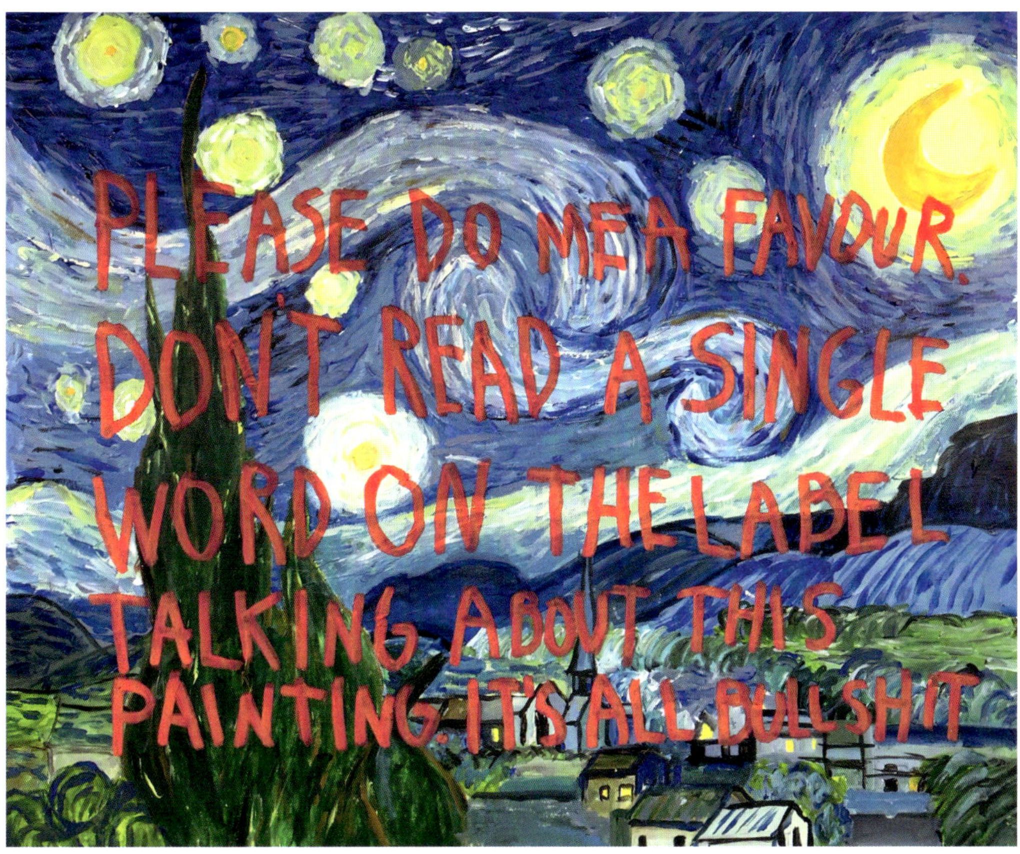

Buy a Fake Picasso,
2018
Acrylic paint on canvas,
150 x 100 cm

It's All Bullshit, 2018
Acrylic paint on canvas,
74 x 94 cm

Page 58
Scream at the Price,
2018
Acrylic paint on canvas,
200 x 150 cm

Page 59
CB posing in front
of *Scream at the Price*
while in the making
in Istanbul, 2018

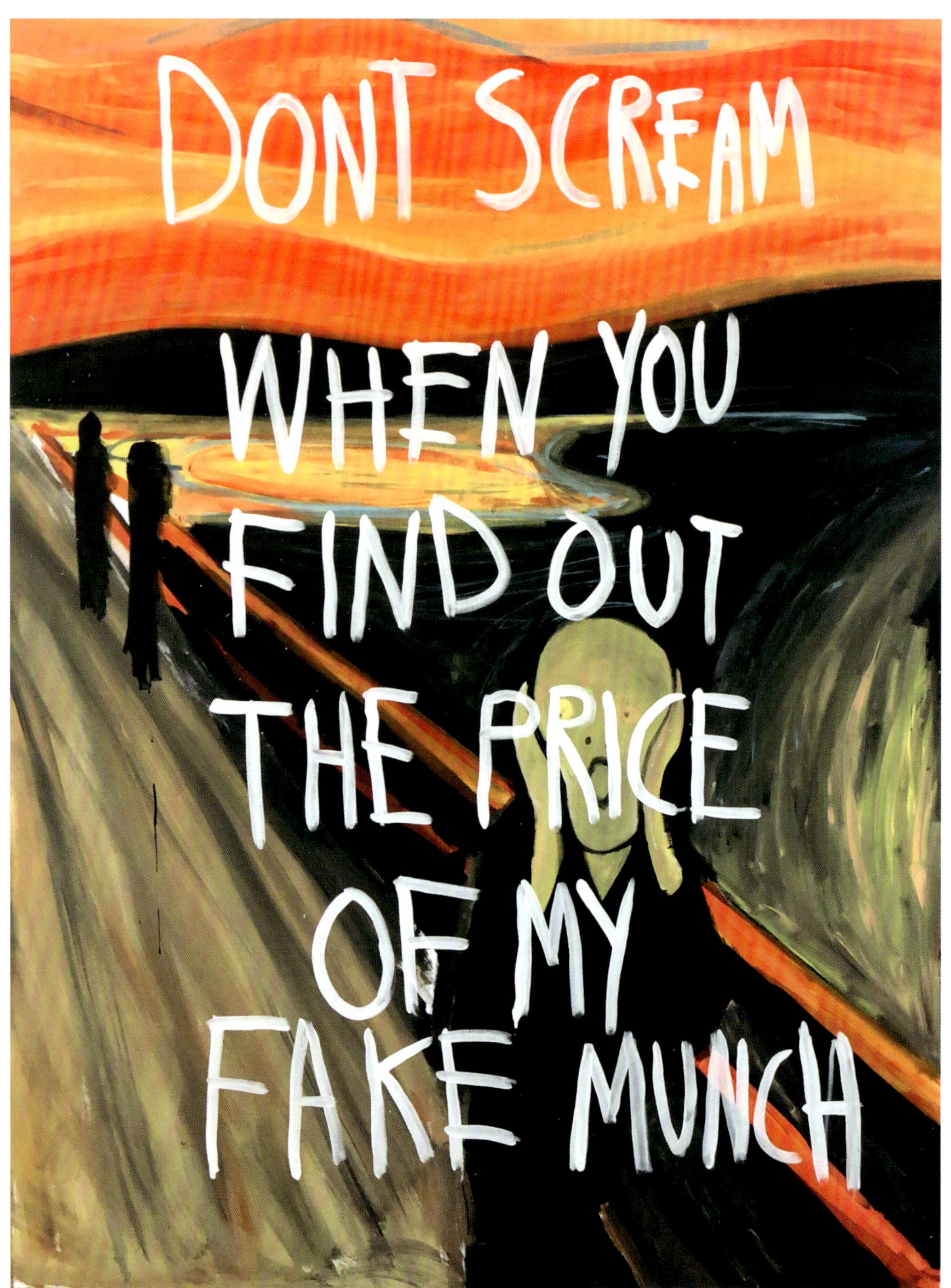

DON'T SCREAM
WHEN YOU FIND OUT THE PRICE OF MY FAKE MUNCH

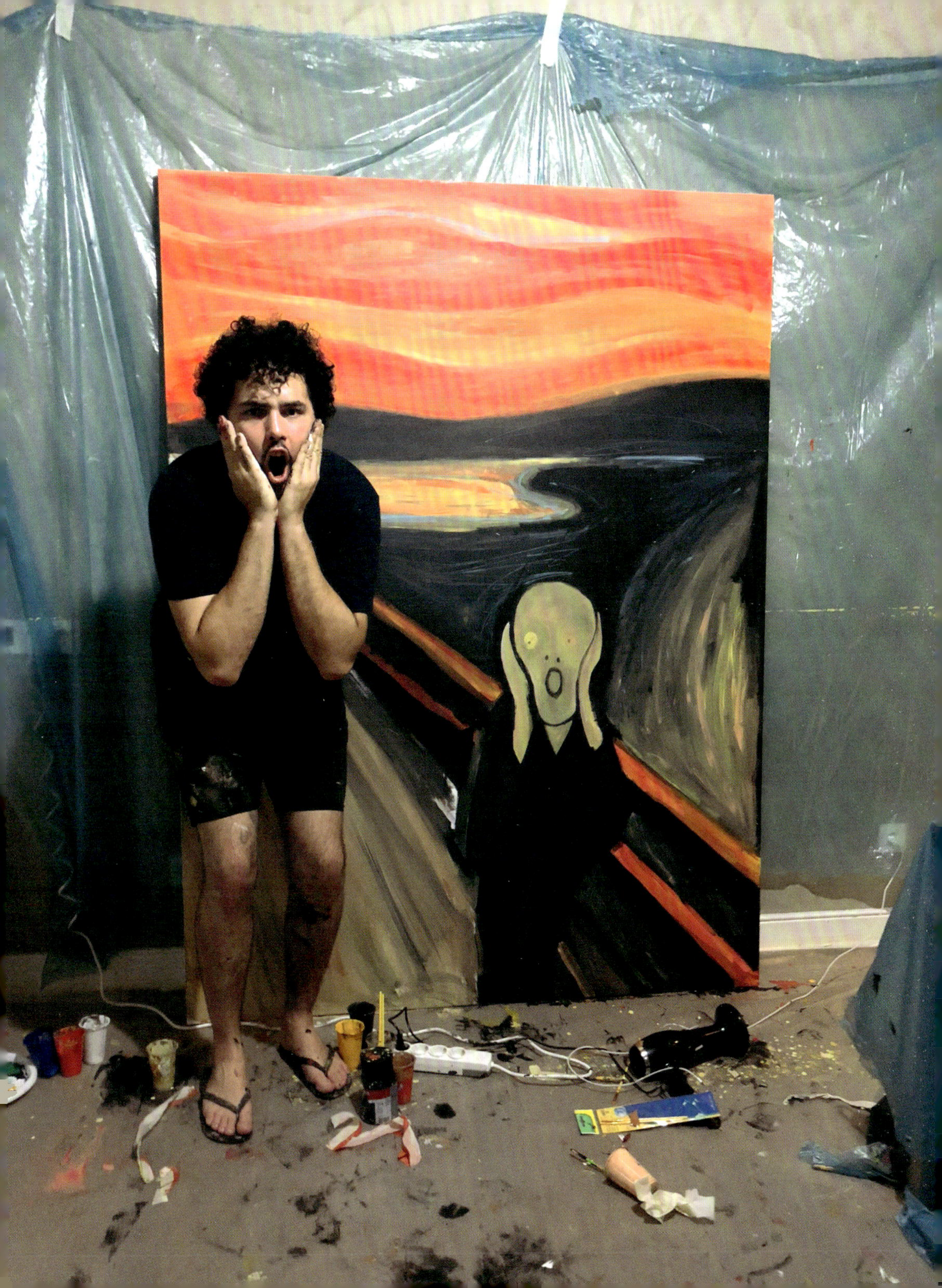

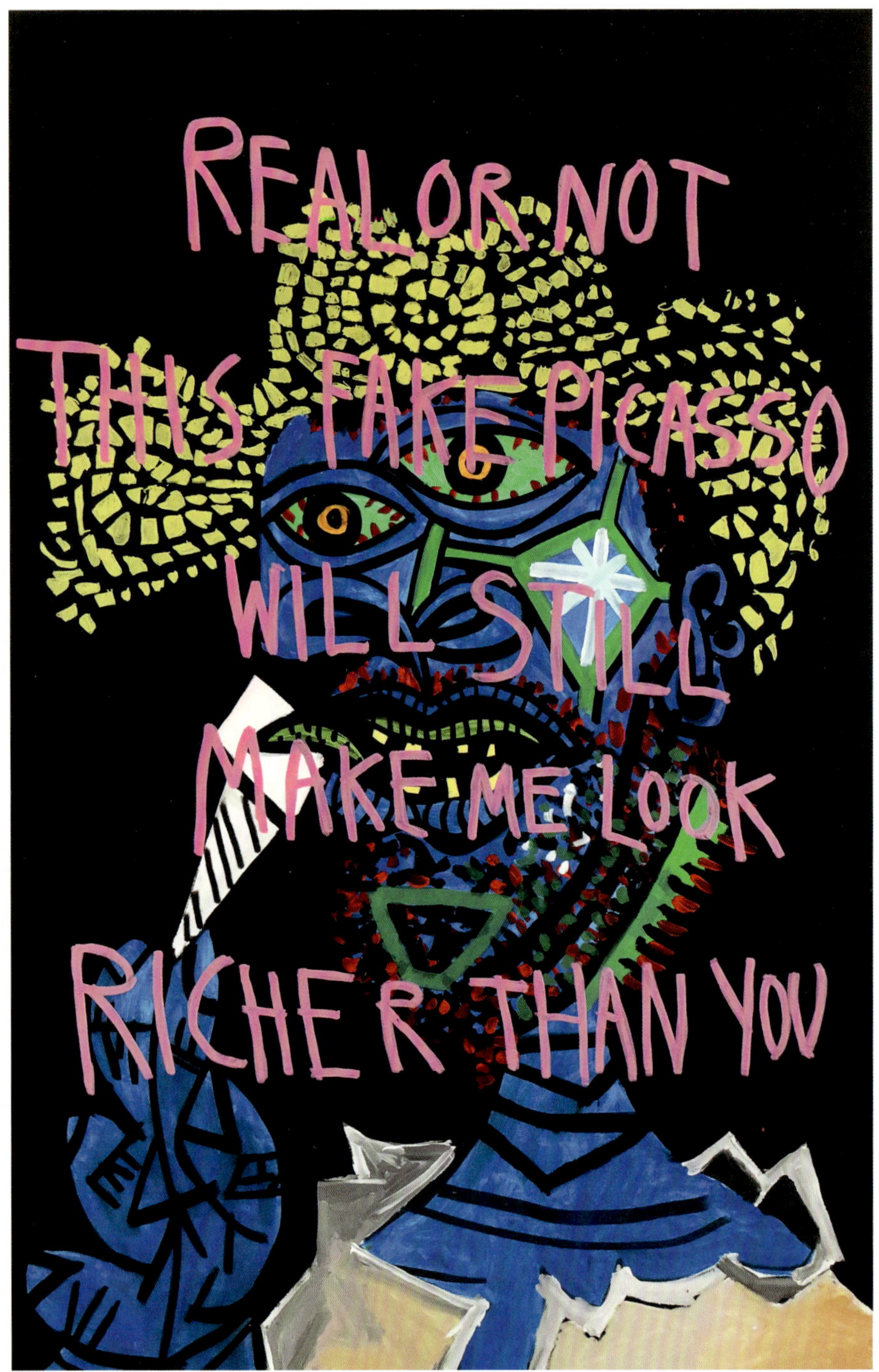

REAL OR NOT
THIS FAKE PICASSO
WILL STILL
MAKE ME LOOK
RICHER THAN YOU

Richer Picasso, 2018
Acrylic paint on canvas,
140 x 90 cm

Picasso Please, 2018
Acrylic paint on canvas,
100 x 80 cm

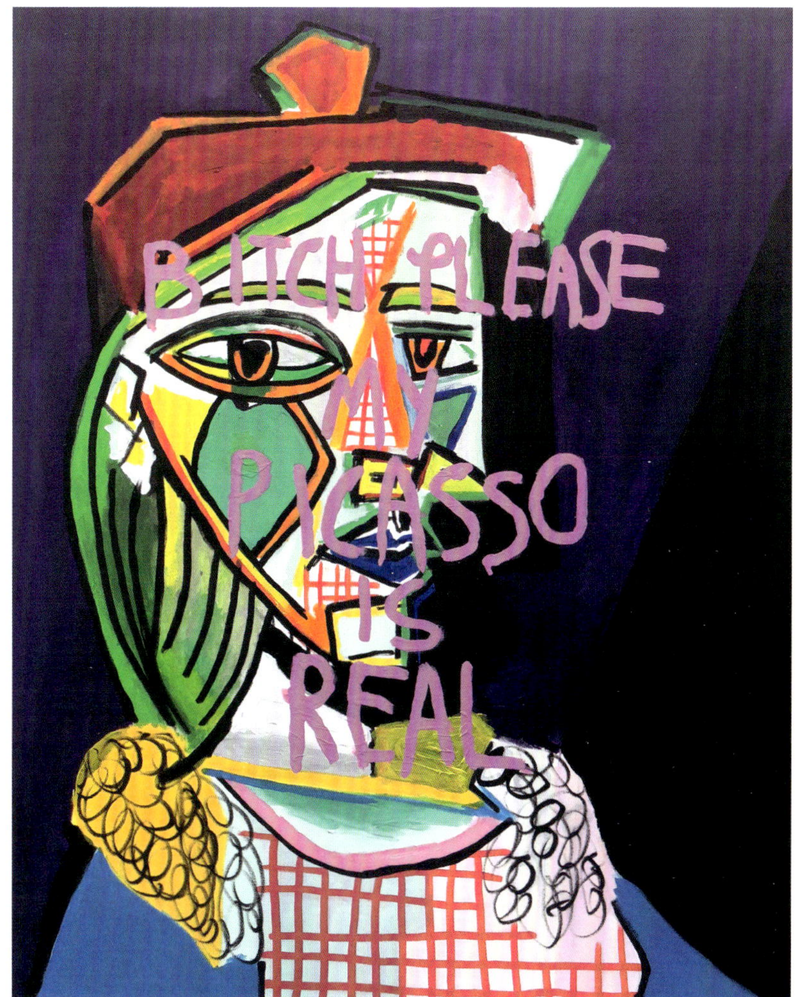

MAKE

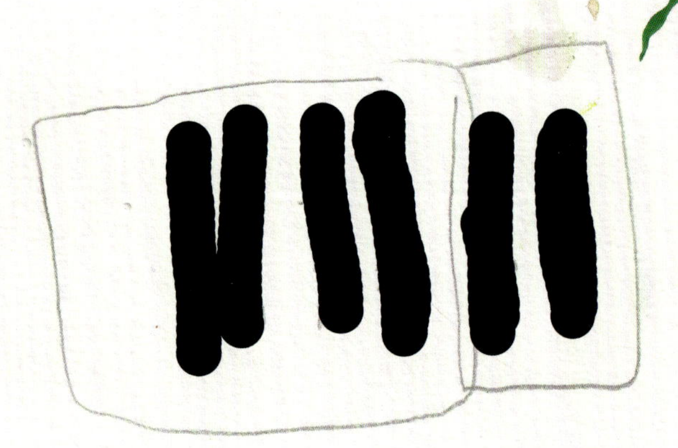

STEPS ON
MAKING MONEY AS
A COLLECTOR 101

1

3 EASY
STEPS ON
MAKING MONEY AS
AN ART COLLECTOR
1- INVEST ON A LIVING ARTIST
2- MAKE THAT ARTIST FAMOUS
3- KILL THAT ARTIST

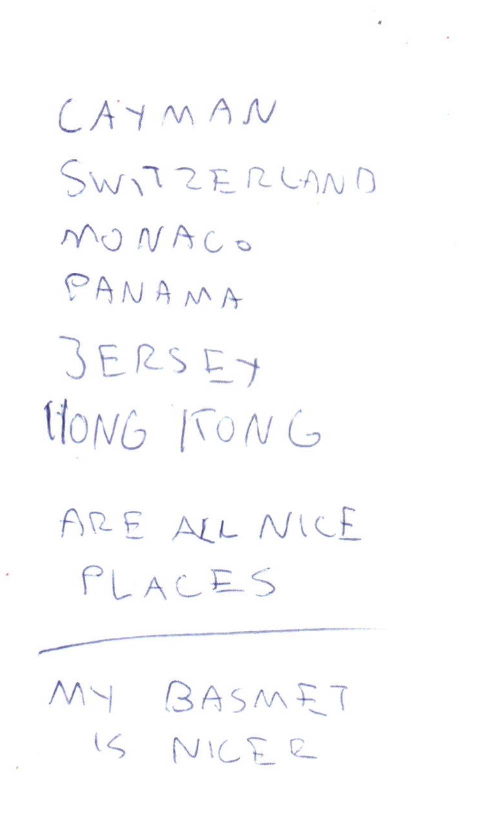

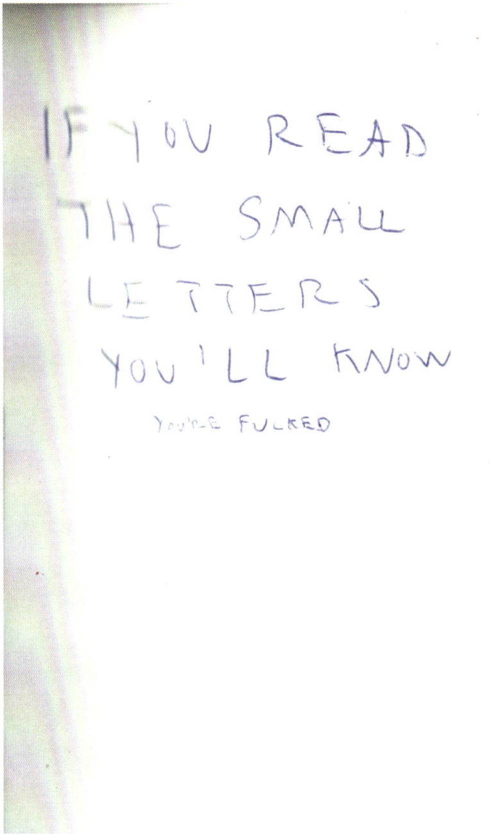

Untitled (Study), 2018
Color and lead pencils
on paper,
29.7 x 21 cm

Untitled (Study), 2018
Pen on paper,
14 x 11.5 cm

Untitled (Study), 2018
Pen on paper,
14 x 11.5 cm

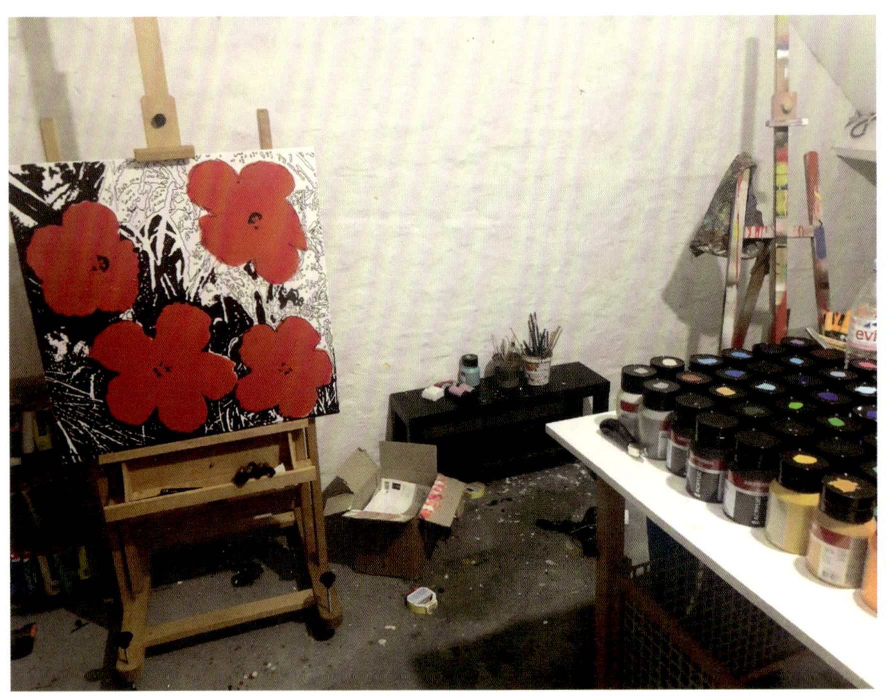

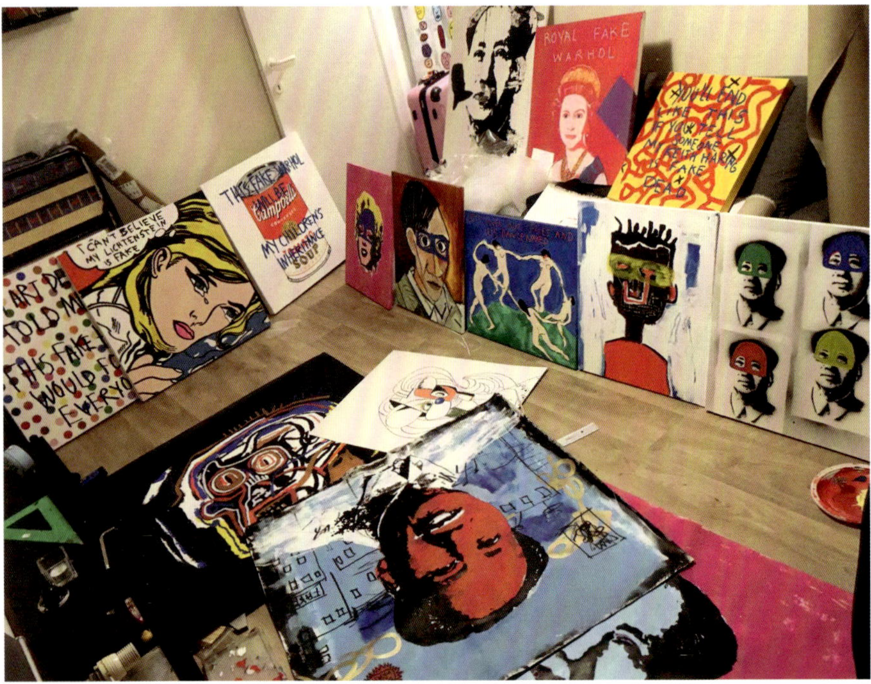
ART DE
TOLD MI
THIS FAKE
WOULD F
EVERYO
I CAN'T BELIEVE
MY LICHTENSTEIN
IS FAKE
THIS FAKE WARHOL
WILL BE
Campbell's
MY CHILDREN'S
INHERITANCE
SOUP
ROYAL FAKE
WARHOL
YOU'LL END
LIKE THIS
IF YOU SELL
MY SOMEONE
IS WITH HARING
FAKE
DEAD

Studio, *No Refunds*
in the making, 2018

Studio, 2018

Untitled (Study), 2018
Pen and oil markers on
paper, 29.7 x 21 cm

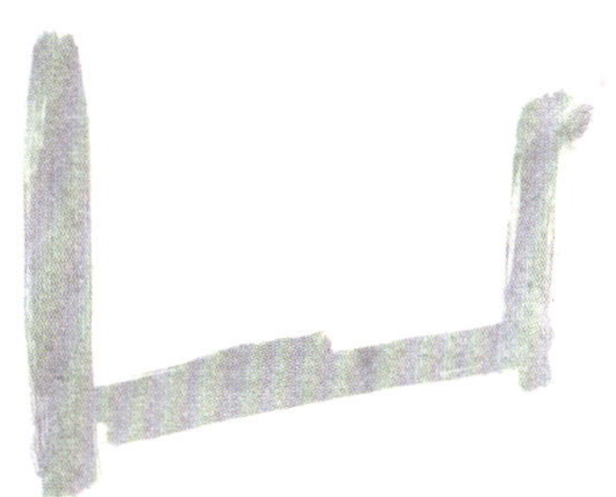

*I Obviously Don't Know
What I'm Saying and
Take You as a Fool*,
2019
Acrylic paint on linen
mounted on aluminum
frame, six pieces each
measuring 50 x 40 cm

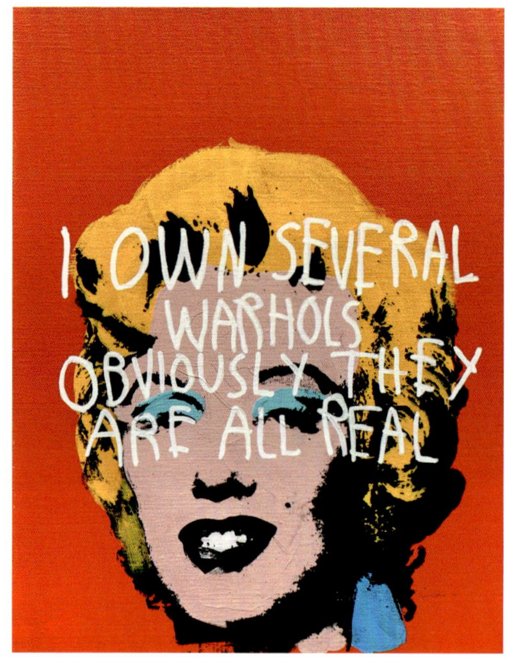

I OWN SEVERAL
WARHOLS
OBVIOUSLY THEY
ARE ALL REAL

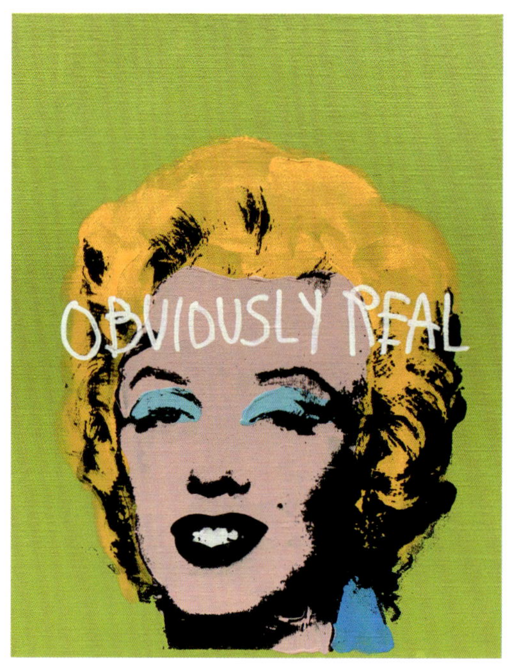

OBVIOUSLY REAL

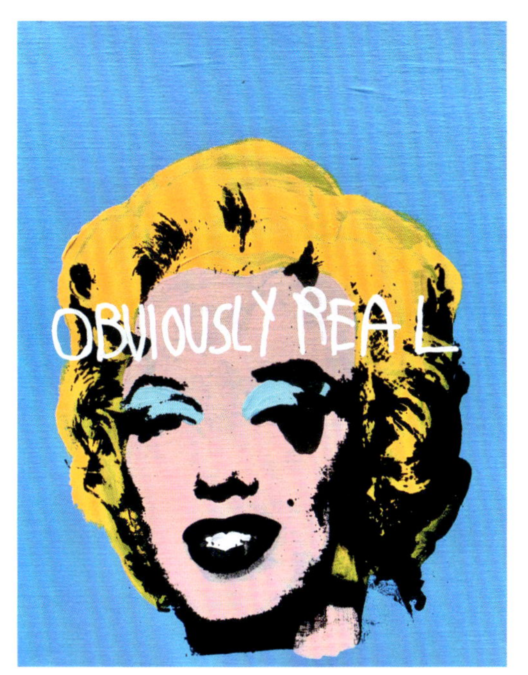
OBVIOUSLY REAL
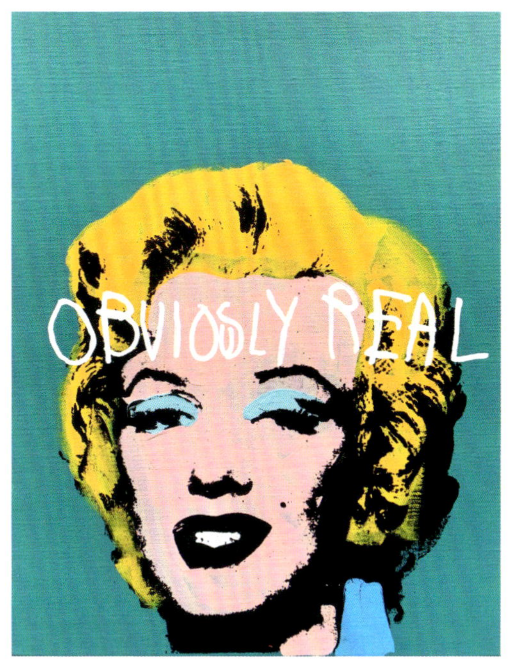
OBVIOSLY REAL
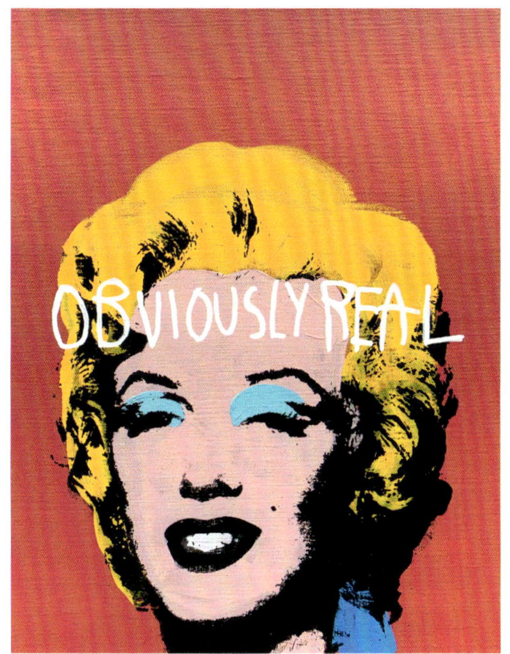
OBVIOUSLY REAL
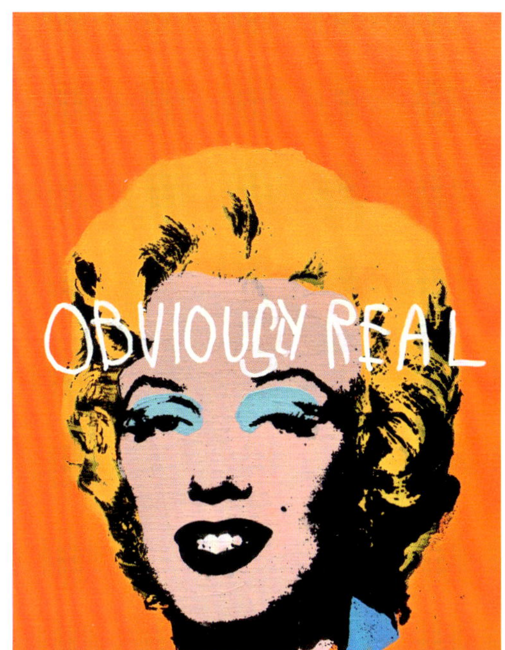
OBVIOUSLY REAL

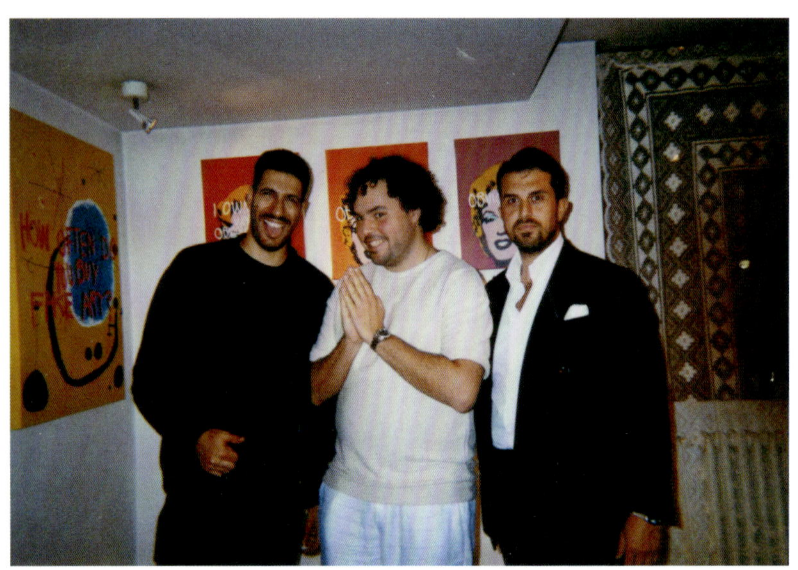

CB Hoyo, Marcello Polito, and Nicolò Stabile in Venice, 2019

Untitled (Study), 2019
Lead pencil and pen on paper,
27.9 x 21 cm

Freaky Collector, 2019
Acrylic paint on linen,
170 x 130 cm

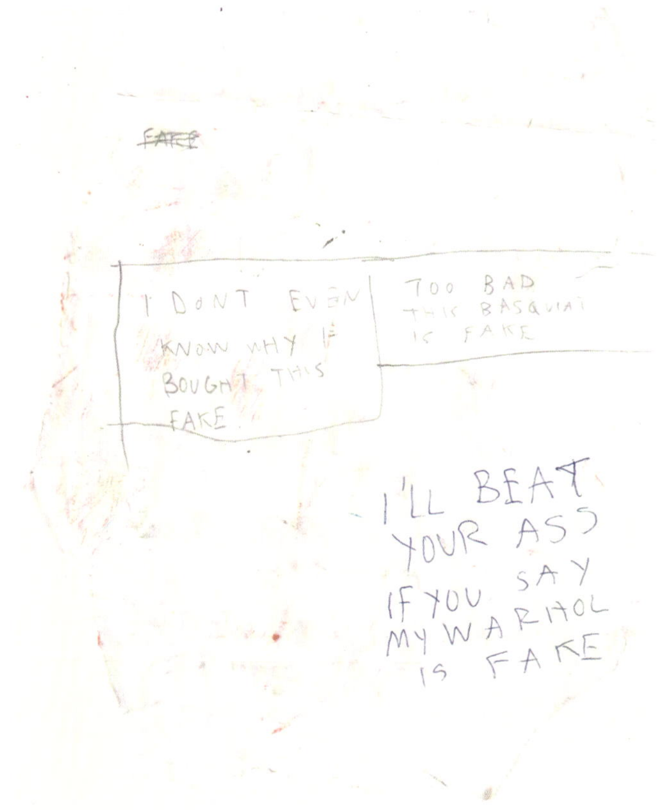

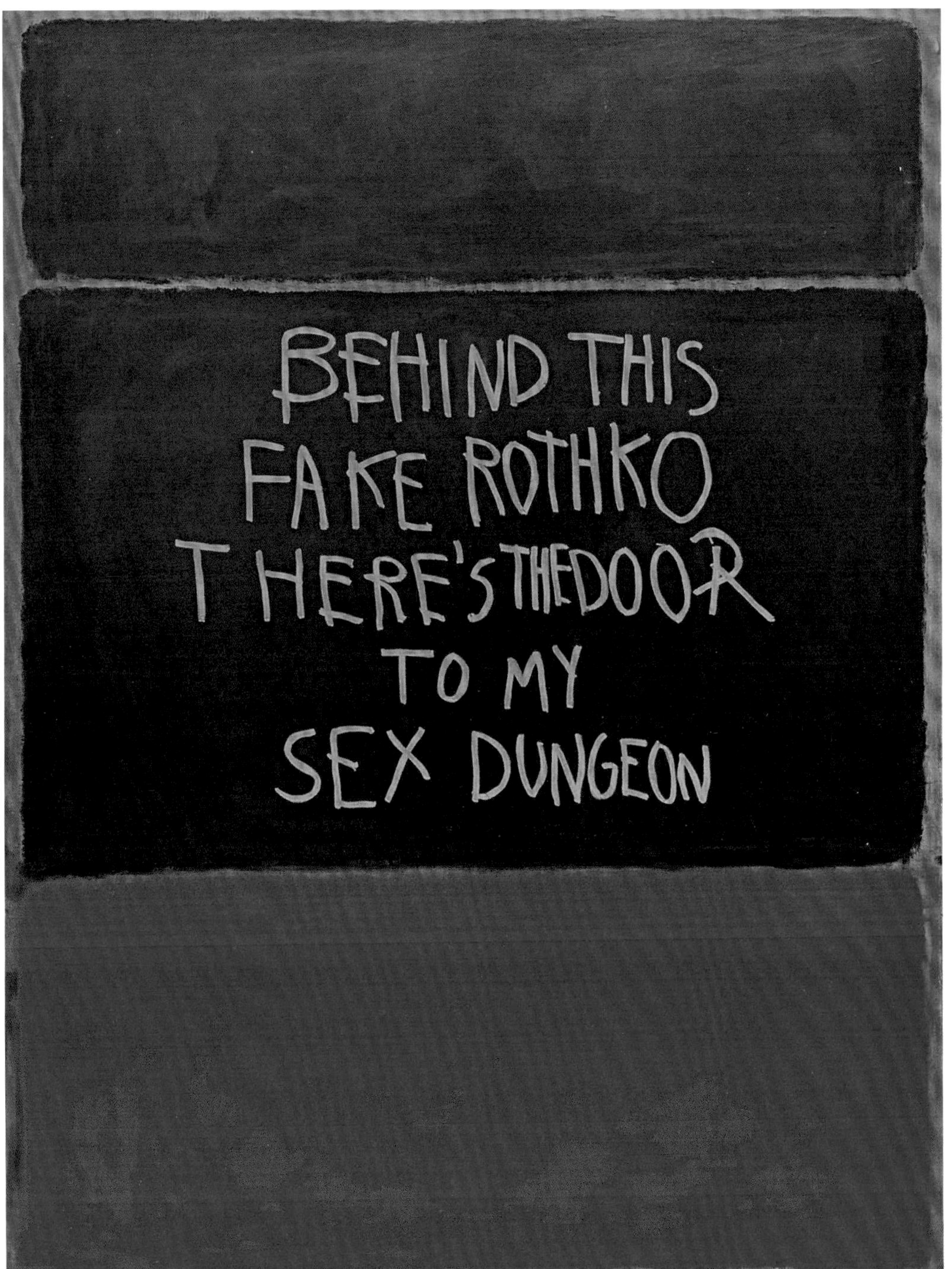

BEHIND THIS
FAKE ROTHKO
THERE'S THE DOOR
TO MY
SEX DUNGEON

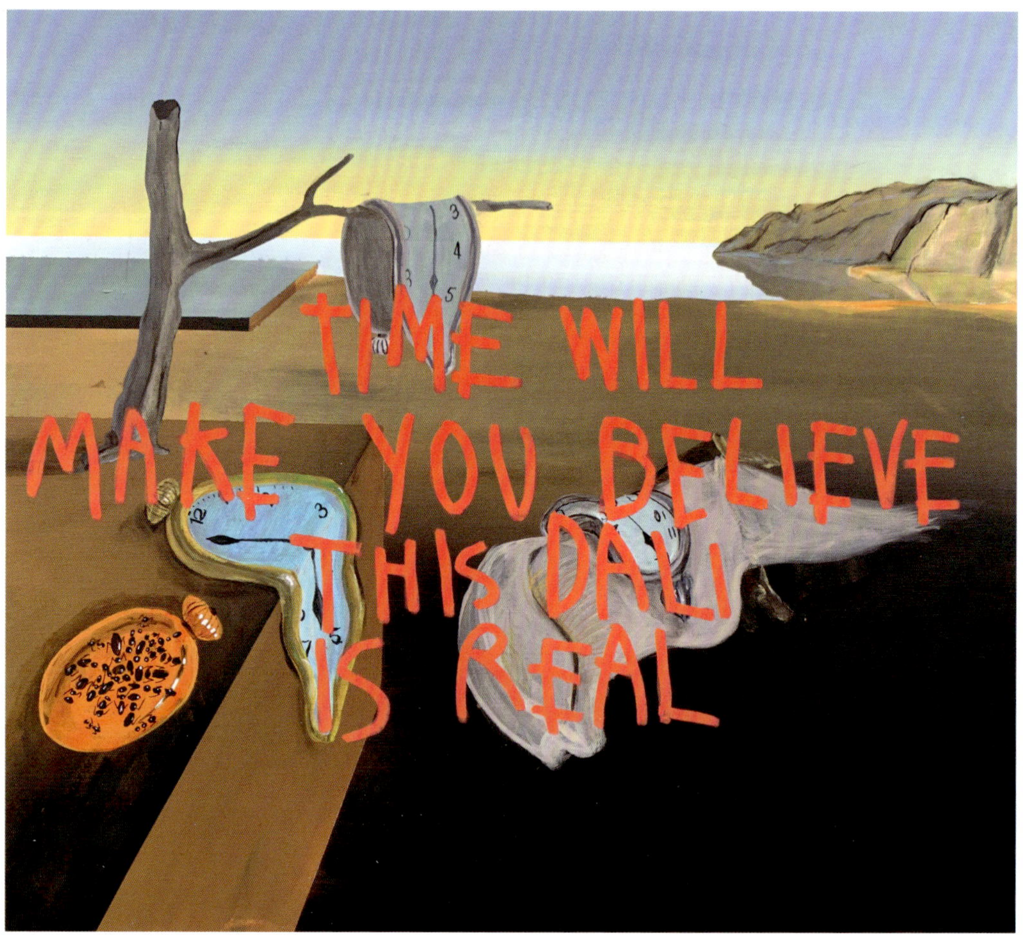

Time Will Tell, 2019
Acrylic paint on linen
mounted on aluminum
frame, 90 x 100 cm

*Van Gogh and Chill
(Van Hoe)*, 2019
Acrylic paint on linen
mounted on aluminum
frame, 100 x 120 cm

*You Have Reached the
Mailbox Of*, 2019
Acrylic on canvas,
60 x 90 cm

Pages 72–73
*I Had So Much Fun
with Pablo*, 2019
Acrylic paint on canvas,
162 x 130 cm

Studio, *I Had So Much
Fun with Pablo* in the
making, 2019

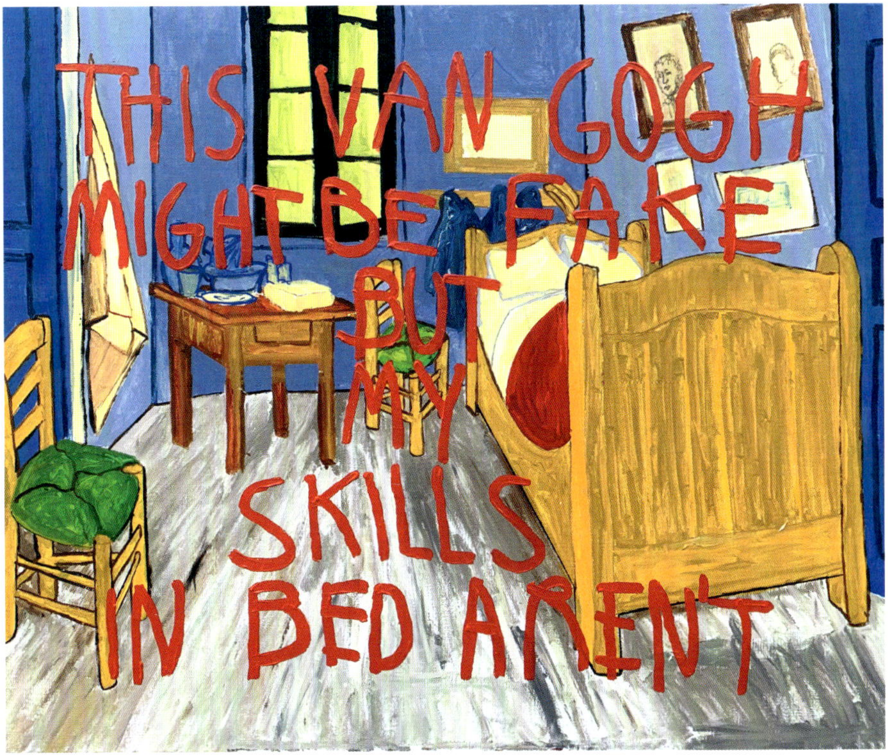

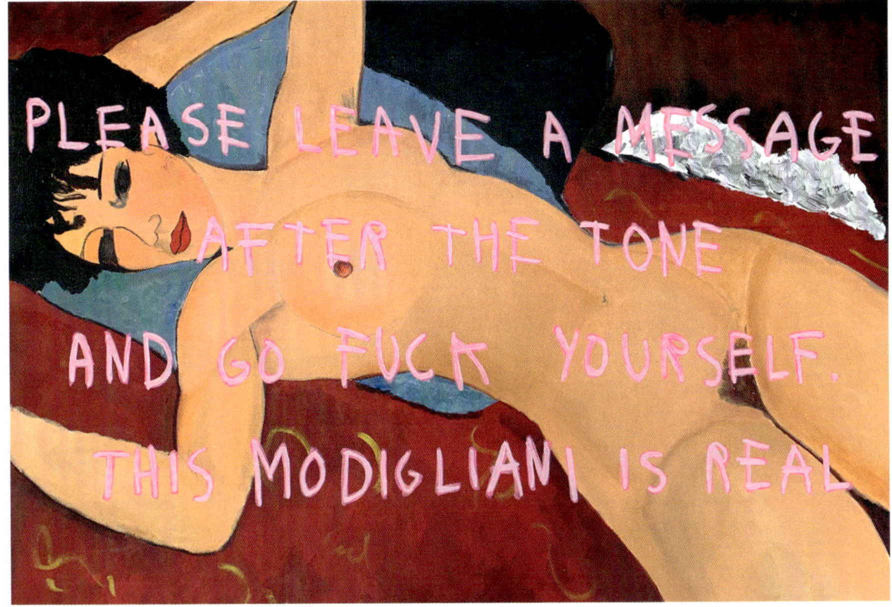
THIS VAN GOGH MIGHT BE FAKE BUT MY SKILLS IN BED AREN'T
PLEASE LEAVE A MESSAGE AFTER THE TONE AND GO FUCK YOURSELF. THIS MODIGLIANI IS REAL

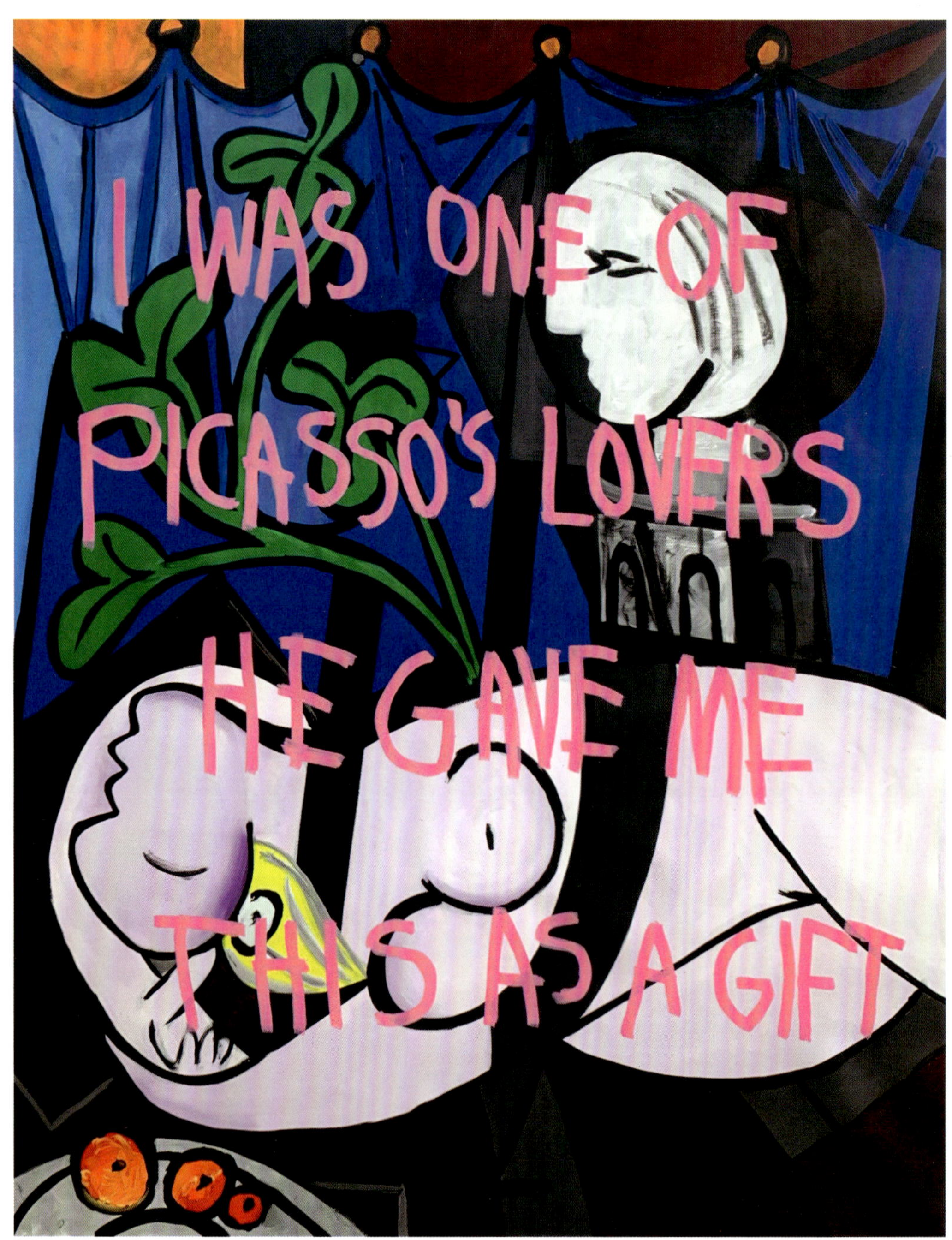

I WAS ONE OF
PICASSO'S LOVERS
HE GAVE ME
THIS AS A GIFT

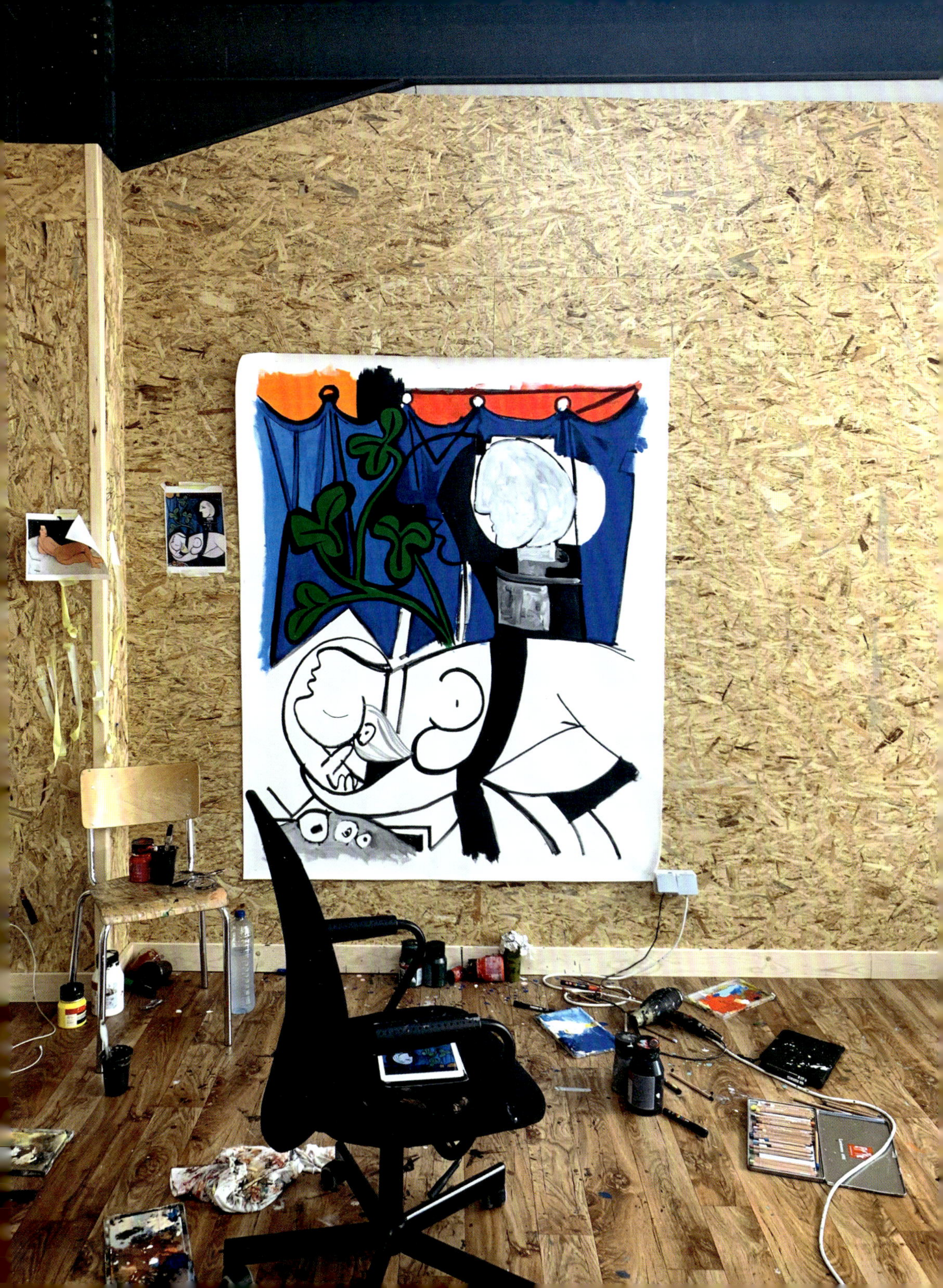

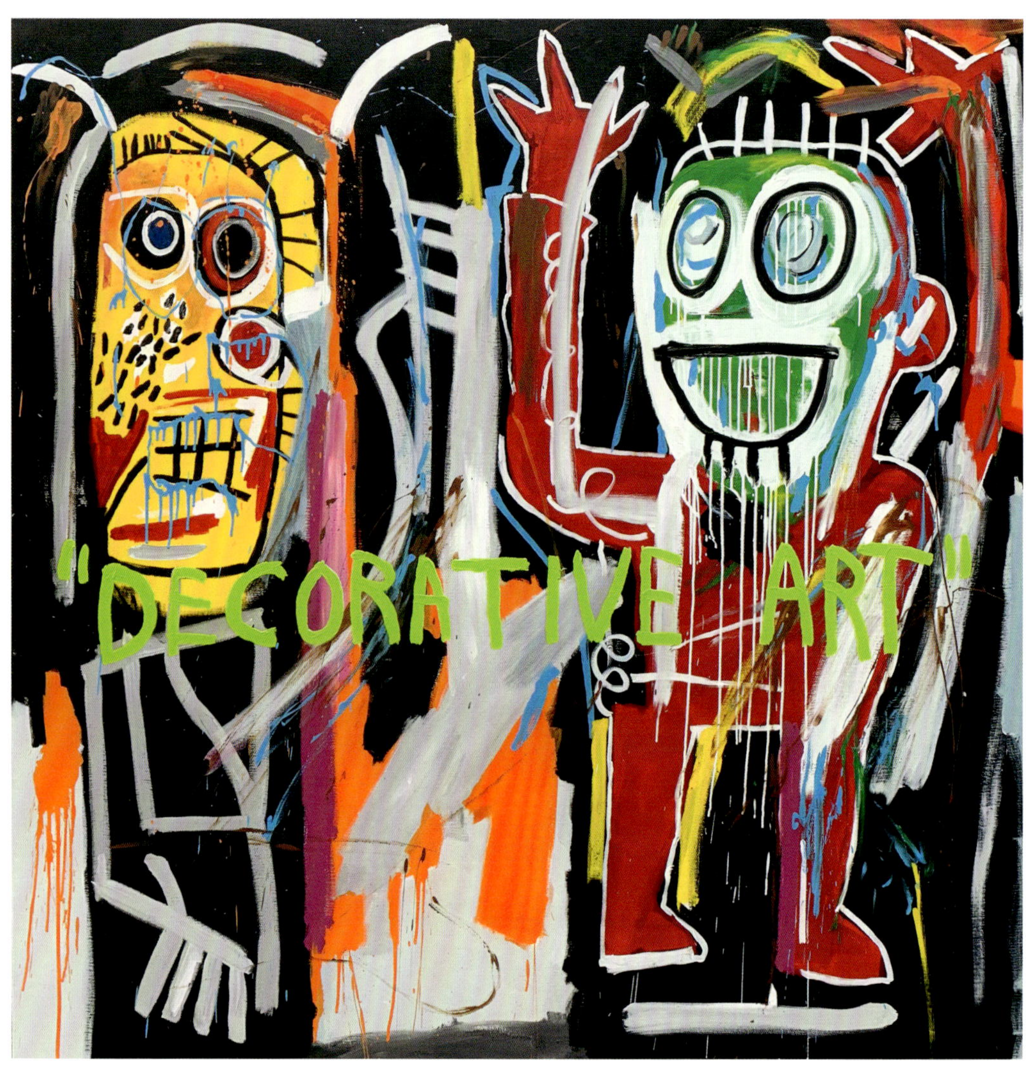

Interior Decoration,
2019
Acrylic paint on linen
mounted on aluminum
frame, 200 x 200 cm

Interior Decoration
in the studio, 2019

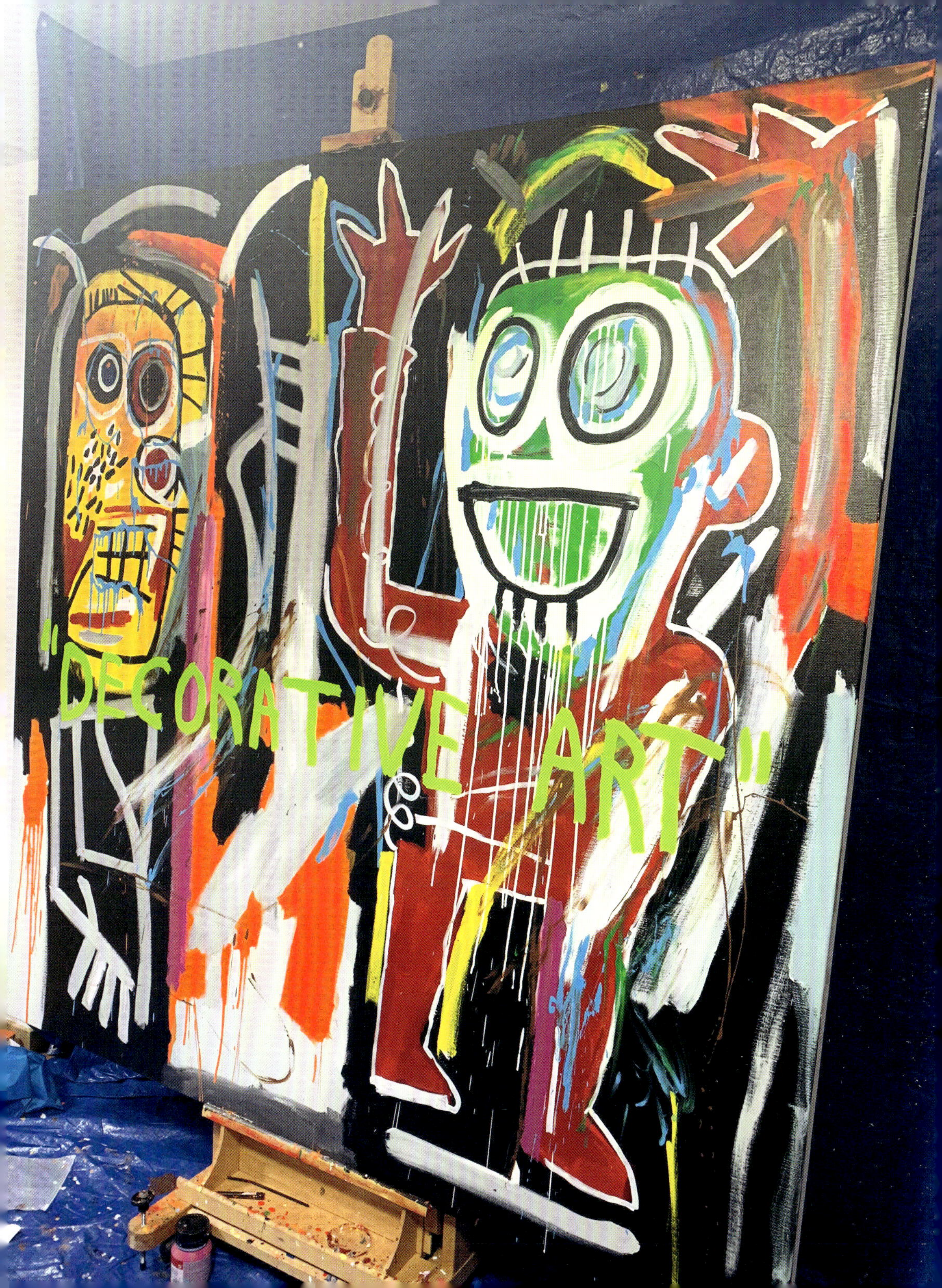

"DECORATIVE ART"

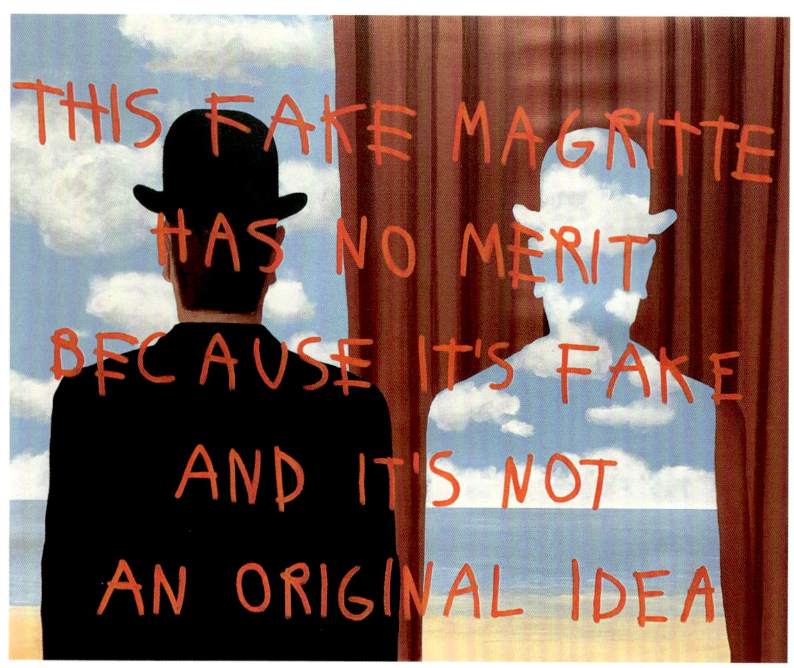

Pure Plagiarism, 2019
Acrylic paint on canvas,
80 x 100 cm

Studio, *Pure Plagiarism*
in the making, 2019

Statement, 2018–2019
Acrylic, wax crayons,
color pencils, ink, gel
medium, soluble oil on
canvas, 150 x 100 cm

Page 78
*Do You Even Know Who
Is Basquiat?*, 2019
Acrylic paint and spray
paint on linen mounted
on aluminum frame,
180 x 120 cm

Page 79
Fuck Your Sensitivity,
2019
Acrylic paint on linen,
150 x 120 cm

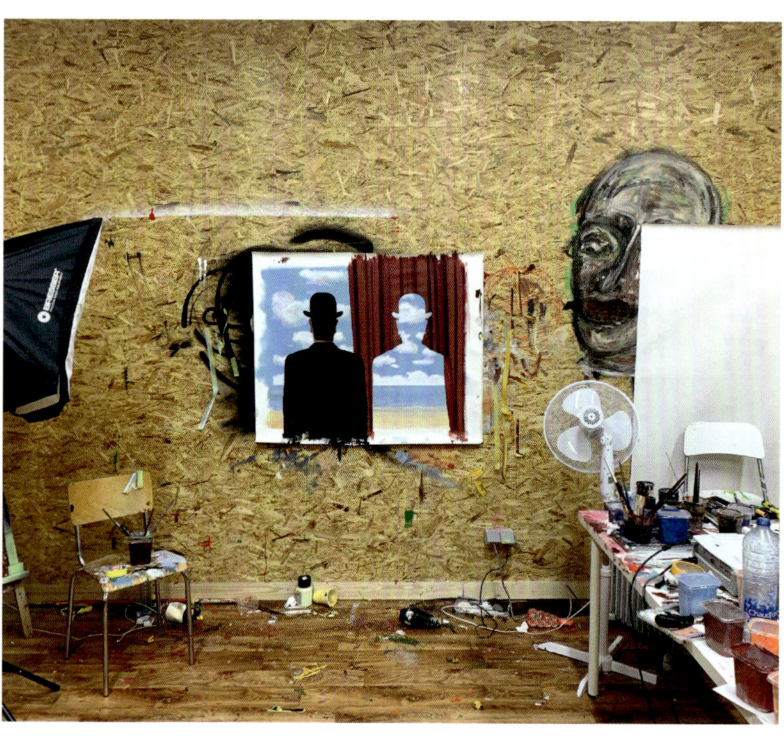

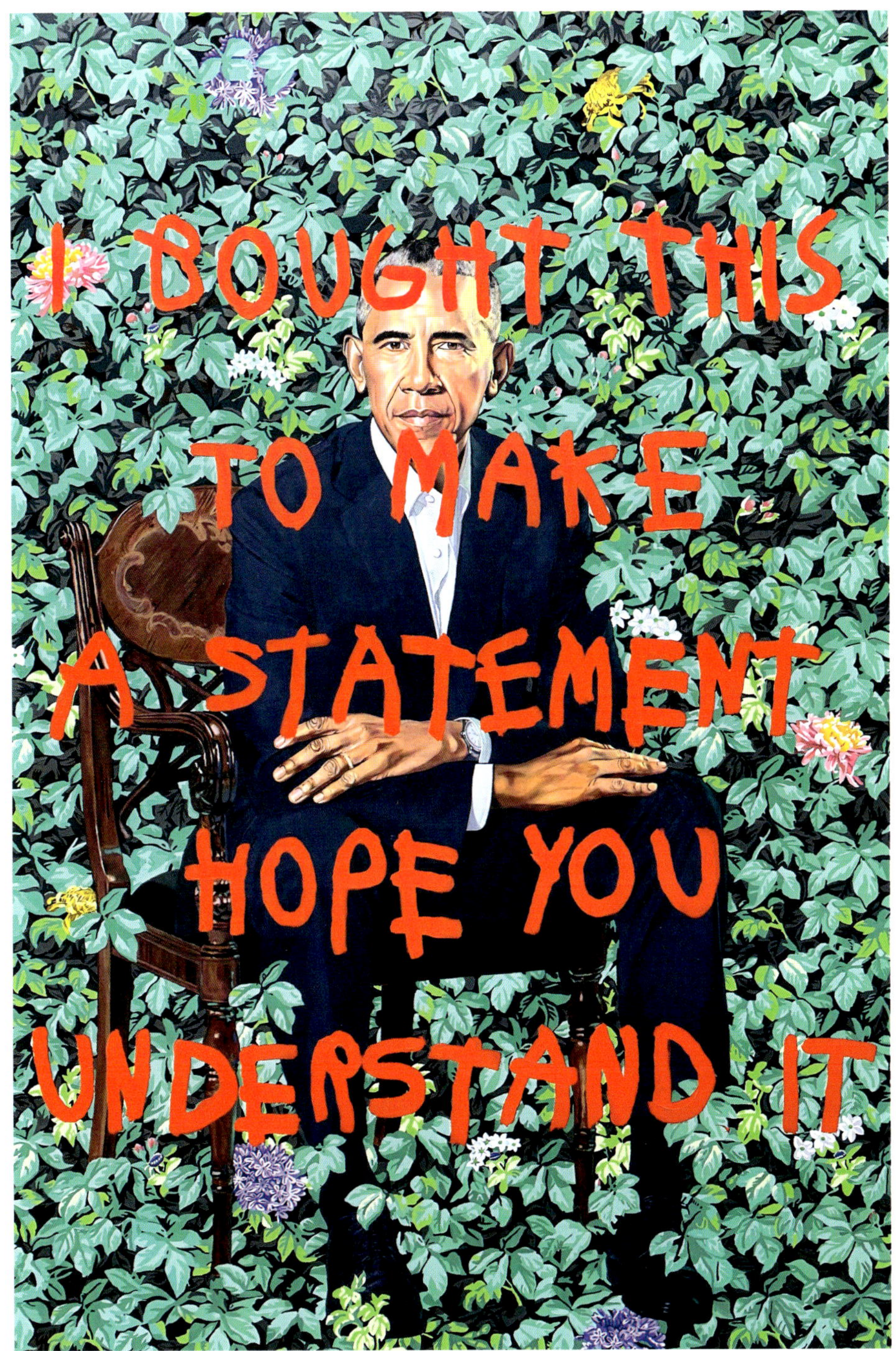

I BOUGHT THIS
TO MAKE
A STATEMENT
HOPE YOU
UNDERSTAND IT

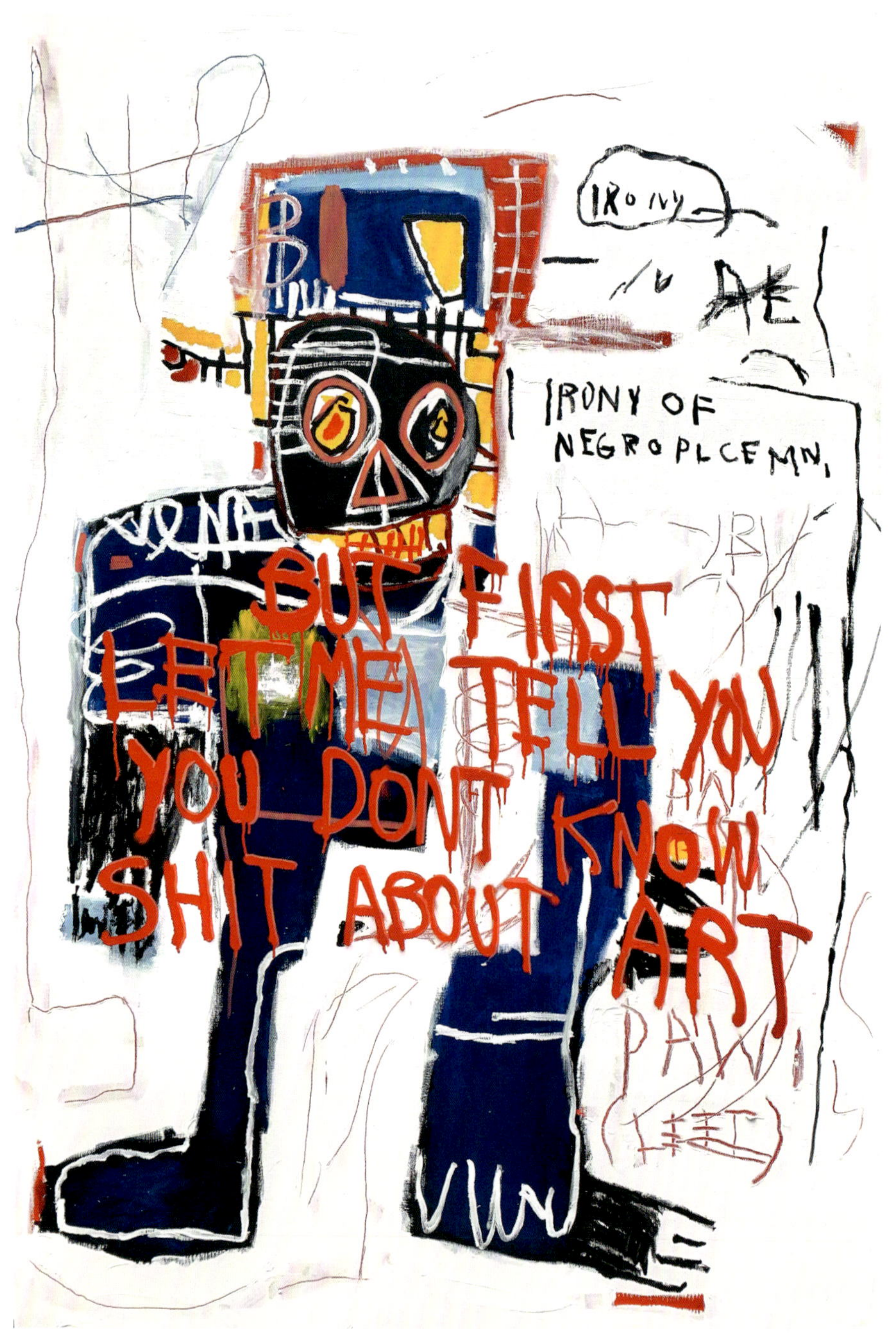
IRONY
IRONY OF
NEGRO PLCEMN,
BUT FIRST
LET ME TELL YOU
YOU DON'T KNOW
SHIT ABOUT ART
PAW

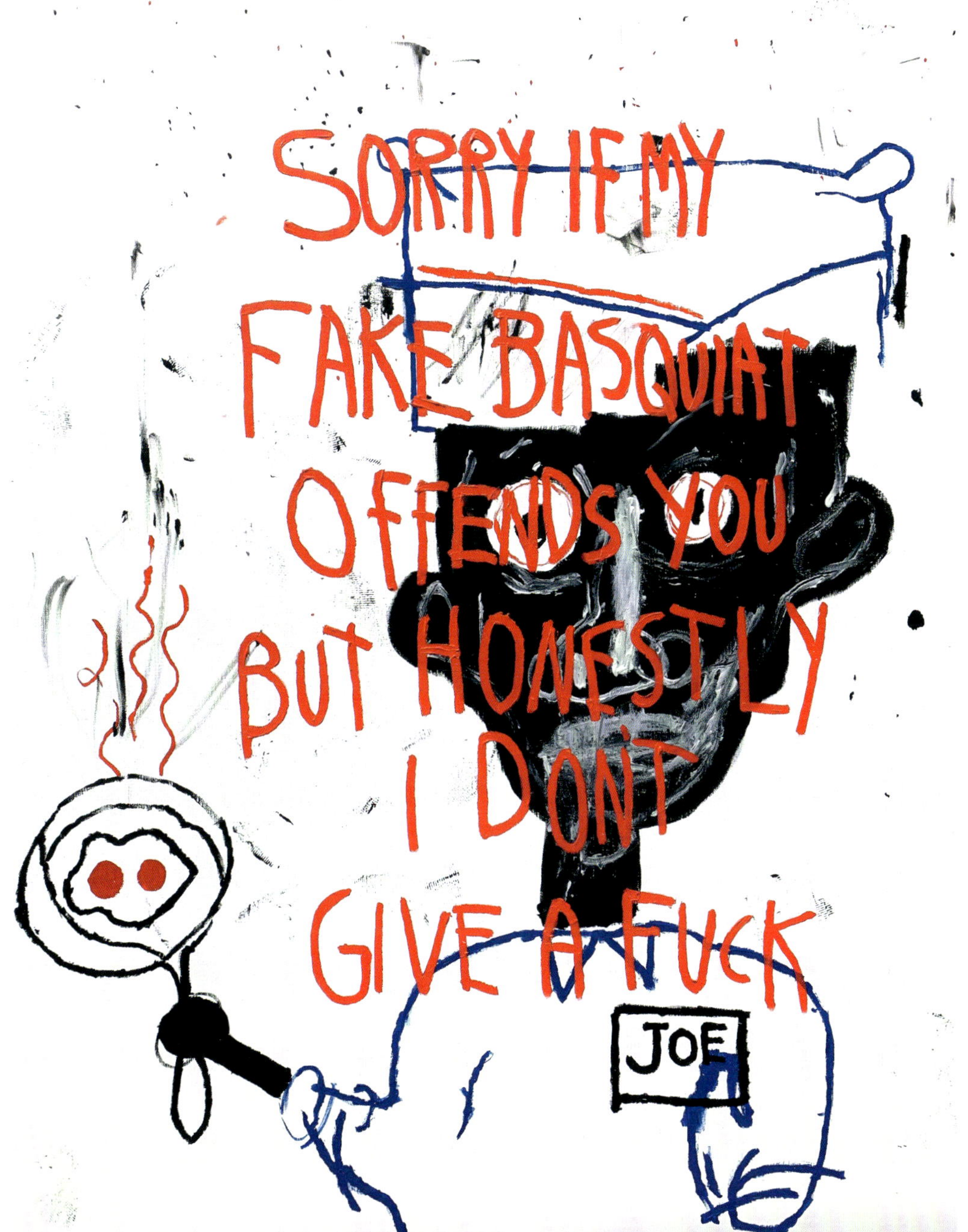

SORRY IF MY
FAKE BASQUIAT
OFFENDS YOU
BUT HONESTLY
I DON'T
GIVE A FUCK
JOE

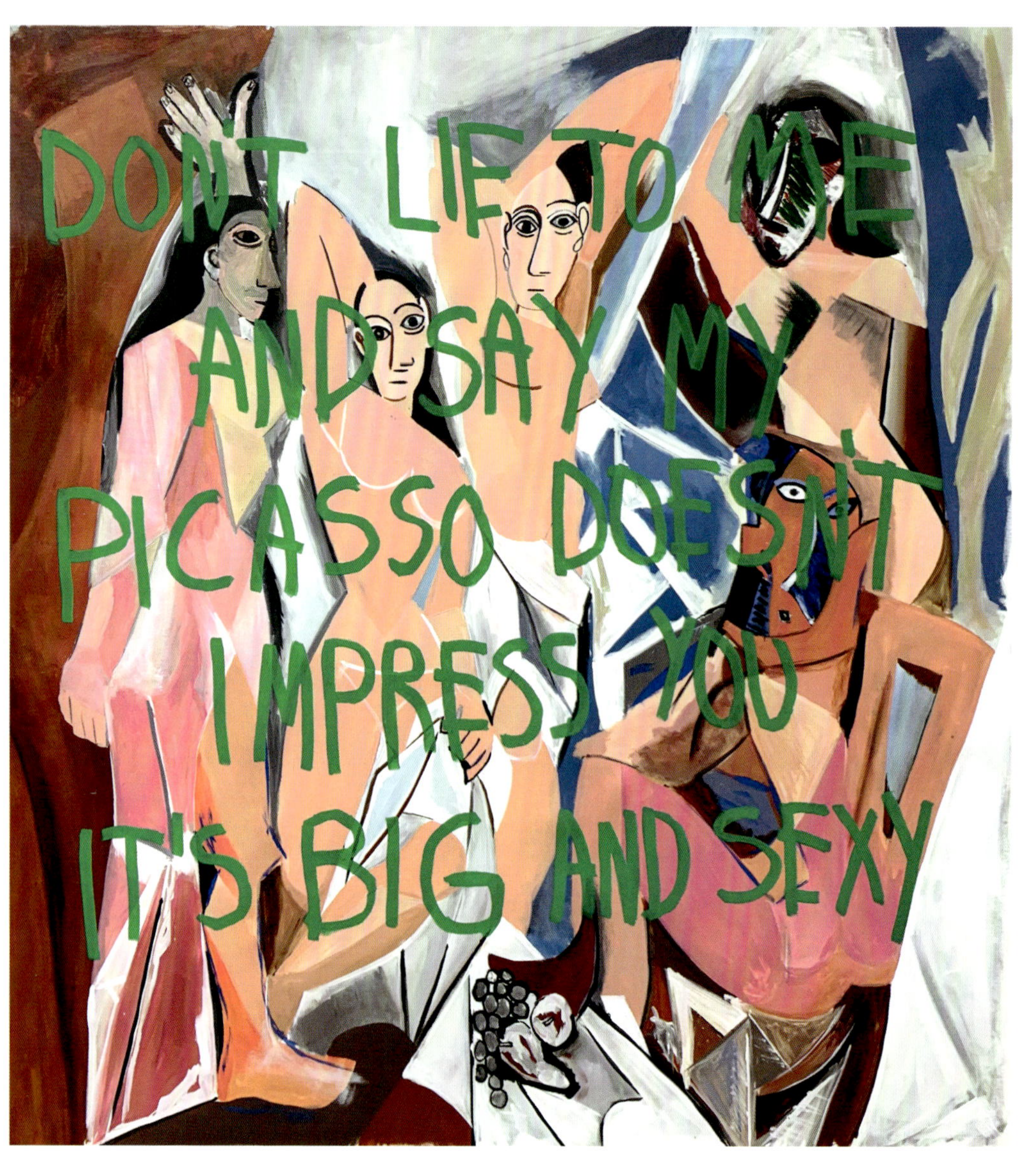

You Know You Like Them Big, 2019
Acrylic on canvas,
150 x 140 cm

Studio, 2019

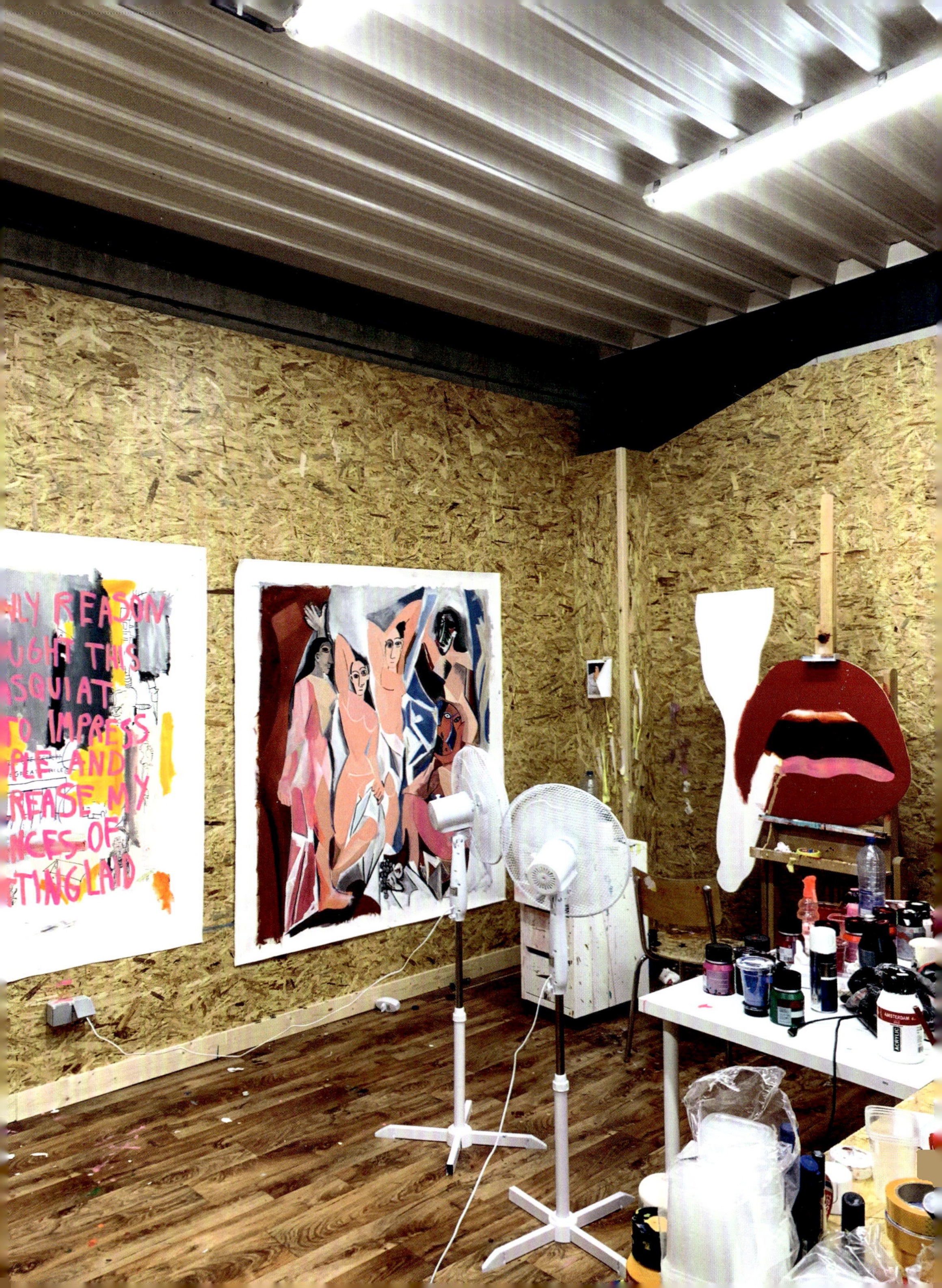

NLY REASON
UGHT THIS
SQUIAT
TO IMPRESS
PLE AND
REASE MY
NCES OF
TING LAID

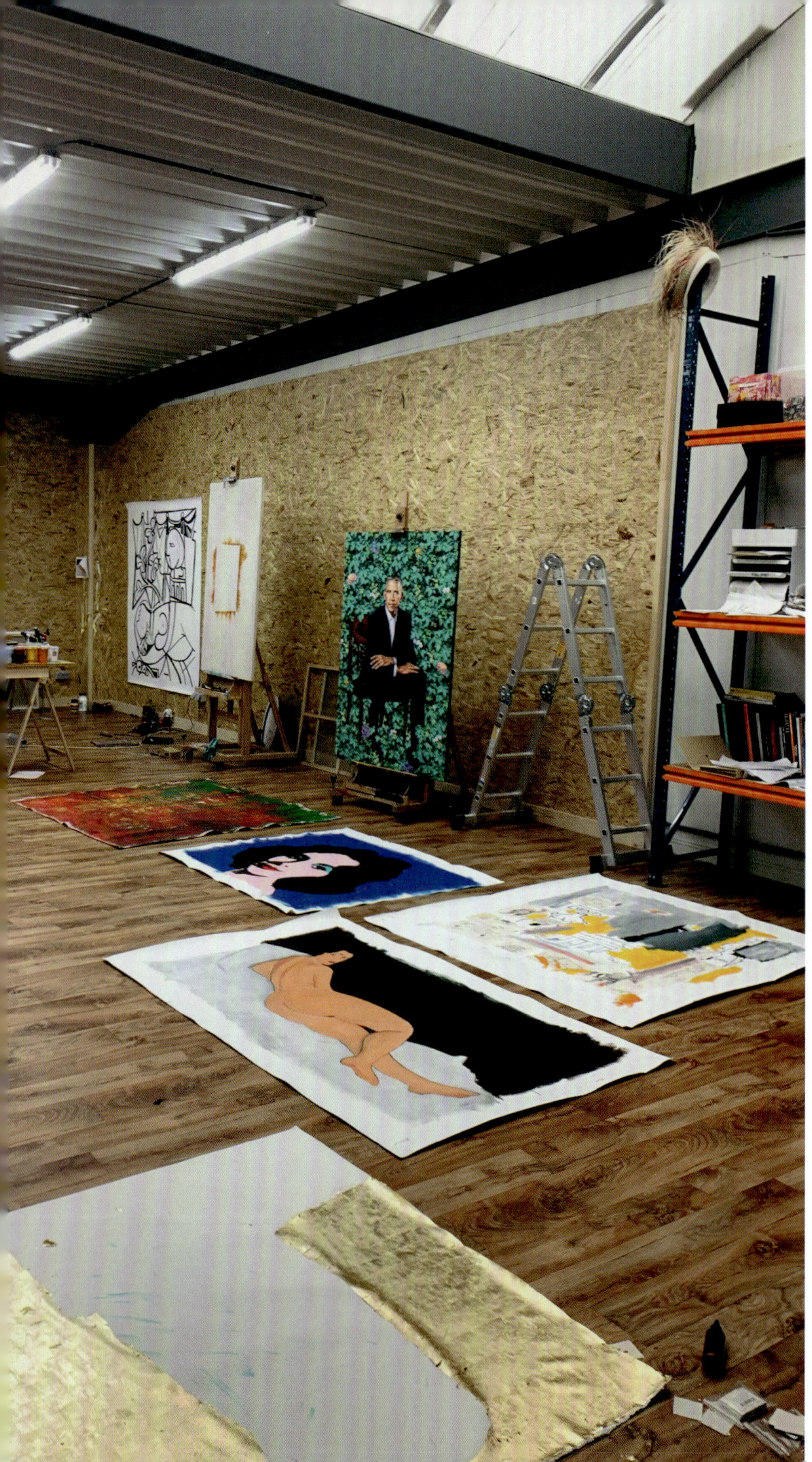

Studio, 2019

Too Provocative, 2019
Acrylic paint on canvas,
89.5 x 146.7 cm

Studio, *Too Provocative*
in the making, 2019

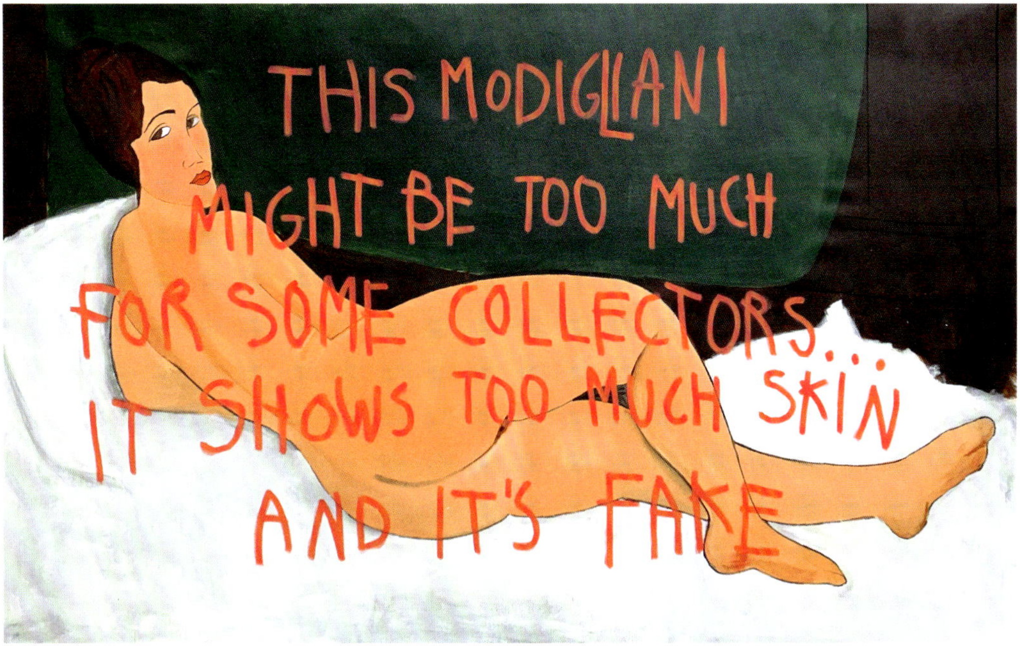

THIS MODIGLIANI
MIGHT BE TOO MUCH
FOR SOME COLLECTORS...
IT SHOWS TOO MUCH SKIN
AND IT'S FAKE

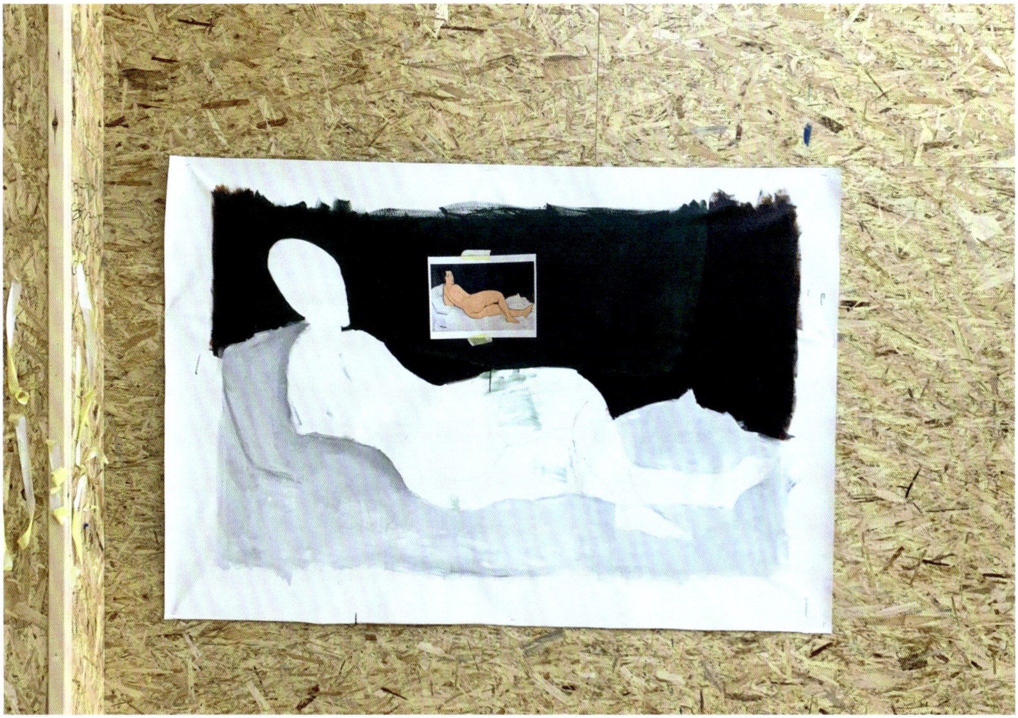

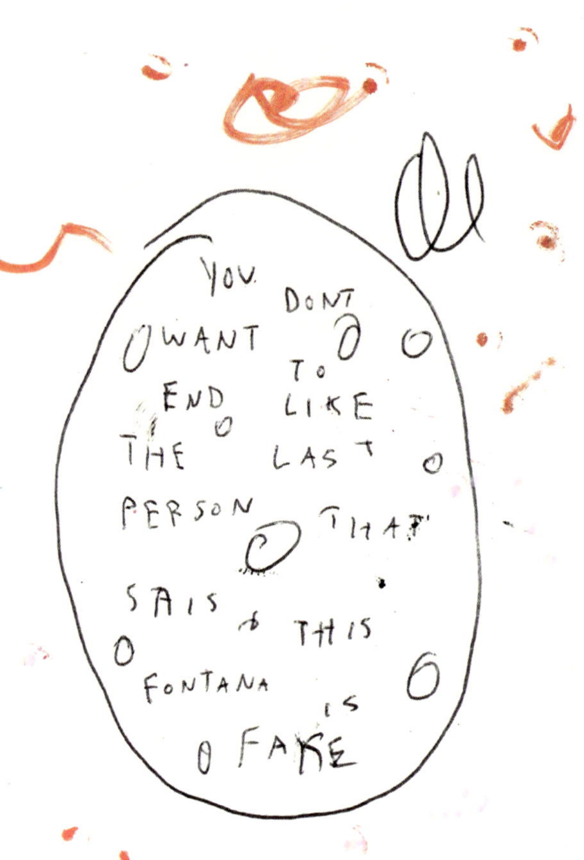

Study for *End Up Like Fontana*, 2019
Pen on paper,
15 x 10 cm

End Up Like Fontana,
2019
Acrylic on canvas,
120 x 82 cm

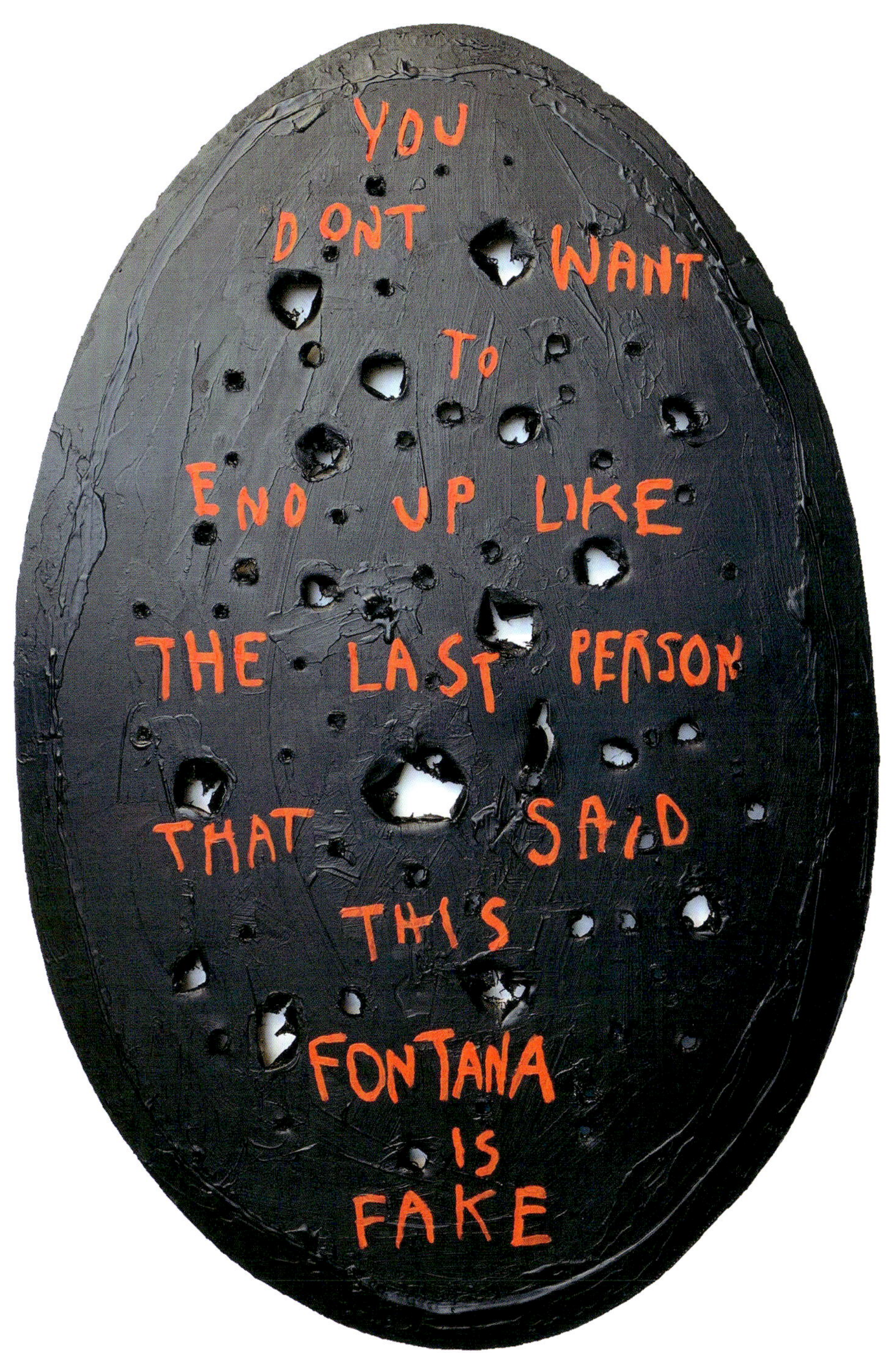

YOU
DONT WANT
TO
ENO UP LIKE
THE LAST PERSON
THAT SAID
THIS
FONTANA
IS
FAKE

THE ART WORLD
IS FILLED WITH SCAMERS,
CROOKS, SOCIOPATHS, EGOMANIACS,

AVANT-GARDE, MY ASS! THIS FAKE PICASSO IS BULLSHIT

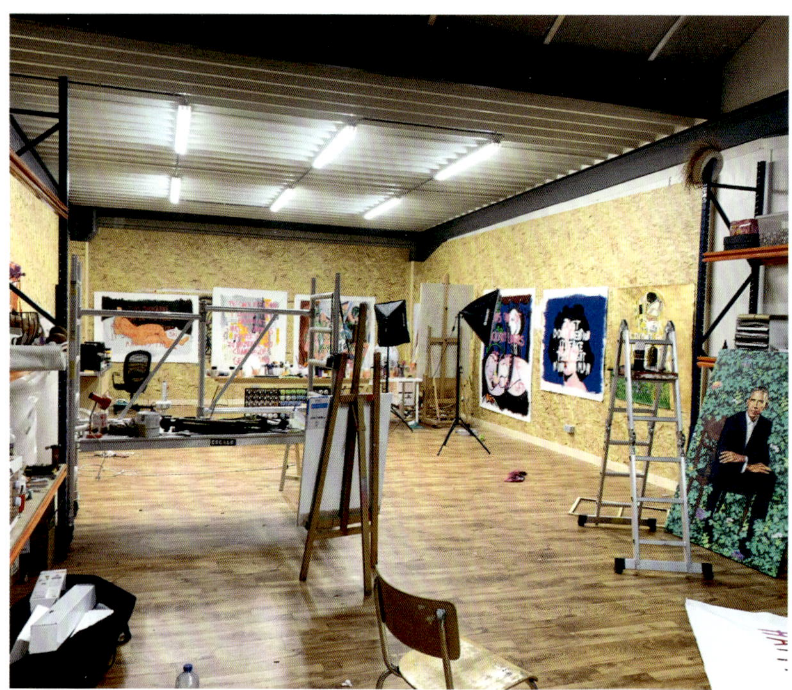

Studio, 2019

Studio, *Elaborated Plan* in the making, 2019

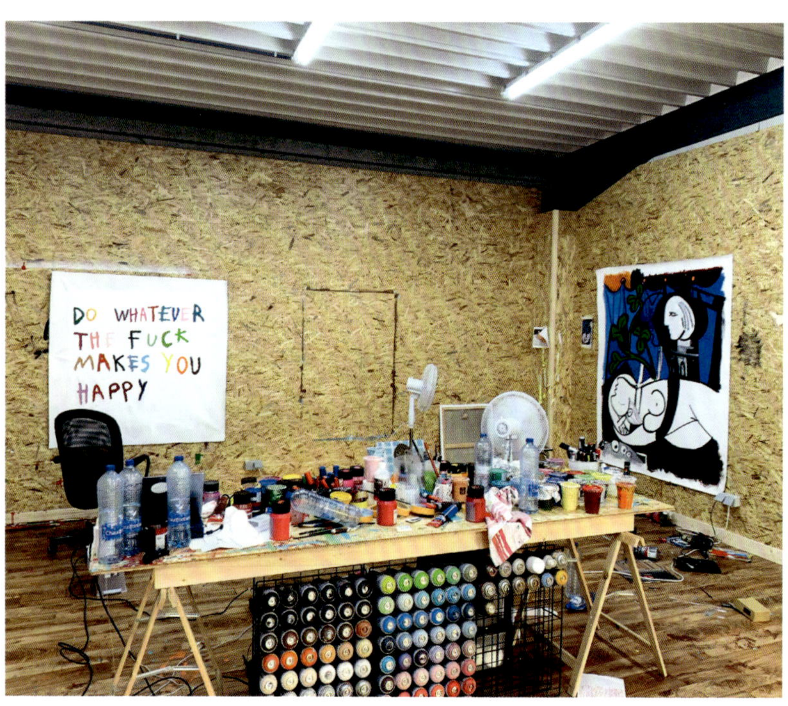

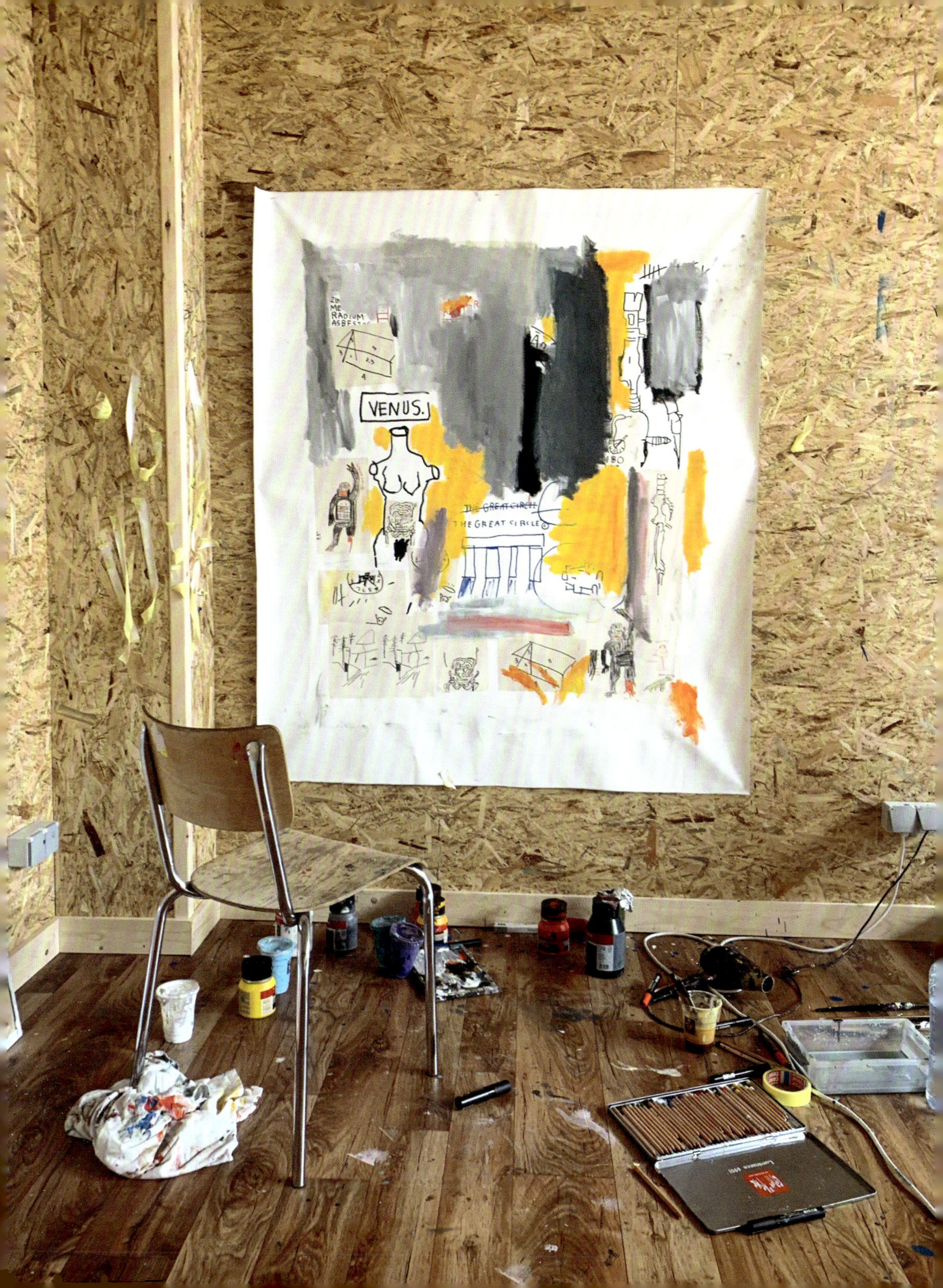

ZIP
ME
RADIUM
ASBESTOS
VENUS.
THE GREAT CIRCLE
THE GREAT CIRCLE

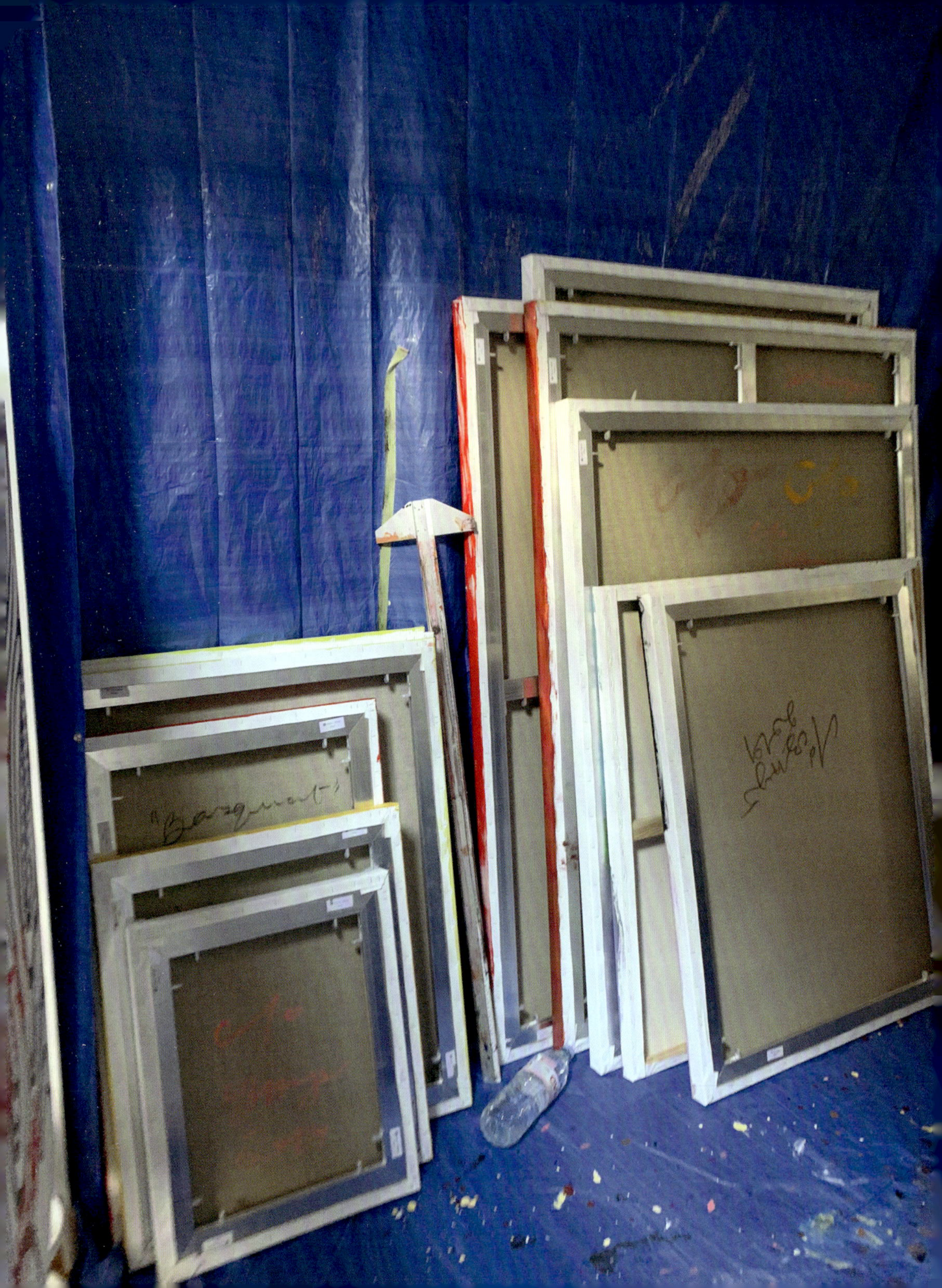
"Basquiat

Studio, 2019

Studio Self-Portrait,
2019
Fujifilm Instax Colorfilm
Glossy, 8.6 x 10.8 cm

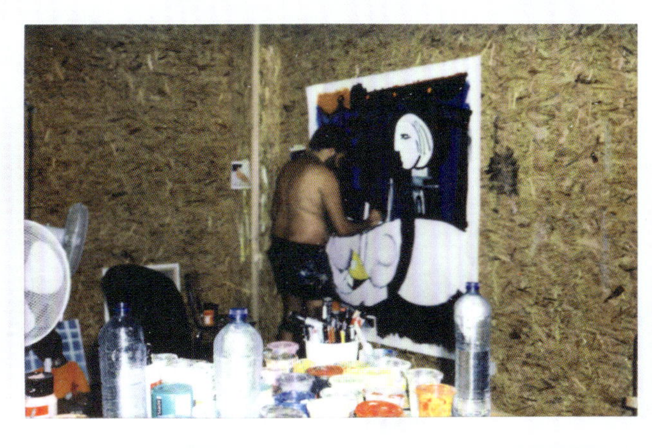

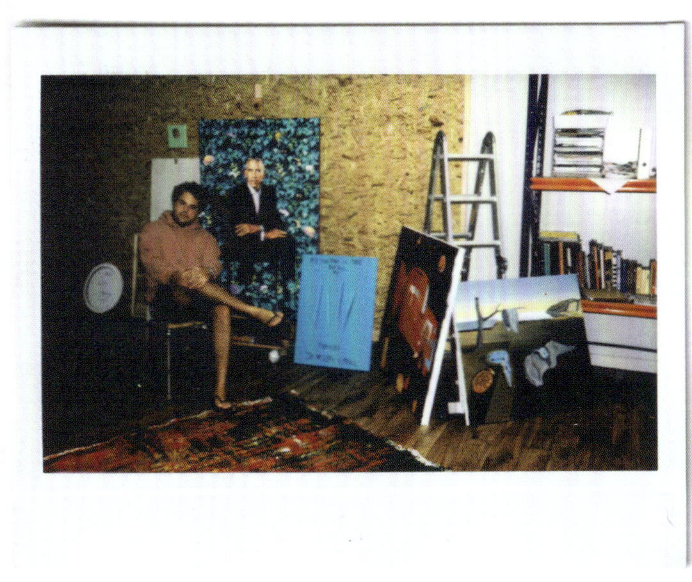

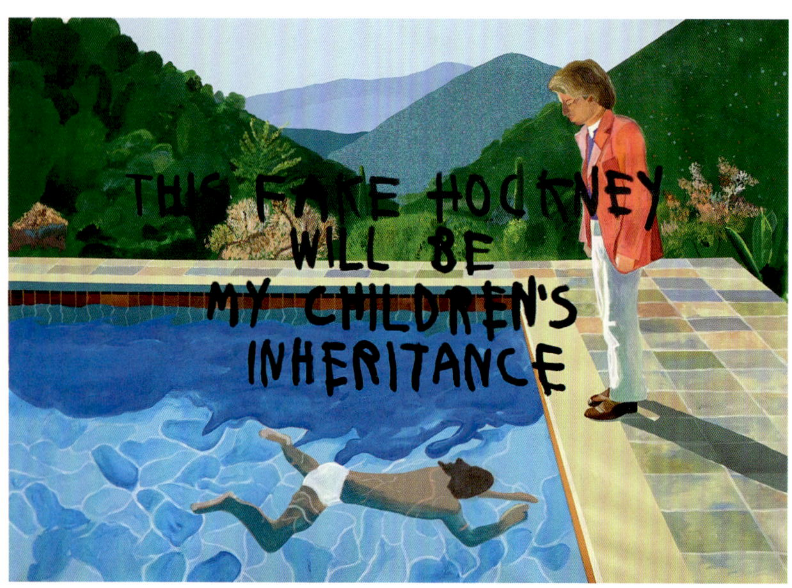

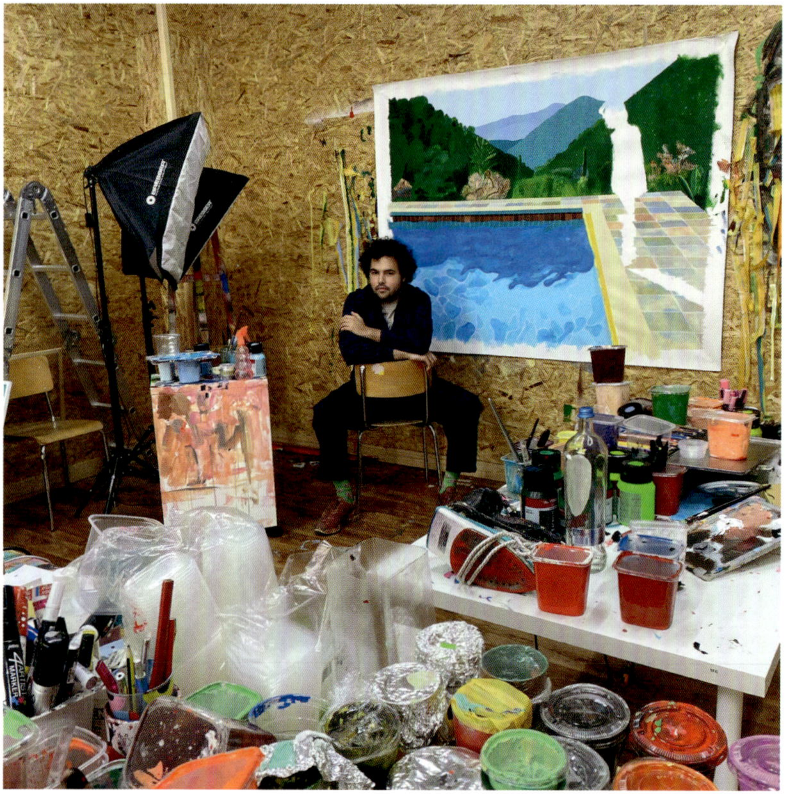

Hockney Inheritance,
2019–2020
Acrylic paint and oil bars
on canvas,
121,92 x 172,72 cm

CB in his studio while
working on *Hockney
Inheritance*, 2020

Forged Magritte, 2020
Acrylic and water-
soluble wax pastels on
canvas, 54 x 73.4 cm

Studio, *Forged Magritte*
in the making, 2020

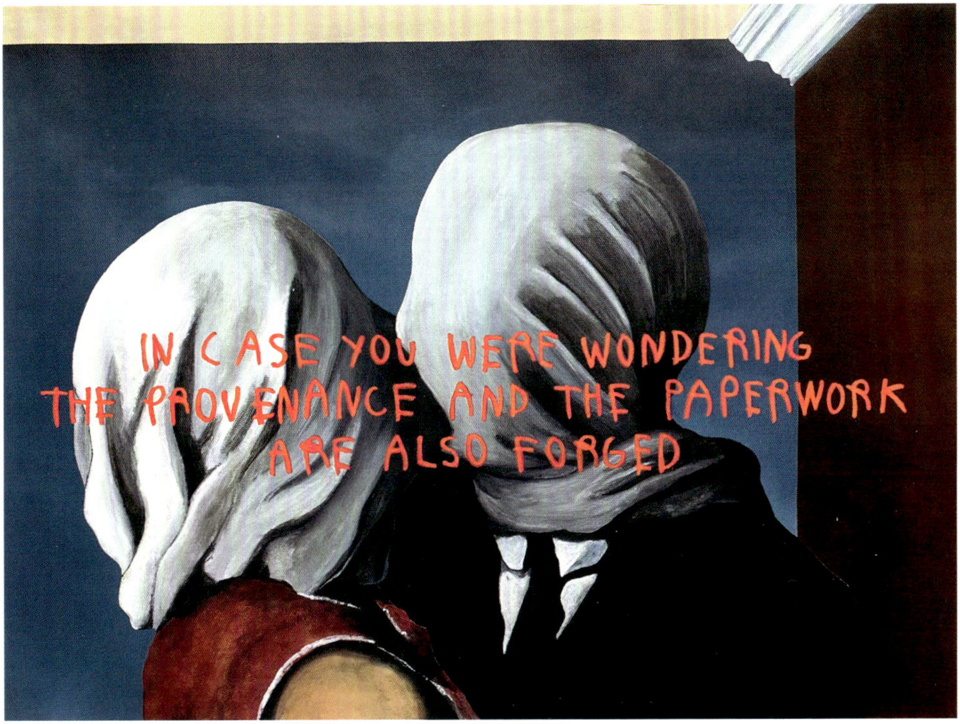

IN CASE YOU WERE WONDERING
THE PROVENANCE AND THE PAPERWORK
ARE ALSO FORGED

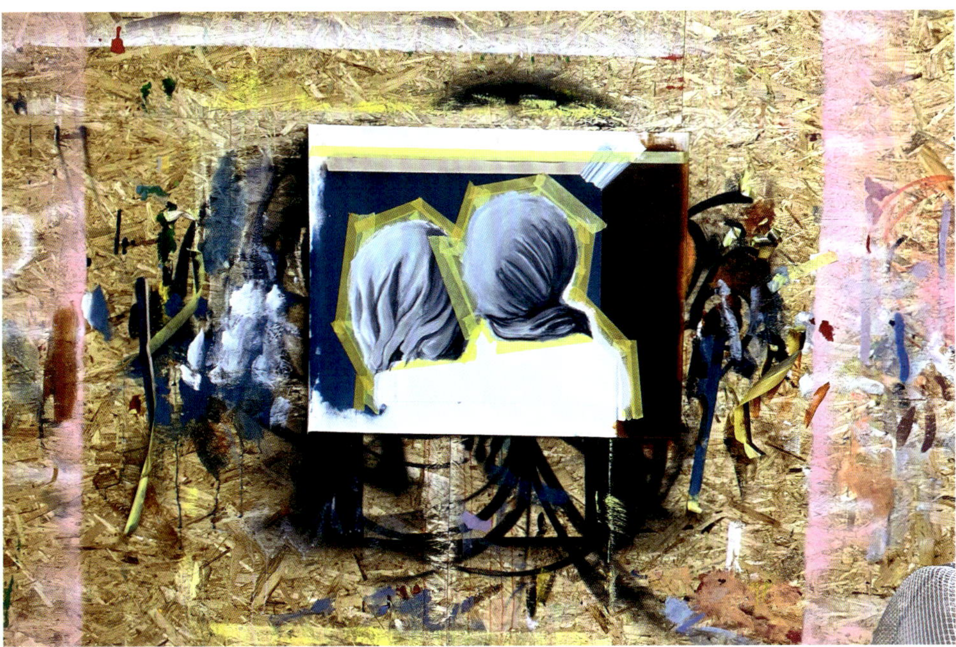

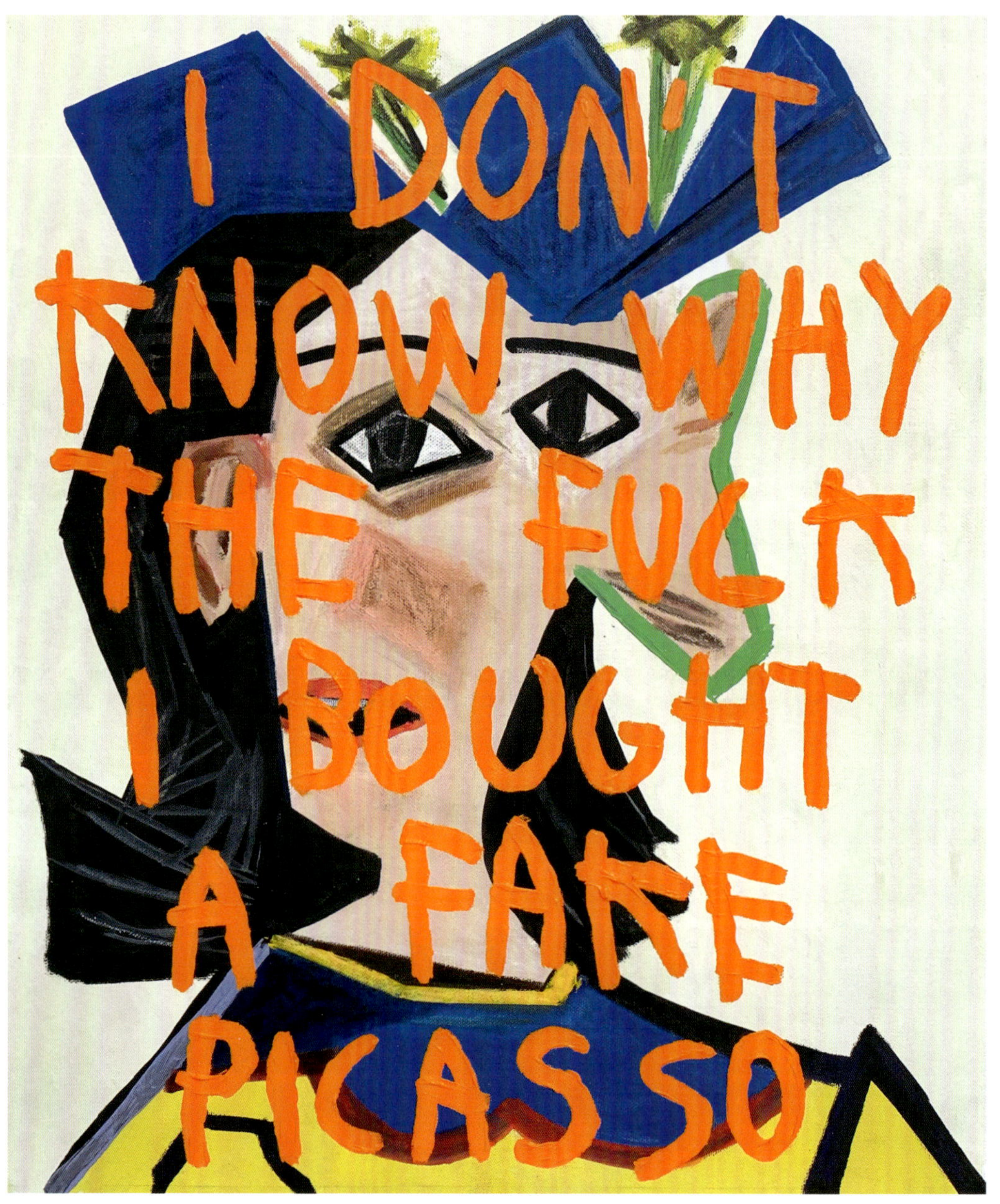
I DON'T KNOW WHY THE FUCK I BOUGHT A FAKE PICASSO

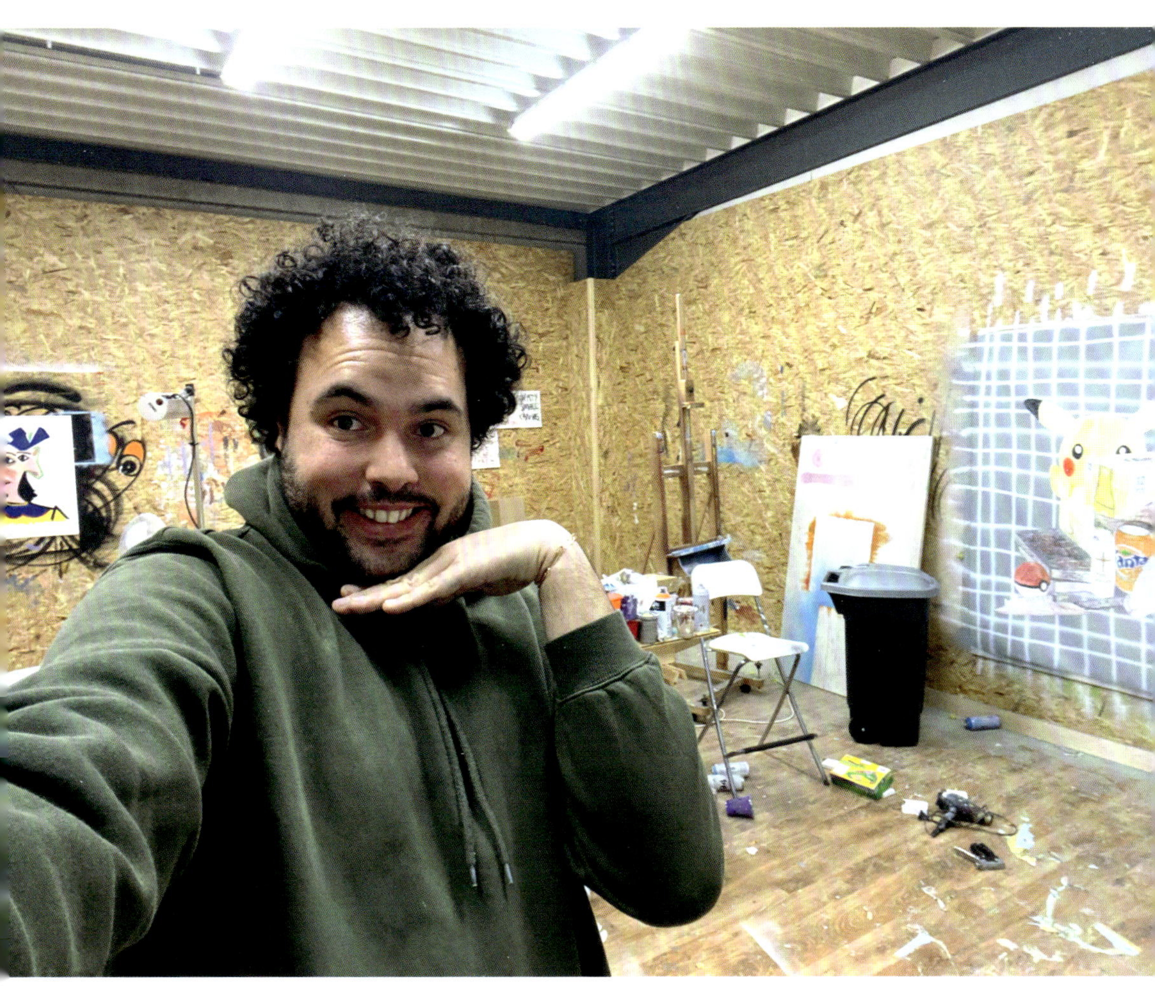

*I Buy Stupid Shit All
the Time*, 2020
Arcylic, wax crayons,
color pencils, gel
medium, water soluble
oil crayons on canvas,
55 x 46.5 cm

Studio selfie, 2020

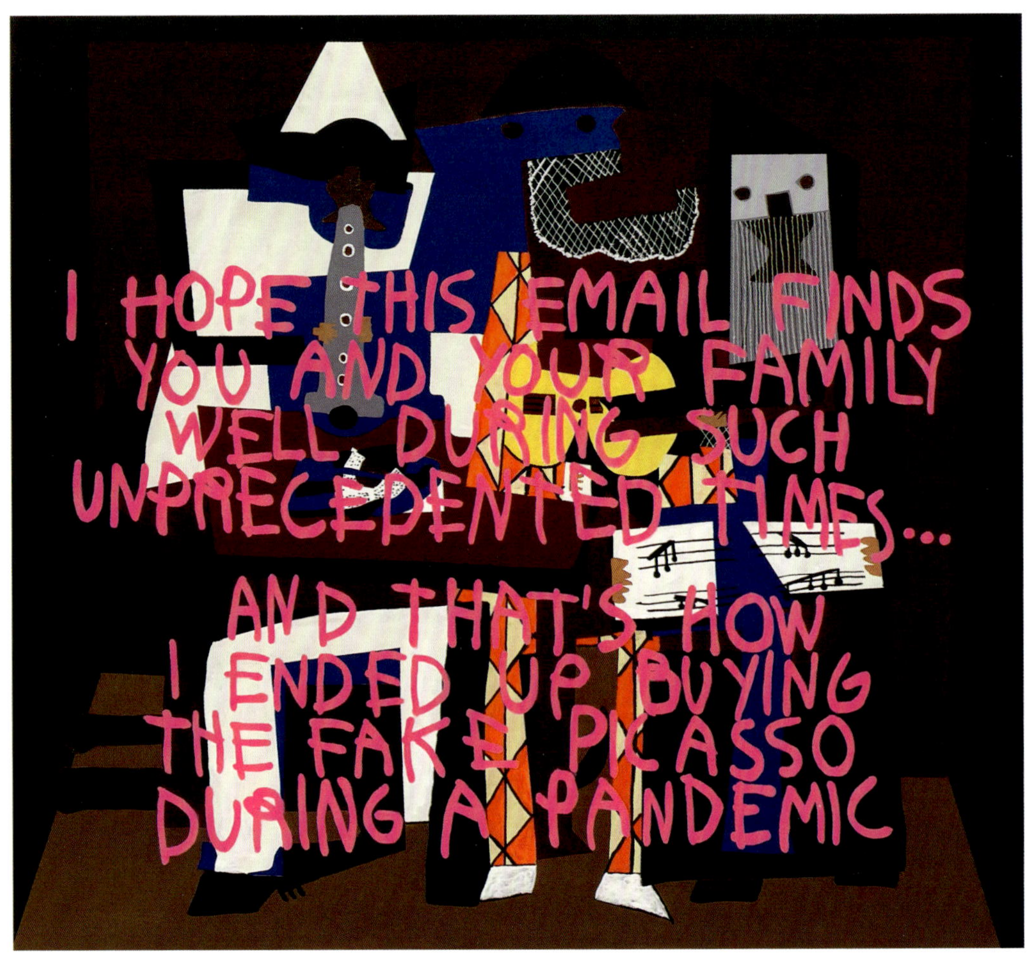

COVID19, 2020
Acrylic on canvas,
90 x 100 cm

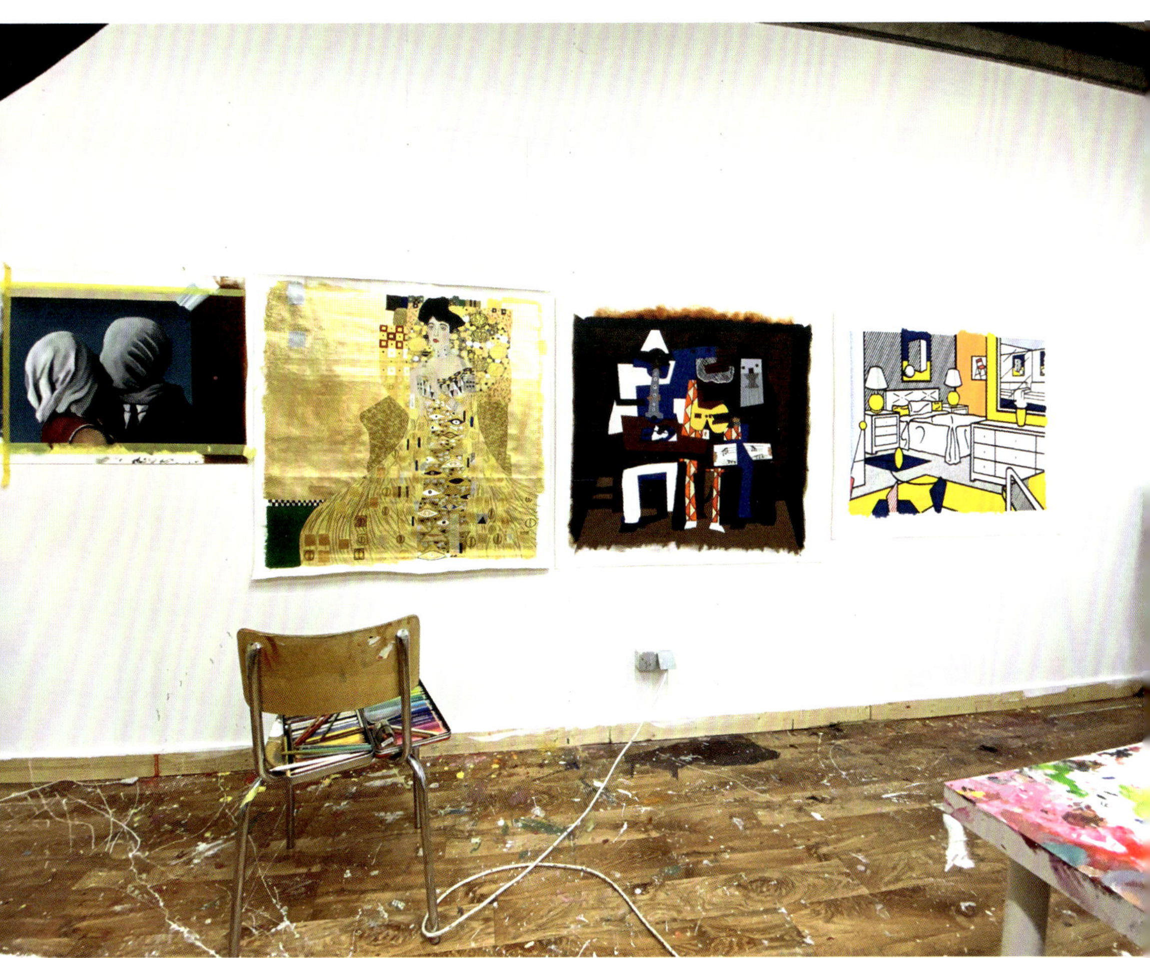

Studio, 2020

Page 98
Self-Portrait, 2019
Polaroid film,
10.752 x 8.847 cm

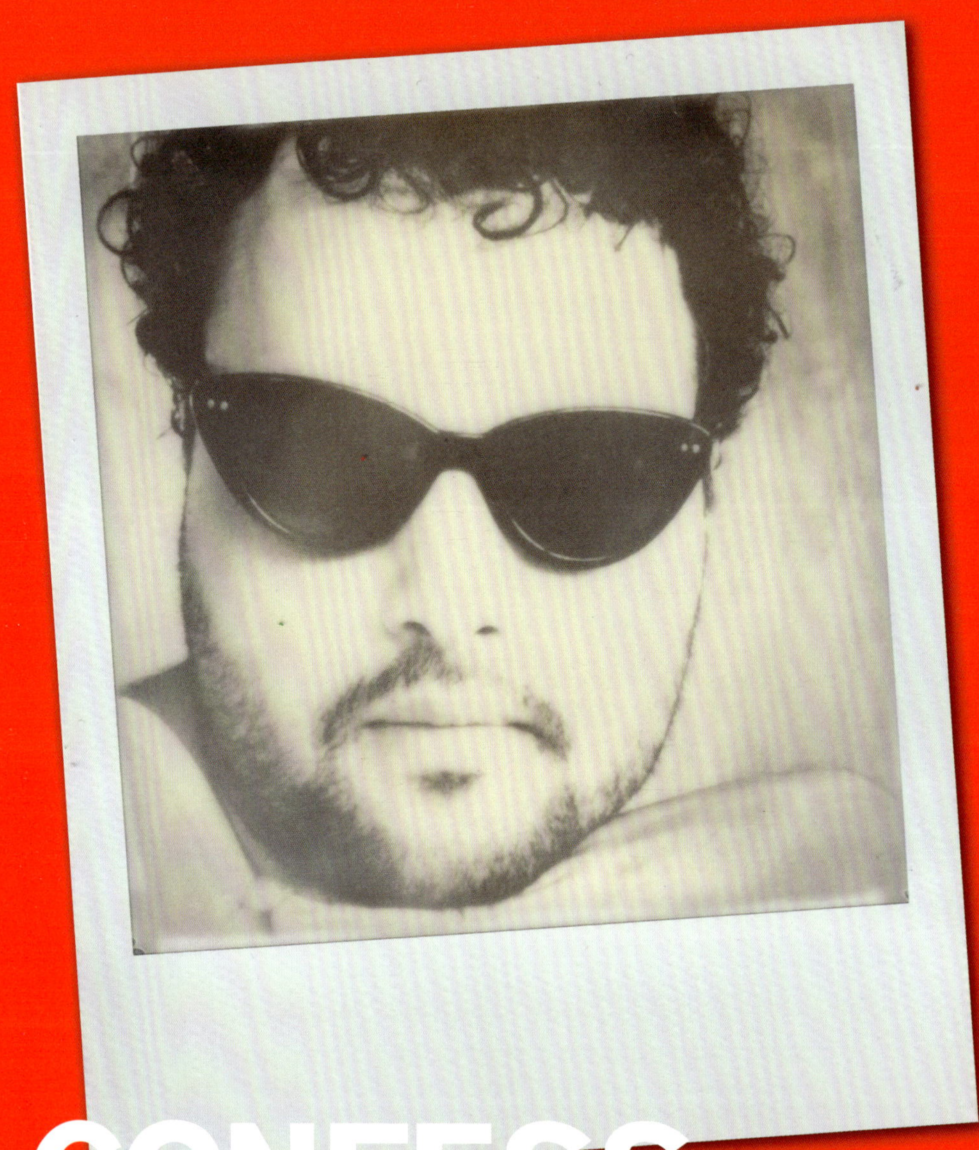

I CONFESS

CB Hoyo **and** Cesare Biasini Selvaggi

in Conversation

HOW WOULD YOU DEFINE CB HOYO?

I am CB HOYO. CB HOYO is me; my artistic name is my real name's acronym. I don't use my full name to keep a certain privacy in my life, something complicated to achieve nowadays because whoever wants to know my full name can easily find it on the internet. I want to be true to myself and use my name to create art, but I feel more comfortable having a certain anonymity level. It gives me some peace of mind.
I am a person who says what he thinks. I am an artist, a preacher, a being... I am me. Honestly, who the fuck knows who they are.
I have been an immigrant my whole life, a citizen of the world. I connect to places but I feel like I don't belong anywhere. I am an outcast. I am far from being orthodox. I do what I want in the way I believe it should be done. I can distinguish between right and wrong; I have values. I consider myself someone who lives and acts outside the box.
The person who stretches my canvases in Italy calls me "the animal" because I have my own way of doing things. Not receiving a formal art education is probably part of this. I experiment a lot; I go through trial and error. I do things how I fucking feel like doing them, even if they are not academically or technically correct. All of this is part of who I am, and it is part of my identity.

YOU MENTIONED THAT DETAILS OF YOUR CHILDHOOD—BEING BORN IN CUBA AND RAISED IN THE DOMINICAN REPUBLIC—AREN'T OFTEN WRITTEN ABOUT, CAN YOU SHARE SOME OF YOUR STORY THAT YOU WISH MORE PEOPLE KNEW ABOUT?

I was born in Cuba in 1995 in the middle of a critical economic moment full of precariousness and scarcity, best known as "The Special Period." I lived there for less than two years until my mother, who had no more hope of freedom or a better future, made the wisest decision ever and we emigrated to the Dominican Republic in 1997.
My mom left Cuba with me in one hand and a bag of books in the other. She didn't have a single dime to her name and raised me the best she

could. She did a great job, actually. We were limited in a certain way. It was a single-parent home, and we could not have everything all the time. But no matter how difficult it was, she gave me a good education and made me a better person.

In the Dominican Republic, I went to school with the country's elite, the country's owners, and I was nobody, economically speaking. I always felt like a fish out of water. However, I found a way to fit in. They were

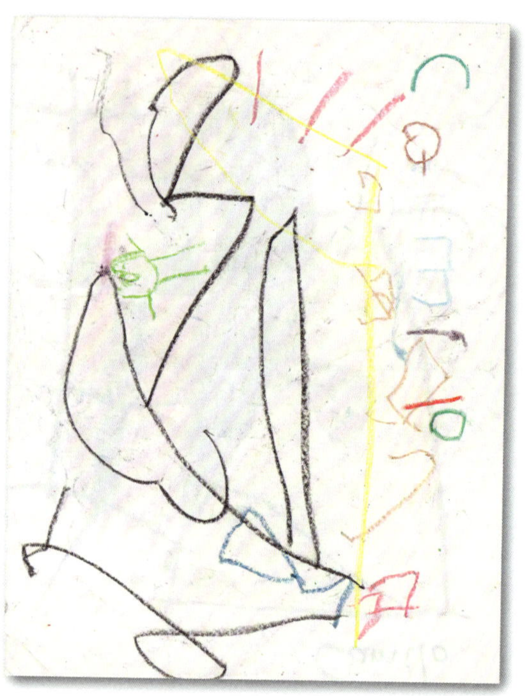
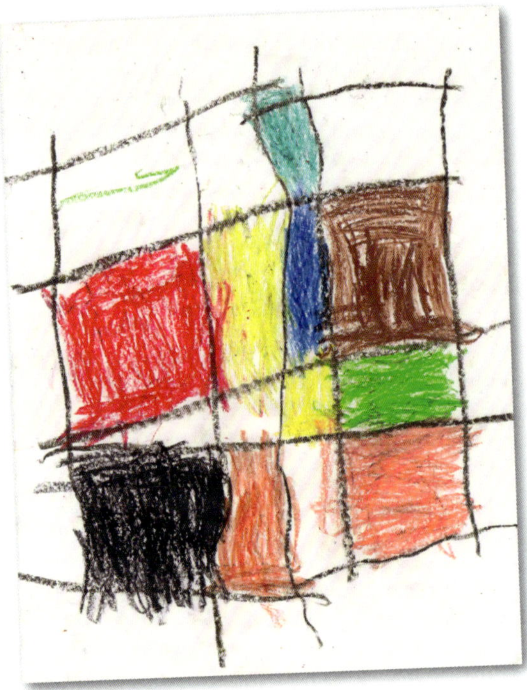

always talking about the things they did, the things they had, and the places they had visited, while I left the Dominican Republic for the first time when I was almost 16. To grow up in this environment and be surrounded by these people made me see things differently, and I learned to take things easy. If I had been somebody else with a different character in the same situation, I might have become depressed.

When I was 17, right after graduating from high school I decided to leave the Dominican Republic and travel to Europe. There was no future

in the Dominican Republic for someone like me. When you have great
aspirations in a place like that, unfortunately, you need money to make
them come true. At that moment I didn't know what I wanted in my life.
But I was certain about something—whatever it was, it was not in the
Dominican Republic.
I left the country with no plans. I went to Europe to visit my family
and see what would happen. I was just a teenager, but I didn't want
to do what everybody else was doing: go to school, study something
I probably didn't like, get a diploma, get a shitty job, work until
I turned 65, and then die. I did know what I didn't want for my life.
Being raised by a single mother in a developing country gave me
a different perspective of life. The ways my mom educated me and the
values she taught me, they protected me and made me stronger.
I was able to keep going on with my life in a positive way.
All of this shaped me into the person I am today. I'm direct. I have a
dark sense of humor, and all this comes from the situations that I had
to face while growing up. You need to let things slide; life is too
fucking short to have worms in your head eating all your thoughts.

WHAT ARE YOUR MEMORIES AND OBSERVATIONS ABOUT THE CUBAN GOVERNMENT?

In all honesty, I have zero memories because, as I said, I left Cuba
when I was almost two years old. The only memories I have come from
photos and my family stories.
The situation in Cuba is unfortunate. The Revolution and the communist
system have only brought disgrace to the country. Cuban people used to
be known as well-educated people. Education, culture, and health used
to be priorities for this system, but now it is not like that anymore.
There are no resources, and people are divided. Families are broken.
Cubans live everywhere in the world.
In its pursuit of progress and social change, it is sad to see how the
Revolution brought calamities to the Cuban people. Millions of families
were divided and are still divided. What's ironic is that there are

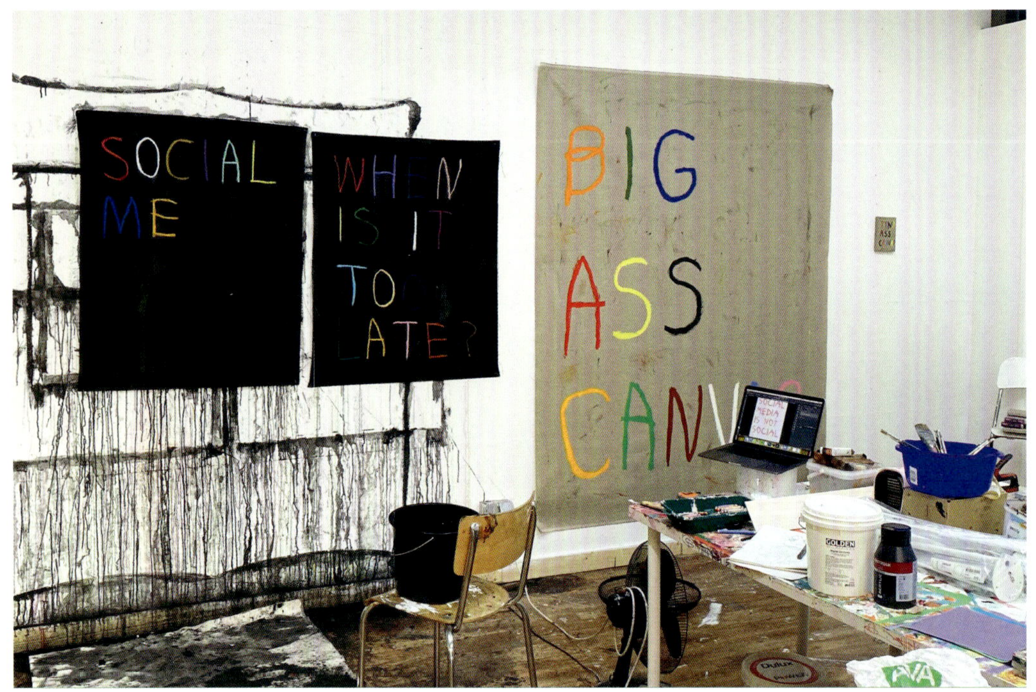

clear social and class differences in Cuba. They talk about equality, but we are not equal. Those in power are not equal to the rest of the population. Power has corrupted them. Humans are living contradictions—hypocrites and corrupted beings by nature. I believe undoubtedly that utopias cannot prosper.

IF YOU COULD CHOOSE, WHERE WOULD YOU LIKE TO HAVE BEEN BORN AND WHERE WOULD YOU LIKE TO LIVE NOW?

I would not choose anything different. I am the type of person who doesn't regret anything because the things that have happened to me have shaped me into the person I am today. Sometimes these things need to happen in order to learn an important life lesson.
Being born in Cuba is a fucking pain in the ass, bureaucracy-wise. Everything takes longer than usual and costs hundreds and hundreds of dollars, but I don't regret the fact that I was born there. I don't

Studio shot, 2020

Studio self-portrait,
2020

Page 100
Untitled (childhood
drawing), 1998
Wax crayons on
paper, 27.9 x 21cm

Untitled (childhood
drawing), 1998
Wax crayons on
paper, 27.9 x 21cm

Page 104
Untitled (study), 2020
Wax crayons on
paper, 27.9 x 21cm

Untitled (study), 2020
Wax crayons on
paper, 27.9 x 21cm

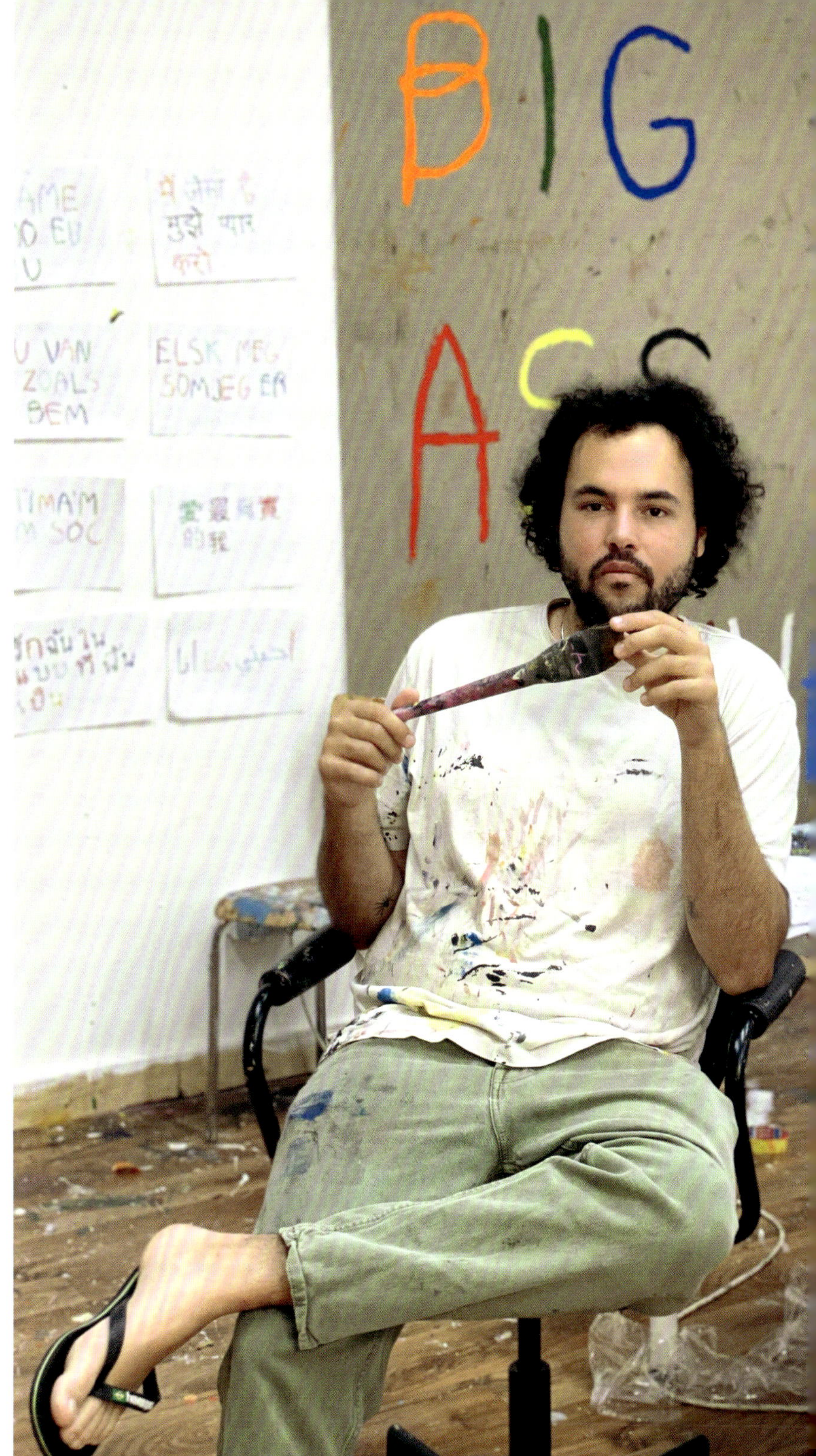

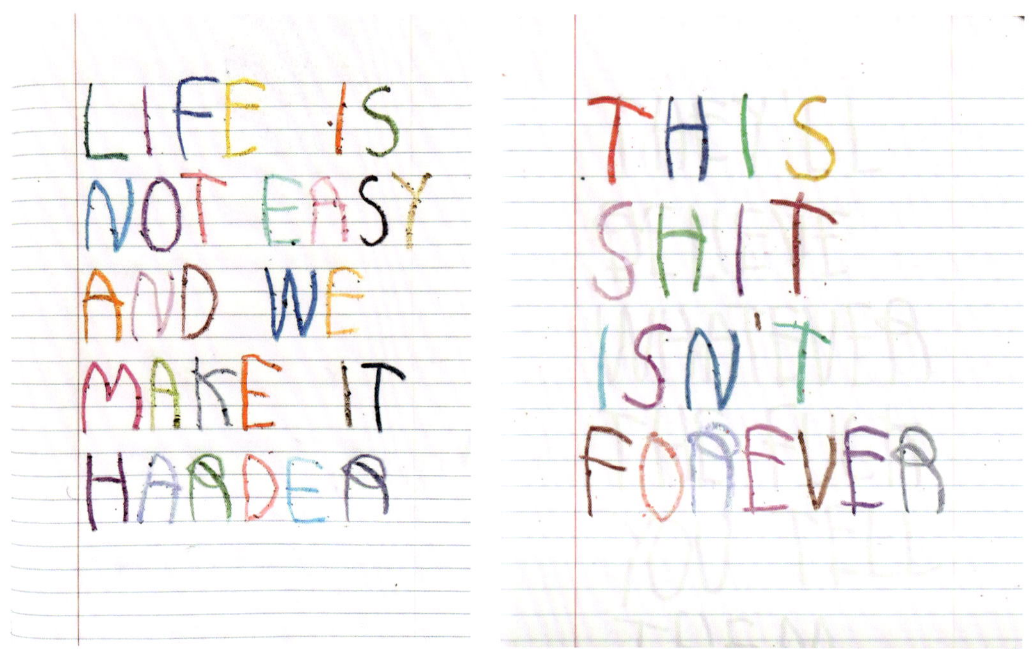

want to change it. That is part of my identity and a significant part of
who I am. Maybe if I were born somewhere else, I would not see things
the way I see them now. I don't know, and I don't want to know. This
is my life, and this is how I know it. Maybe I would have been another
person, or perhaps I would not have been born at all. I have no regrets
in this sense, and I would not have changed anything.
Ideally, I would like to live in a place where there are no people.
My dream is to move to the jungle with no one nearby. Close enough to
a big city and an airport with good connections, so that when I want
to see people I can see them, but where I am also far enough, so nobody
can bother me.

HOW AND WHEN DID YOUR INTEREST IN ART BEGIN?

Art has always been a part of me and I've always been a creative
person. My mom says that I was painting before I could even walk.
She took me to museums, ballets, operas, theaters, art biennales,

all sorts of cultural happenings. I enjoyed them. I was a weird kid.
Usually, kids like to go and play in arcades and parks. They play
video games. I did that too, but I always had an interest in cultural
things. I've been exposed to culture at all times, even before I was
born—my mother would stick a radio on her belly for me to listen
to classical music.

When I was around seven, I briefly took art lessons, but that didn't
go well. Even at an early age in my life, I felt that my creativity
and spontaneity were killed during those painting lessons. I was not
free to create. I had to paint boring oil still lifes and landscapes.
I could not express myself freely. I did learn how to mix colors
though.

Moving to Europe in 2013 awoke something in me, artistically speaking.
I started painting again; I became more active and painted every single
day of the week. I was studying culinary arts, working a job, while
still painting late at night. It became a habit, and I wanted to share
what I was creating. So, in March 2015 I decided to create an Instagram
account. At that time, I was creating and experimenting without a defined
intention, without a personal voice. You can look at some of the pieces
I produced then, and you will not find CB Hoyo on them. I was creating
many different things simultaneously, and they didn't share common
traits. My identity as an artist was non-existent. As a matter of fact,
I am still finding myself. Evolution doesn't stop—it is a continuous
process. The difference between that period and today is that my work is
now recognizable. You see it, and you immediately see me. Now my work
contains my essence. It has this uniqueness that makes it mine.

Between 2015 and 2016 I was creating without a clear purpose, just for
the fun of it. My artistic identity and voice were not born yet. There
was no clear message in what I was making. Somehow I started evolving,
I started writing, and for the first time, my style as an artist came
to life. Writing put me on the right path.

In 2017 I was working at a restaurant and was not happy. I was working
for too many hours in an unhealthy environment, and art was the only

escape I had from that tedious reality. In March 2017, I decided to quit my job and took a leap of faith. I knew what I wanted, but I did not have any type of security. I threw away a stable job to chase a dream. It was a risky plan to quit my job, create for six months, and see where it might take me. If things didn't go as planned, I could always go back to cooking, after all, I already had a profession. I gave myself a trial, and four years later, I am still on trial. Things aligned well, and I haven't had to go back to the kitchen. Quitting my stable job was not an easy decision. Family and friends thought I was crazy. I didn't get much support from them and many were questioning my actions. My girlfriend, Andrea, and my mother were the only two people who truly believed in me and gave me their unconditional support. That's a little bit of the story.

You can say that I started making art professionally in 2017. Before, it was more of a stress reliever, to have fun, enjoy, but, don't get me wrong, I am still enjoying it and still releasing stress. But now it is no longer a hobby; I am not part of the audience; I am exposing for an audience now.

WHAT WAS THE MOST IMPORTANT ENCOUNTER FOR YOUR FORMATION AS AN ARTIST?

I was seven when I had my first conscious encounter with contemporary art. We were doing a science fair in school, and they took all the kids to the National History Museum in Santo Domingo. I was sick and I could not go. I threw a tantrum and insisted so much on visiting that weeks later my grandma tried to take me to the museum, but it was closed because a lethal virus had killed one of the employees and the entire staff was in quarantine. So guess what, I was taken to the Modern Art Museum (MAM) instead. I remember that they had this photography show in the temporary exhibitions—pictures of toilets and shit everywhere. Literally, I lost my shit. I was expecting to see animals, insects, scientific artifacts and, instead, I ended up looking at shit. It was my first encounter with contemporary art.

From that moment, I started questioning art and what can be considered
art. It was eye-opening. If toilets full of diarrhea were exposed
as art in the most important art museum on the island, why couldn't
something else also be considered art? It made me appreciate art from a
different point of view. Everything and nothing can be considered art.
It was an enlightening experience. That triggered me.

WAS THERE AN EVENT OR ACQUAINTANCE THAT CHANGED THE WAY YOU SEE THE WORLD? IF SO, CAN YOU DESCRIBE IT?

I cannot recall a particular event or events that have happened in the
last ten years politically and economically speaking. I have realized
that people are full of shit, corrupted, and selfish. We think about
our own benefit instead of thinking about the entire society. Political,
economic, and environmental issues have been filling up an imaginary
glass and make me talk about a lot of things. I was actually tired
of seeing a lot of shit and not voicing my opinion. All events are
important in one way or another. They are all interconnected and have
changed my perspective.

The shitty people I have met have disappointed me and have affected
the way I act with people. They have changed me as a person. Now I am
more cautious. I think twice before doing anything, before opening up
to other people. I have had bad experiences: people who stole from me;
people who made me believe in them and deceived me; people who scammed
me. I am not going into detail because I don't want to give them the
importance they don't deserve. Life goes on. They have opened my eyes
and have taught me valuable lessons.

In times of crisis there are situations that make a positive impact
on you. They make you act and react. They are not necessarily
a curse but a blessing in disguise. They fuck you up, take away your
sleep at night, create anxieties, put you in bad emotional and mental
states. However, if you beat the situation, they will make you
stronger. As corny as it sounds: what doesn't kill you, makes you
stronger.

When I was eleven, I had my first encounter with Picasso. It was an exhibition at the MAM in Santo Domingo organized by a Latin American bank. There were sketches and prints displaying people fucking. I became obsessed with Picasso and started researching his work. It was one of my first encounters with faking, me faking something. I learned how to forge his signature and even adapted my own signature to his. I was still a kid, and for some reason, I needed to have a personal signature. I decided to write my first name in Picasso's style. Nowadays, it is still my official signature.

When I was thirteen, I started taking French lessons. I have French origins, and my mom always pointed out the importance of learning the language. She used to question me and always said, what kind of French citizen are you if you cannot speak French? I started studying at the Alliance Française in Santo Domingo. There, they had a huge médiathèque, full of art books. They had this big blue book, a Taschen book, a monograph about Picasso released in the 1990s. It contained excerpts from Picasso's Catalogue Raisonné Zervos. I immediately fell in love with that book. It was 1000 pages and I literally rented it for almost two consecutive years. Years later, I bought the book in Europe.

WHICH ARTISTS OR PARTICULAR WORKS HAVE INFLUENCED YOU THE MOST?

Warhol and his way of transforming everyday popular culture into art. I genuinely enjoy the art style from the late nineteenth century, medieval art, and religious iconography. I also love Hieronymus Bosch and Pieter Bruegel, the Elder. They are masters of the Dutch and Flemish Renaissance and were doing Surrealism even before Surrealism was formally defined. They were ahead of their time. Their way of capturing things is impressive. Their paintings tend to be really dark, and a lot is going on. New details will come to life whenever you look at them. Their works tell stories, and it is too bad I cannot buy any

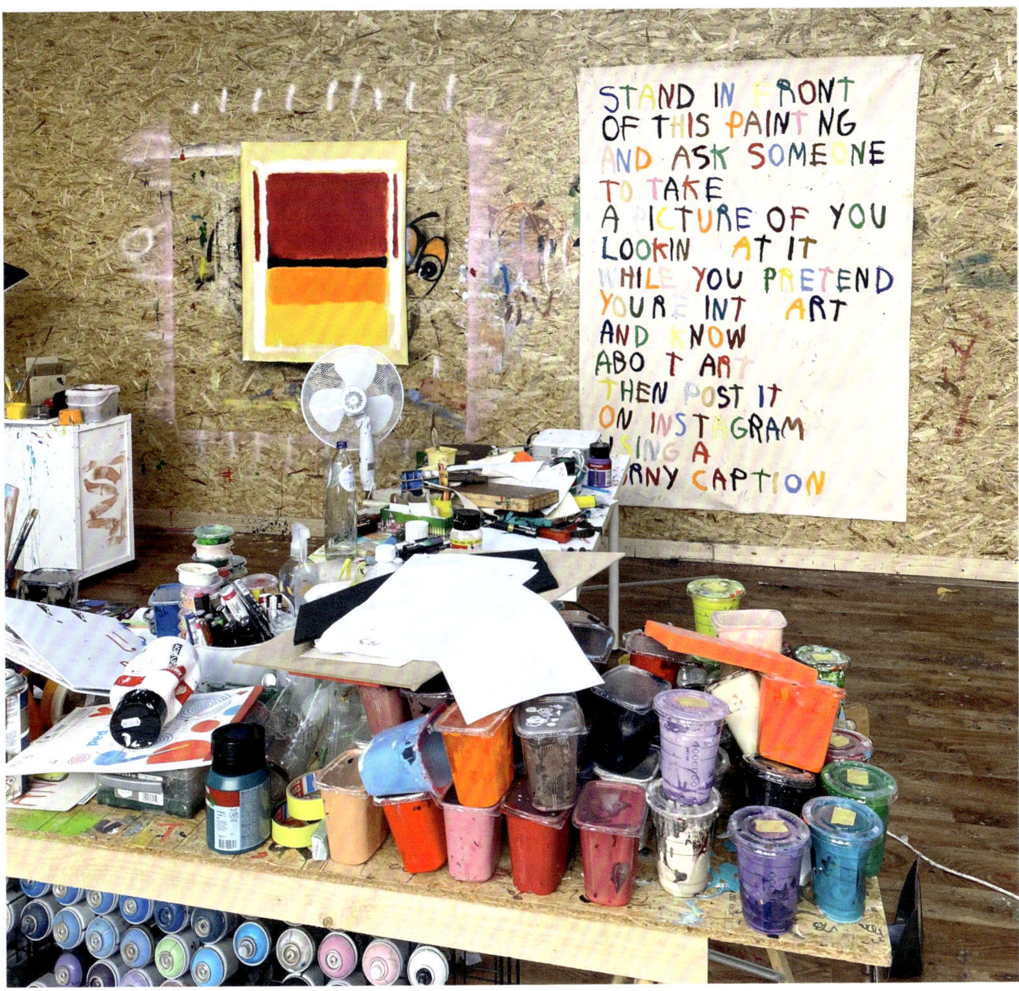

Studio shot, 2020

Page 110
Studio shot, 2020

of them. Unfortunately, they are not for sale, and just a few are in private hands. I enjoy their work a lot; they bring me happiness, which makes me approach things differently—my vision changes. Being an artist is like having a special pass to say and do things in a different way. If "normal" people were doing what artists do, they would be put in a mental institution.

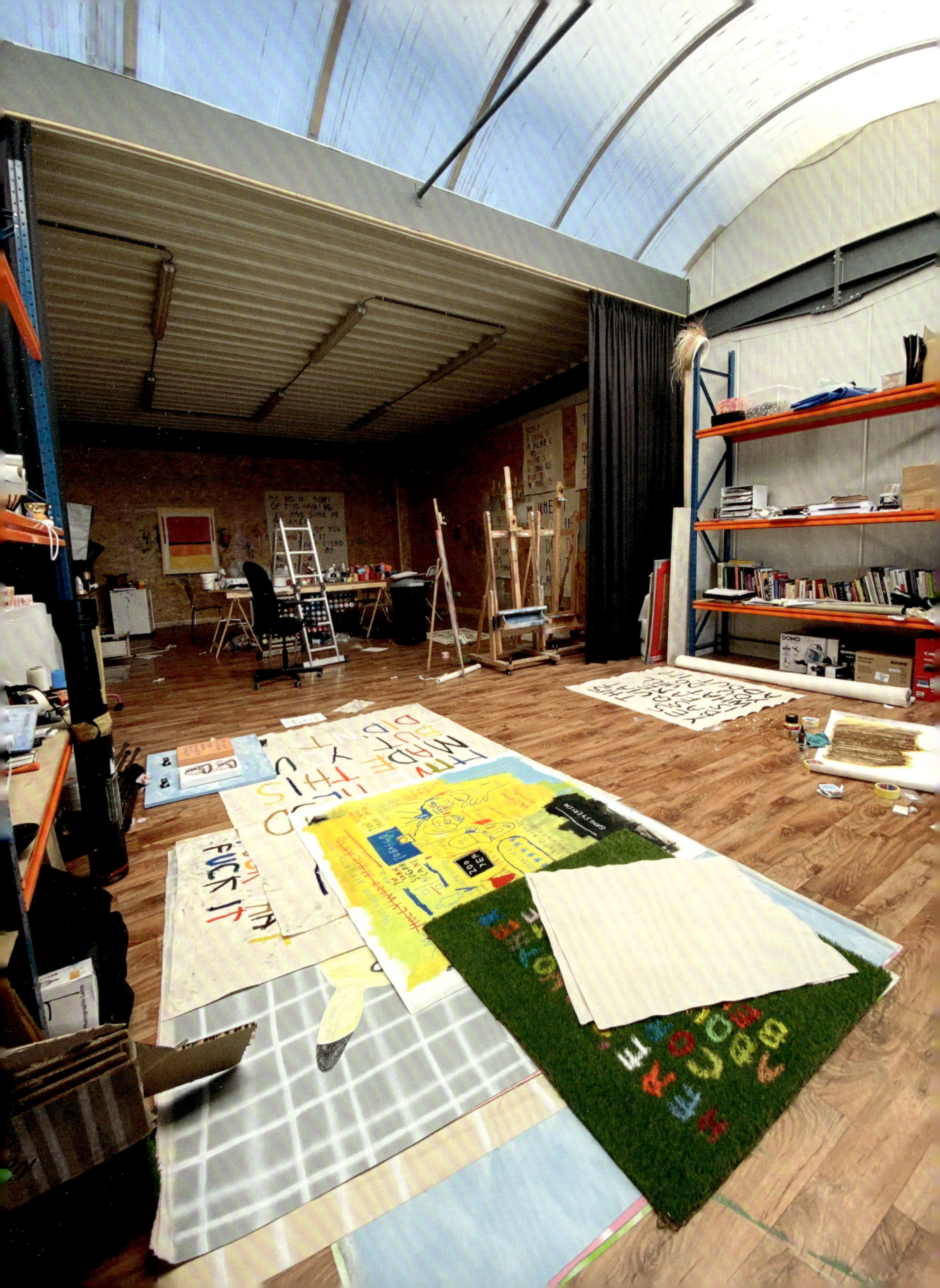
I'LL MAKE ART BUT I AM SAD THIS
FUCK IT

WHAT DOES YOUR TYPICAL DAY LOOK LIKE?

I hate schedules; I hate routines. I cannot wake up with alarms, that ruins my day. I sleep the number of hours my body tells me to; it could be 2 or 12 hours; it all depends on what I need at the time. I cannot be bothered while I sleep.

I usually wake up with the sunlight; I like it. I don't have breakfast, I would rather have lunch. I go to my studio and stay there for around eight hours, sometimes more. Sometimes I just come for half an hour and then leave. I go back home, eat, read the news, play with my phone, and go to bed at around 3 in the morning. This is when I'm home.

I said I hate schedules, but I do have a plan or a way to manage my time when I go to the studio. I just don't like to feel like it is something mandatory. I am the master of my time; I decide when to go to work or when I break my schedule, so it is very flexible.

If I'm traveling, it's the same thing, but obviously, I don't go to the studio. I visit people or places. I like to do what I want when I want. It's a roller coaster. Every day is a little bit different.

Before doing art, I was trapped in a routine—wake up, go to work, sleep, and repeat the cycle over and over again. Sometimes I had just two days off in the week and didn't have time to travel that much or do new things. That made me say fuck the 9-to-5. It was like living in a box; that was not life.

DO YOU HAVE ANY SPECIFIC RITUALS WHILE YOU WORK?

Yes, I need the internet while working to see what's happening in the world and to watch memes. I consider memes a representation of our current society. It's a humor that captures society. I think that they are one of the most powerful forms of contemporary art, even if they are not seen like that by many. At the end of the day, what is art? For me, it is something that makes me feel some emotion and captures the time when it was created. Memes do that perfectly well.

I also need music. Let's talk about my musical taste. I am a rollercoaster when it comes to music. I enjoy all sorts of genres

except modern Christian pop-rock music, which I find a bit annoying.
It's nothing against religion; it is just the music that annoys the
living shit out of me. Other than that, I could be listening to
reggaeton and then to opera, classical music, death metal, or hardcore
techno from Berlin. My taste depends on my mood. I need music to work.
Sometimes when I want to create new ideas or feel saturated, I like
to sleep. I take these weird naps where I'm half awake, but I'm also
sleeping, and that is when the best ideas come. When I'm sleeping,
I need tons of silence, my phone, and nothing else. I need to be with
me, myself, and I.
I need my phone because I write everything on it, it is more practical
than writing on paper. Sometimes, ideas come out of nowhere, and
I don't have a paper sheet to write on, so I write almost everything
on my phone now. It is eco-friendly, and texts are easier to be
located on the phone. The problem I had before was that I was writing
everything on paper, and I would lose the sheets of paper and notebooks
I used. There were times in which I would buy three or four notebooks
in the same week because I kept on losing or misplacing them, and
I always needed something to write on. Now and then, I randomly find one
of these lost notebooks with just two or three pages of notes, and it
feels like winning the lottery.
When I get to the studio, I take a shit for 40 minutes and watch my
phone. Then I go upstairs, sit on my chair, and stare at the walls for
hours while listening to music. Then when an idea pops up, I execute
it or I don't. There are some days in which I go to the studio, stay
there for ten hours, and maybe work for 20 minutes. The other 9 hours
and 40 minutes are still considered work because they're part of the
creative process, but what you would call working—like painting,
physically creating something, or anything like that—can sometimes
just take 20-30 minutes. It is my creative process.
Before the pandemic, I traveled a lot, and most of the ideas came while
I was flying. I would sit by the airplane window, stare outside at the
clouds, and ideas would start coming.

Untitled (study), 2017
Pen on paper,
29.7 x 21 cm

Untitled (study), 2017
Pen on paper,
29.7 x 21 cm

Untitled (study), 2020
Color pencils on
paper, 27.9 x 21cm

Untitled (study), 2017
Color pencils on
paper, 27.9 x 21cm

Page 114
Untitled (study), 2018
Color pencils on
paper, 14.8 x 21 cm

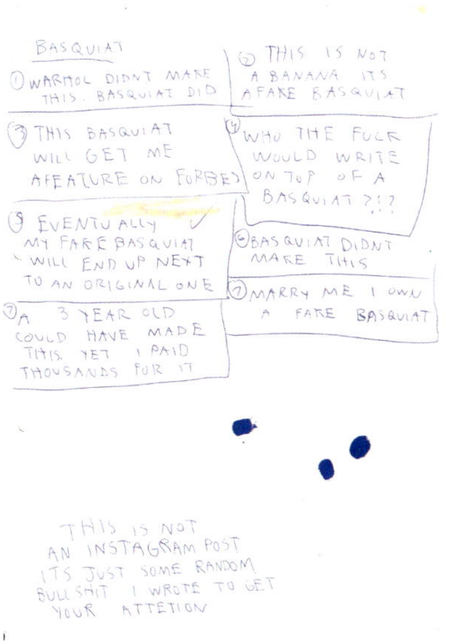

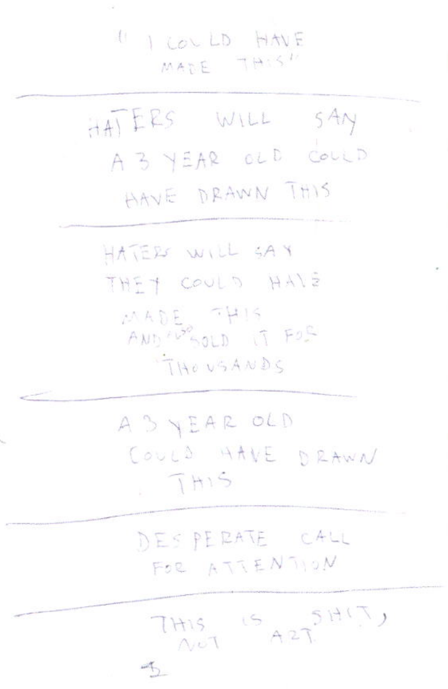

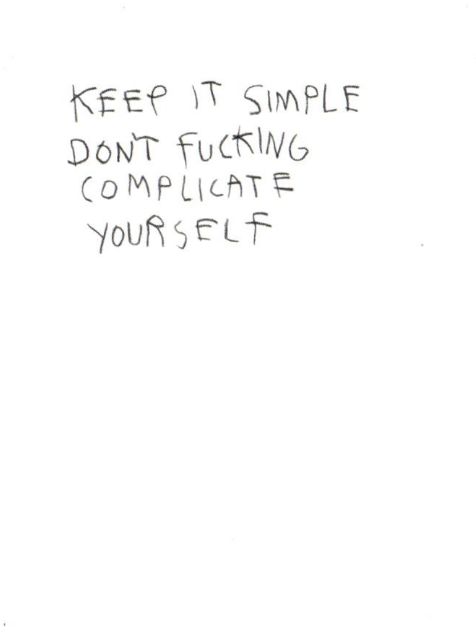

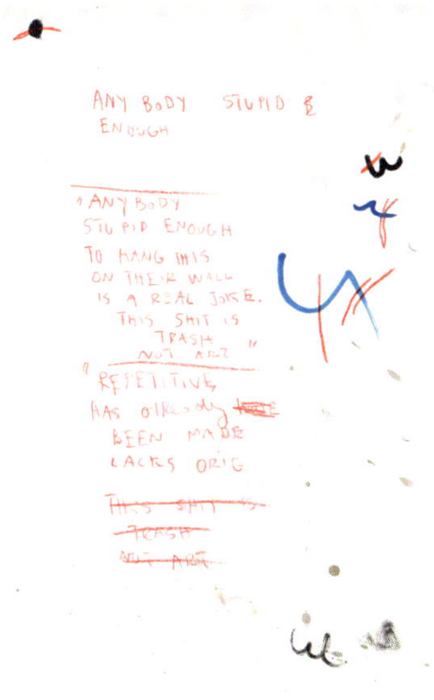

DO YOU LEAVE ROOM FOR THE UNFORESEEN WHILE YOU WORK?

There is always room for the unforeseen; shit happens. You need to know that nothing is permanent in life; things are constantly evolving.

If you think that things will last forever and you will always have the hen with golden eggs, then you are fucked up.

I have gone through many shitty things in the past few years, so I know the unforeseen can happen. I started in the art world as a very naïve person. I would believe anything. But I have been disappointed by many people so many times that now I don't expect anything from anybody.

I rely on actions. They speak for themselves. Anything positive that happens is welcome, and if nothing happens, life keeps on going. No deceptions and no expectations.

DO YOU HAVE ANY PARTICULAR FEAR OF WHAT YOU DO?

My greatest fear is to become blind. That's what I fear the most—not seeing colors and things. Life is already too complicated. Sometimes I feel I am in a limbo, unsure about things' actual existence. Being able to see is an escape from your thoughts. Can you imagine if that escape is taken away from you and you get stuck in the darkness of your mind? That would be terrible. I would keep creating, but I don't know or don't want to imagine how that would go. I don't even want to put myself in that position. Death is not even a fear for me because that is the only thing in life we know for sure will happen; everybody eventually dies. I obviously don't want to die now, but when the time comes, the time comes, and there's nothing I can do about it.

Not being relevant scares me just for a few seconds, but in the end, it is not even important. As long as I can say what I have to say and feel happy, being relevant is not essential.

Humans always have these insecurities that pop up, and it is up to us to ignore them or let them materialize. We all fear failure at some point in our lives that what we do is not going to come out as expected, but that is a temporary feeling. You keep on moving and overcome these obstacles. In the end, it is just my mind playing games. There is always a solution.

HAVE YOU HAD ANY MOMENTS OF CRISIS DURING YOUR ARTISTIC CAREER? AND, IF SO, HOW DID/DO YOU OVERCOME THEM?

I am an artist, most of the time a painter. What do you call what PAINters do? PAINtings. Can you dissect the word? PAIN tings. Pain is there everywhere as well as obstacles. We artists suffer moments of crisis. Yes, many of them. I always overcome them with the support of the people I love and cherish. Sometimes it is just by realizing that what I'm thinking is just another obstacle in my mind, and it is not worth thinking about it. So I just let it go.

I have had crises just like everybody else: lack of inspiration, people I cannot trust anymore, people who owe me money, people who backstabbed me and ran away with my money—you name it. In the end, losing your mind won't solve it. You need to face it and keep on going. I have nothing in this world, so I've got nothing to lose. I lose more by not doing anything, so I take action and get out of the crisis.

HOW WOULD YOU DESCRIBE YOUR PAINTING PROCESS?

Lately, I have not painted that much. Or, at least painted what most consider a painting. Let's call it, instead, my creative process. I paint, I use paint all the time.

It is a spontaneous process; sometimes, it just happens by accident. As I didn't have any formal artistic education, I tend to make up a lot of things. I experiment with materials and processes that, if you were to use in an academic world, they would consider you an outcast, a lunatic, or an animal.

My process is based on trial and error, inventions, and accidents. Something small has always led me to something bigger. That is how life works. Sometimes the smallest things will make you realize a bigger meaning or find greatness.

I go with my emotions, what I'm feeling, what I think I should do, and try to experiment. Sometimes I am successful; sometimes, it doesn't go well at all. Sometimes I mix the wrong paints and chemicals. Sometimes I use materials that don't go well together. I would say that my painting practice is more about experimenting, a trial and error process. I like to innovate, although sometimes I'm just defying chemistry and science laws.

An anecdote: back in 2019, while working on one of my Fakes, a Wesselmann, I was faking one of his lip paintings in some wood that I had to prime, and I used the wrong primer. After painting everything on top of the primed wood, the paint started to fall off. The paint and the primer reacted chemically, leading my work to disaster. I ended up having to buy a sander to remove all of the paint and the primer from the wood and repaint everything. The worst part of this experience was that the painting needed to be finished in less than 15 hours from when this happened. So in 15 hours, the piece had to be ready, dry, and crated on a plane to Lima, Peru. Luckily for me, I'm good at working under stress and pressure; I'm a natural-born procrastinator, so leaving things for the last minute has taught me how to work under adverse time conditions. My procrastination has sometimes gone too far... When I was

studying restaurant administration in the final year of the course, I had
to write a thesis. I had an entire year to write it, but guess what...
I decided to write it literally two days before it was due, and to make
matters even worse, I had to write it in Dutch, a language I had just
learned and barely dominated. I ended up pulling it off.

DOES YOUR WORK BEGIN WITH RESEARCH? IF SO, WHAT KIND OF RESEARCH HAVE YOU DONE AND IN WHAT WAYS HAS THIS SATISFIED YOUR EXPECTATIONS?

Not always because many of the things I create come from spontaneity.
But many times, that same spontaneity comes out of research, by being
surrounded by all sorts of people, by reading the news, the things
I see and hear, research comes from my everyday life.

Regarding the Fakes, I research the artist. At the beginning of the
series, I was not doing it that much. But as the series started
evolving, I would examine the paintings I was making and the artist
themselves. It was a mixture of both.

My most extensive research comes from living life, analyzing the news,
and meeting people; that's my real research. Sometimes when I want to
go in-depth into a particular subject, I ask my followers on Instagram.
I create polls and ask about their thoughts and opinions on a specific
topic I am interested in.

Research is one of the most critical aspects of art creation. Through
it, I learn new things every day, capturing the human experience.
That is enough satisfaction.

WHAT ARE THE OVERALL THEMES THAT YOUR WORK SEEKS TO ADDRESS?

The human condition, what is being human, the fears and joys of being
human, our contradictions. We are living contradictions. We are a game
of ping-pong against the wall. I want to aim for what is human, our
mundanity, the thoughts that we all have but we don't release. That is
what I try to capture with my work. I do it in a raw and natural way,
being true to myself.

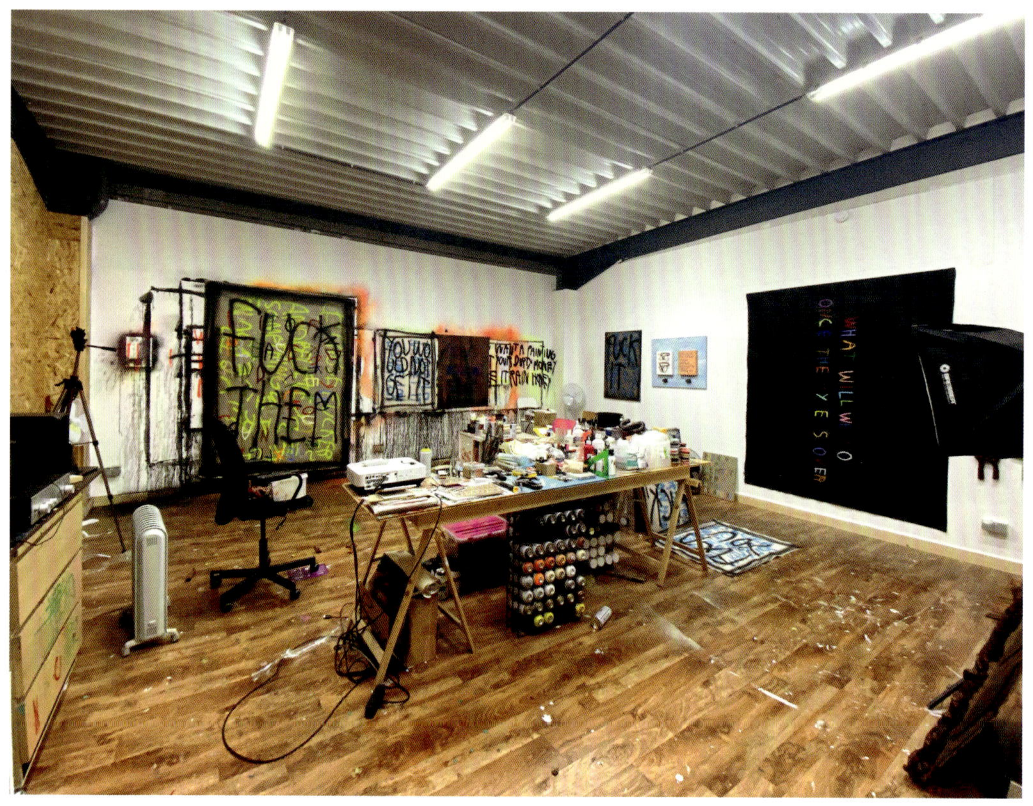

Studio shot, 2020

YOUR WORK HAS BEEN CALLED A NUMBER OF THINGS—A CRITIQUE OF THE ART WORLD, A TONGUE-IN-CHEEK JOKE THAT WE CAN COLLECTIVELY ENJOY AND NOT TAKE TOO SERIOUSLY, AND A CELEBRATION OF LIFE. DO YOU SEE THEM IN A PARTICULAR WAY?

I see my work as an expression of what I'm feeling and seeing. Life cannot be taken so seriously. You need to let things slide and not affect you. My art is all they say it is and more. It is an expression of my thoughts, a way to channel what's happening in the world and in my head. I enjoy creating conversations and sparking feelings that were dormant or were non-existent in my audience.

CAN YOU DESCRIBE THE SERIES FAKES? WHEN AND WHY IT BEGAN, WHAT IS ITS PURPOSE?

It all started in January 2017. I was faking a Warhol for fun. After several hours of work, I messed it up. It was a Mao. I tried to recreate the silkscreen print process on an inkjet printer, a regular house printer. I took high-quality papers and tried to align the ink with what I had painted, with the painting's black part. I had done it multiple times without success. I thought that this intent could be the right one, but unfortunately, the papers didn't align once more. I put so much time and effort into it that I decided not to throw it away. I decided to use it and embrace the fact that it was a fake Warhol.

Around that time, I had read an article about forgeries. It was about how half of the art that goes into auction is counterfeit. It was something I didn't know at the moment. I researched this topic, and I found out that forgeries in the art world are a big issue, that many have passed unperceived.

I decided to take my fake Warhol and showed it to the world. So this is how the Fakes series was born. It started from an accident, and it became bigger than itself. I started creating more fakes, doing more research and writing more messages on them about the fact that they were fake. One thing led to the next one. I started talking about society and the art world. It evolved into something bigger; I started addressing everyday life in my texts.

HOW CLOSELY DO YOU TRY TO REPRODUCE THE FAKES, IN TERMS OF SCALE, SURFACE, PAINT TYPE, AND SO FORTH?

When I started making the Fakes, I was recreating them, faking them however I wanted to. My first fakes were all small works on paper; I was afraid of going into a bigger scale or even switching to canvas. I also didn't have enough space in my studio to do larger works. Around May–June of 2017, I decided to jump into working with canvas and scaling up the pieces. I was tired of working on a small scale.

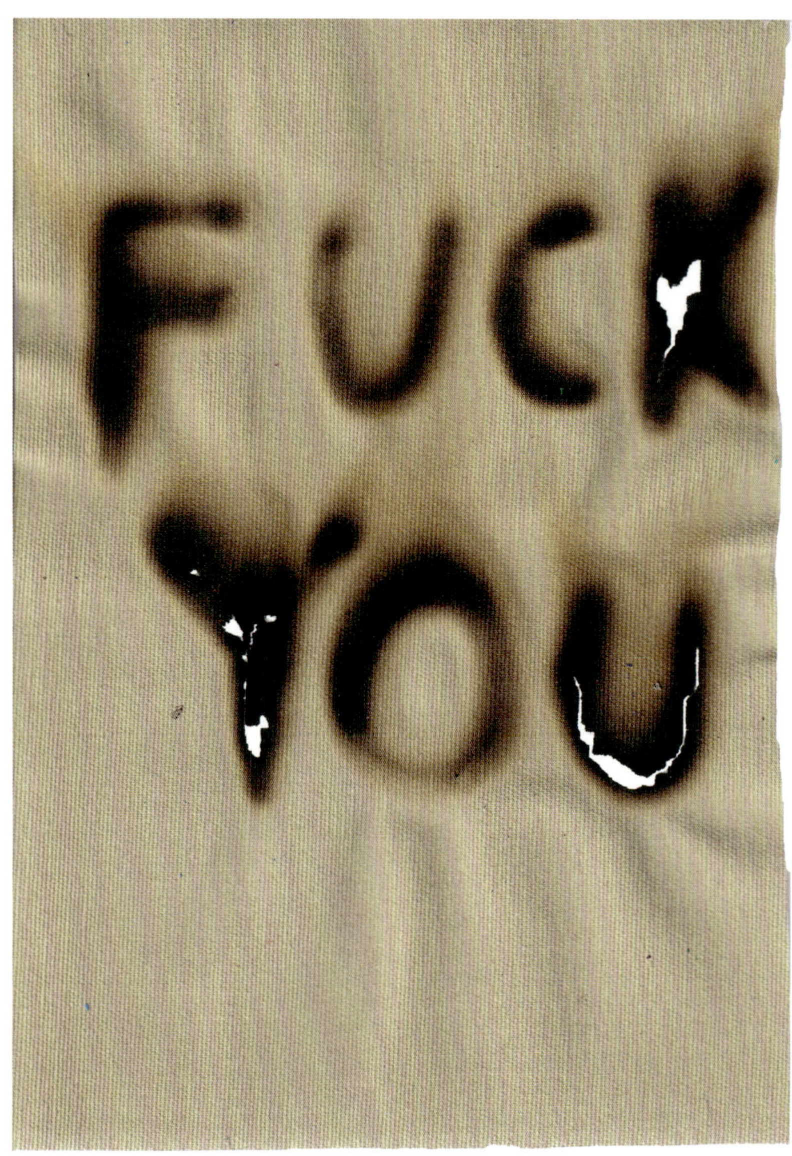

Fuck You, 2020
Blow torch on canvas,
27.9 x 21cm

FUCK, 2020
Corrugated fiberboard,
isocyanate /polyol resin,
plaster, acrylic paint,
and UV varnish

Page 125
Studio shot, 2020

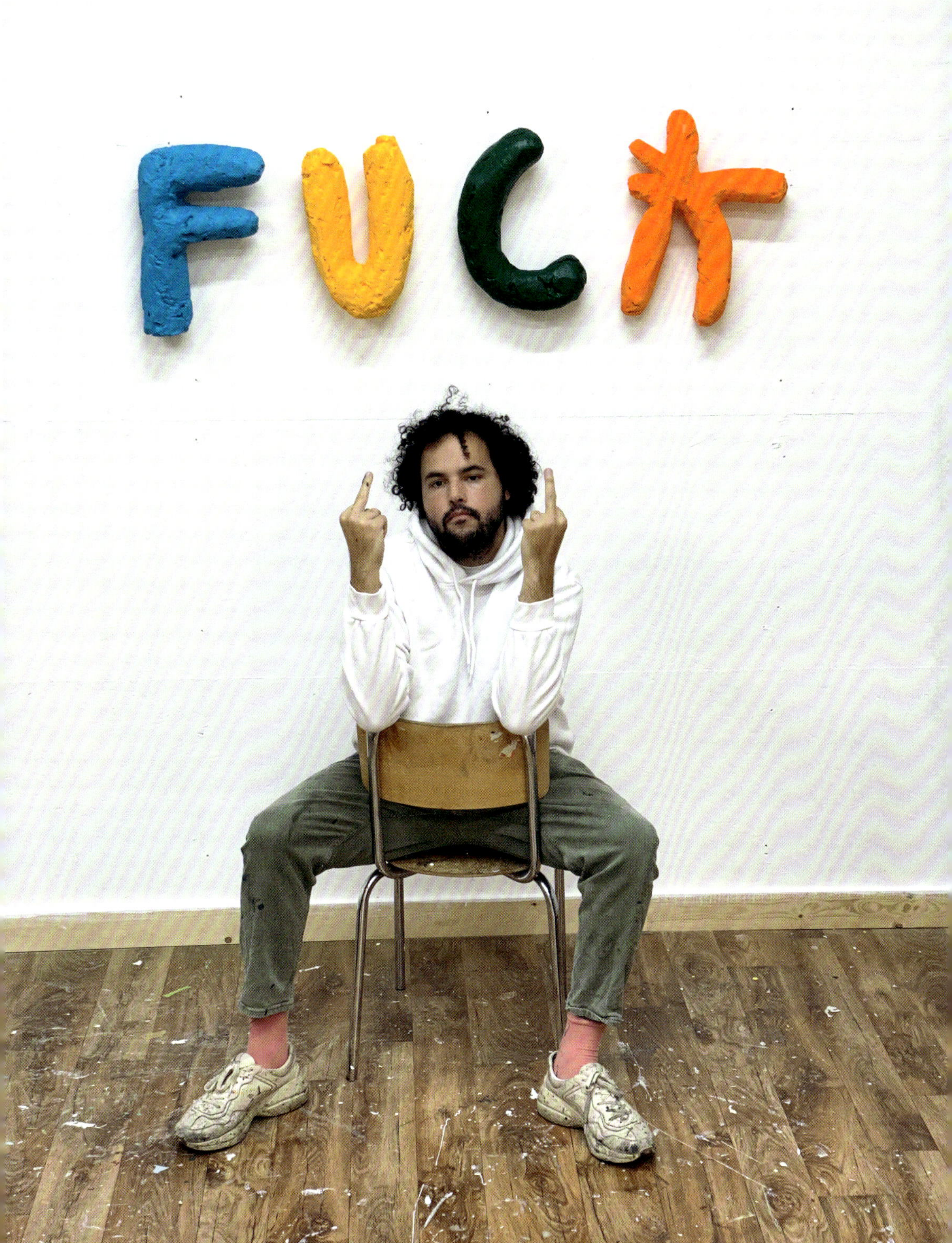

FUCK

Sometimes I would even stretch the paintings to give them a weird
appearance. I didn't respect dimensions or analyze them in-depth.
I would just translate what I saw from the original into my canvas.
And that went on for about a year.
By 2018 I started to consider the pieces' original sizes and did more
research. I checked their provenance and studied the history behind
each artwork. In 2019, I started recreating the Fakes in the original
paintings' exact sizes.
In the beginning, I didn't care too much about making the Fakes
as an exact copy of the originals because when something is fake,
there has to be a fake factor about them.
When I fake something, I don't try to make it exactly like the
original; you need to know it is fake because otherwise, what's the
point of just forging them. They would be only replicas. If there is
something off about them, then it is a fake. Some of my Fakes look
like the original pieces, but there is always a detail that makes
them an original imitation. You need to own what you are doing, or it
won't serve its point.
When I started faking the Rothkos, I worked with spray paint. In 2018
I switched my method. I started researching more on Rothko and his
practice.
I studied his method of creating several oil paint layers to create
the perfect texture he wanted. I started doing the same thing but
with acrylics reduced with water. I cooked them with a hairdryer and
high heat. The last Rothkos I made probably had nearly twenty to
thirty thin layers of paint that would give them the depth of a real
Rothko.
Another artist that I studied and analyzed was Basquiat. When faking
his works, I studied them for a couple of days to see how he painted
them. It was the reconstruction process of the painting. I was not
doing everything exactly as he did it.
His art is highly explosive and spontaneous, a true challenge if you
want to recreate it.

YOUR FAKES SERIES BEGAN AS A JOKE ABOUT THE ART WORLD, AUTHENTICITY, AND VALUE OF ARTWORKS, BUT NOW IT HAS AN ENTIRELY NEW LEVEL WHEN CONSIDERING FAKE NEWS. DOES THIS INSPIRE YOUR WORK?

Fake news affected how I created my works. I was creating counterfeit things while recognizing they were fake. Fake news has been around for years.
By the time I started producing the Fakes, there was a fake news boom. It was around the time that Trump became president of the US. People were always talking about what was fake and what was real. News authenticity was questioned at all times during this period; I was doing the same with my art.

WHAT DO YOU THINK ABOUT THE RELATIONSHIP BETWEEN CONTEMPORARY ART AND POLITICS IN GENERAL?

Contemporary is what's happening right now. There is a close relationship between art, politics, and everything taking place nowadays. Contemporary art captures contemporary society. Whatever happens in society goes hand in hand with art. Not every single artist uses politics as the main subject of their work, but the subject of their work is definitely influenced by politics whether they want it or not. Most aspects of our lives are impacted by politics, reflecting in our creative work.
Being confined or in lockdown during the COVID-19 pandemic has to do with politics. Politicians have decided what you have to do or not. The emotions that are born during this period have influenced my work, directly or indirectly. Even if politics is not the main topic of one's creation, it plays a role in what has been created.

DOES CENSORSHIP PLAY INTO YOUR WORK AT ALL?

With my work, I try to be as raw as I can. I try to say what I think without putting myself in an uncomfortable position. Being direct is one thing; acting stupid is another. Not everything needs to be said when you are thinking about it. There is a moment and time for everything.

Sometimes you need to sit down and analyze things. I don't like to say things in the heat of the moment. If I still have the same opinion about something after a while, I will say it. Even though I work with emotions and I capture them through my work, I don't let them control everything. It would be best if one thought before they talked. One can consider this as censorship to a certain extent because I am not generating the work, but I am still thinking about it. I will say what I have to say, but there are specific occasions in which a certain degree of caution and tact is needed.

I say what I think and how I think it, but I protect myself too, avoiding being placed in a compromising position.

YOU HAVE MENTIONED THAT YOUR FAKES SERIES IS FINISHED, AT LEAST FOR NOW. HOW DO YOU KNOW WHEN A WORK IS FINISHED OR WHEN A BODY OF WORK IS FINISHED?

A work is finished when I am satisfied with it. I feel that I don't need to keep adding to it, and I feel happy with the results. Sometimes there are some pieces that I start today and put away for a year to get to where I want to get. There are occasions when I simply have to discard the work because it is not taking me anywhere. It is more a quest for personal satisfaction. The Fakes were finished when I was done with the background, and I would write the text on them.

With the new line of work I am busy with right now, it is something else. I need to feel it. I need to channel the emotions of what I am writing on top of the canvas.

My Fakes are over; I am not making them anymore. If I ever feel like making them again, I will but I won't exhibit or share them. It would be a matter of personal satisfaction. No compromises will be made.

IS THERE A WORK FROM THE FAKES SERIES THAT YOU NEVER MADE, BUT WISH YOU HAD?

I wish I had faked more work from Dalí, Rembrandt, Rubens, or Van Gogh. I just made one Dalí. One of the reasons I stopped with the

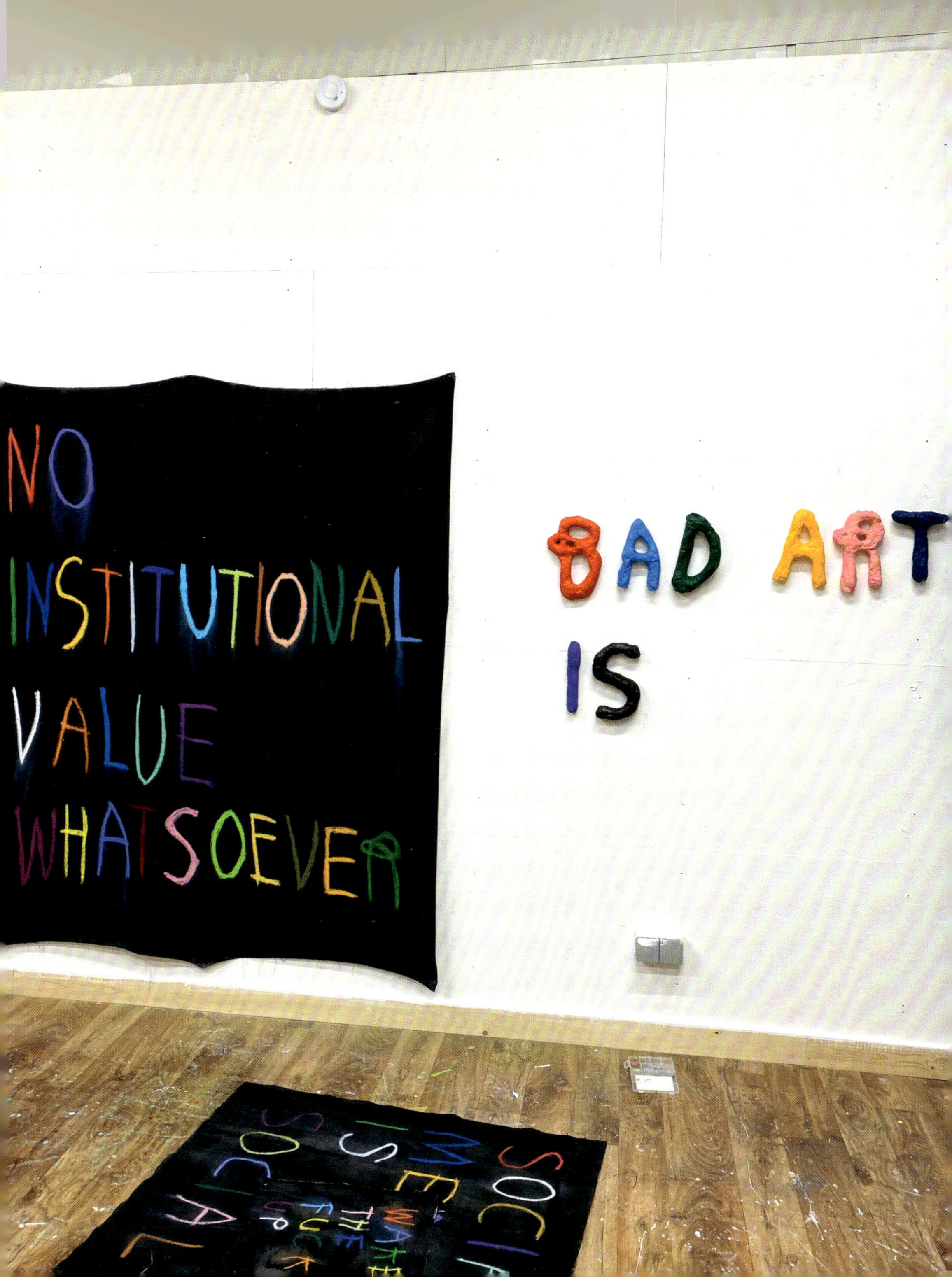

NO
INSTITUTIONAL
VALUE
WHATSOEVER
BAD ART
IS

Fakes is because faking them became a cycle that didn't let me grow
as an artist. Everything became very time scheduled. It was show
after show, compromise after compromise, and I did not have time to
do other things I wanted to do. I suddenly found myself trapped in a
routine; there was no time flexibility. Due to time reasons, I didn't
have the freedom to experiment and fake masterpieces. You cannot
fake a Rubens or a Rembrandt in two days. That takes more time and
dedication.

I had a crazy rhythm, and I needed to find my pace. I would knock out
ten paintings in a week. Sometimes I could take a few hours or weeks to
fake a Magritte. It depended on my mood and emotions.

Obviously, more complex pieces required more time, and at the moment,
I was not having enough.

YOUR INITIAL SUCCESS CAME FROM FAKES AND ENGAGEMENT WITH INSTAGRAM—DO YOU USE THE PLATFORM DIFFERENTLY NOW THAN YOU DID THEN?

Now I try to engage more with my audience, my followers. I post every
week, I do some type of exercise on my Instagram stories. Every
Wednesday, or when I remember it is Wednesday, I do my polls, about
100 yes or no phrases that people might answer. I am actually not
asking anything; I'm just posting about subjects that have come to my
attention during the week. It is a way of capturing what's happening
in the world, what's happening in my mind. Sometimes it is just about
random things that don't make sense. I just throw them out there to see
people's reactions. I play around with these things and try to create
contradictions. The results are amazing.

I engage more and use the platform to analyze what's going on in
people's minds. I use this interaction to connect more with my
followers. It becomes a social experiment in a certain way because
I have access to half a million people's emotions and thoughts. You
can see that most of us, regardless of our personal characteristics,
are all going through the same shit at a certain point in life.

THERE IS SOMETHING INHERENTLY "FAKE" ABOUT MAINTAINING
A SOCIAL MEDIA PRESENCE, I'M CURIOUS HOW YOU NEGOTIATE THESE
CONTRADICTIONS.

I totally agree with the fact that social media is fake. We portray ourselves how we want to be seen, the nicest side of our personal stories. We don't show the nasty side.

Sometimes you cannot negotiate with it. It is human nature to show the best side. We share what we want, the rest we keep to ourselves. Sadly, we cannot see the realness of a situation. We don't see the dark side. That doesn't sell, so probably that is why it's not shown. That's the way we are.

Social media is a lie, a distraction from our reality that makes us feel better. It is like a drug and an addiction.

I just post when I feel like doing it, and it is not necessarily the best side of me. I choose to be present when I want to be present. We look for realness on social media, but not everything needs to be shared on social media. Some people overshare in their quest to get approval from others. They should devote all this energy, instead, to enjoy life.

**YOU CREATE A WEEKLY INSTAGRAM POLL THAT HIGHLIGHTS VARIOUS
CURRENT GLOBAL ISSUES, WHICH OFTEN LEADS TO DIRECT ENGAGEMENT
WITH YOUR FOLLOWERS. WHEN CONSIDERING THE INDIVIDUAL
AND SOCIETY AS A WHOLE, WHAT INTERESTS YOU ABOUT THESE
TWO WORLDS? HOW DO YOU SEE THE CONNECTION BETWEEN EACH
OF THEM AND WHAT IS THE CONNECTION BETWEEN THEM AND YOUR
OWN WORK?**

Individuals and their ways of acting form society. What one individual feels is often reflected in the whole society. We are social creatures, and we tend to feel the same things and go through similar situations. We react in similar ways. This makes up a society. These two worlds rely on each other.

In my work, I talk about society. Therefore I am referring to multiple individuals, the feelings of the collective. My work is

about my feelings as an individual and my position in society, and
how it reflects on all of us. The narrative starts from me as an
individual, how I think, and how I see what's happening in the world.

YOU'VE LIKENED ANOTHER ONE OF YOUR INSTAGRAM PROJECTS, THE SECRET DEALER, TO A CONFESSIONAL—DOES SPIRITUALITY AND/OR RELIGION PLAY INTO YOUR WORK AT ALL?

I believe in everything and in nothing. I do not have a religion, but
I consider myself a spiritual person. I wonder a lot about life, its
meaning. I deal with essential questions, and I separate my mind and
body to get lost in this weird trance. I believe that people should
live and let live, just respect each other.

That is one of the reasons behind The Secret Dealer. Through it, I try
to normalize what everybody does, but that is often considered taboo.
Every Friday, or whenever I want, I share the stories that many of us
have in common. For example, depression is a common denominator for
all of us. Everybody gets depressed, has been depressed, or will get
depressed. It is part of our human condition, yet we don't talk about
it. Instead, we label people as crazy or outcasts without helping them
with something so ordinary as breathing or being.

AFTER FAKES, YOU BEGAN CORNY QUOTES. SAME QUESTION: WHEN DID IT BEGIN, WHY, AND WHAT IS ITS INTENTION?

Before starting with the Corny Quotes, I was writing my thoughts in
black and white on paper. I used to call them Shit CB Says. I changed
the name when I started using colors to write the texts.

It all started as an accident. Back in August 2019, I was in Miami
visiting my grandfather. One day I went to Target to buy shampoo—I buy
my shampoo in the US because I cannot find it in Europe. They had this
back-to-school sale, and I stumbled into the crayon section. They had
these huge boxes of 150 crayons that reminded me of my childhood. I
decided to buy a couple of those boxes even if, at the time, I didn't
know what I was going to use them for.

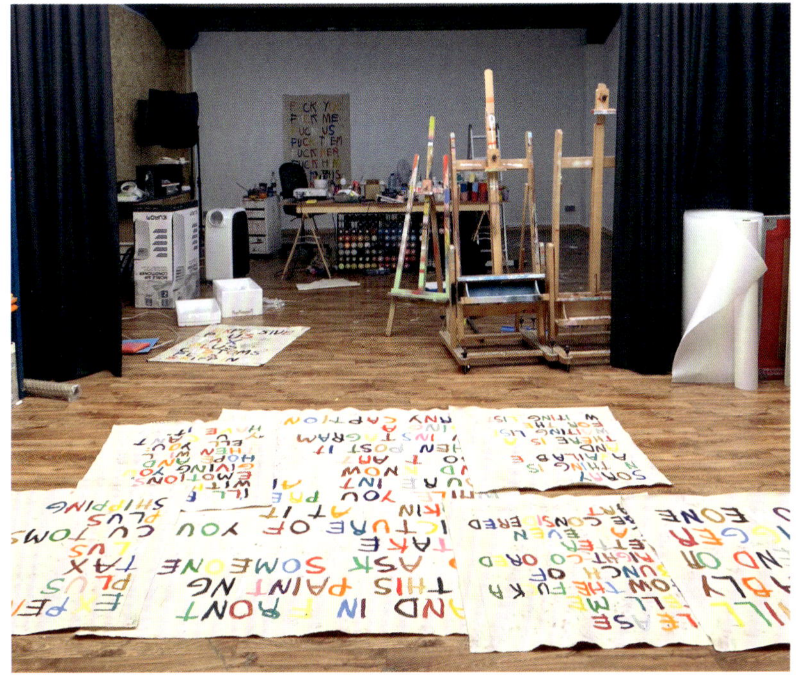

A few days later, I was in the Dominican Republic visiting my grandma.
We started going over some of my childhood paintings that my mom had
carefully kept through time. To my surprise, I found one that had my
name or something written in different colors with crayons. The idea
just popped up immediately in my head. I decided to recreate my three-
year-old self. That's how the corniness started.

I added subjects to my narrative and dialogue. With the Corny Quotes,
I started portraying human feelings rather than just writing about the
art world. I started talking about my feelings and decided to talk more
about the human condition, corny things. Through them, I express my
inner thoughts and feelings while also portraying society.

You have not asked yet, but I will answer this now: Why do I write
instead of just painting? Things can be better understood if they are
written, even if people interpret them in their own way. It is a better
way to get my message across. My handwriting is peculiar and dear to
me. As a kid in school, my teachers often told me that my handwriting

sucked, that it was awful, and it would take me nowhere. I had to do tons of calligraphy in school, but there was no way to tame my letters. My dyslexia didn't help too much either. I was a late writer and reader. I learned how to read when I was around eight, and I still cannot write correctly in any language. Often, my dyslexic condition gets in my way. Sometimes I let it be; I scratch out the mistake or draw arrows pointing to the letters' right position. In other cases, I just carry on and make something new. Even nowadays, writing is difficult.

Listening is a different story. I learn and understand better when I listen. I am proficient in several languages now, at least in the oral and listening part. However, I cannot write any of them correctly. Sometimes I even make up words. Unconsciously I do crossovers with words in the languages I know and create new terms that make sense in my head. When I use them in my conversations with other people, they always wonder what I'm saying. I often get the same reaction—that is not even a word. What are you saying? It is something I have always done. As a kid, I would combine Spanish and English words and would come up with a new expression. Fortunately, technology helps me correct my written mistakes.

This is how life works. Just look at what I am doing now. I use my handwriting to make a living and express myself—ironies of life. At all times, you just need to embrace yourself.

CONSIDERING THE CURRENT HEALTH CRISIS OF COVID-19, HOW DO YOU SEE YOUR ARTISTIC WORK AND YOUR OWN ROLE AS AN ARTIST? AND HOW HAS THE PANDEMIC PERHAPS CHANGED OUR PERCEPTION OF ART AND LIFE IN GENERAL?

What is happening right now is extremely sad; many people have died; many people have lost their jobs; others have lost everything. It is a crisis in every single sense for all humankind. We are living in a lockdown, living differently for more than a year. It is pure horror. Everything changes in times of crisis. These times are not an exception. Change is the only permanent thing in our lives. Change is the only thing we have to get comfortable with because things change whether we like it or not.

My work has been clearly affected by the pandemic. At the beginning of the crisis, I had many projects canceled. On the other hand, I had more time for myself. Therefore I decided to stop with the Fakes. It was the perfect excuse to stop with what I was doing and start something new. Now I have more time to experiment and think about things. It is more me-on-me time.

Before the pandemic, I traveled weekly, taking two flights per week. My life has drastically changed since everything started. It has brought positive and negative changes into my life.

My mental health has suffered greatly with all the restrictions, rules, and confinements. I cannot stay still in a place for more than two weeks. I need to be exposed to new things; I need to meet new people, be in new places, go to restaurants, have a drink, and do something that keeps me out of a repetitive cycle. With the lockdown, I got stuck in a routine, not being able to go out or socialize. I am not a very social person, but I enjoy going out and seeing new things. I enjoy living life, and with all these limitations, my mental health has suffered. The pandemic has imposed a drastic change of lifestyle for me. I am still struggling to adapt. In the end, we all have to adjust to this new living; otherwise, we will perish. I have been more creative; I have been writing and expressing my ideas more often. Art has definitely changed by the spirit of times. It is capturing the moment we are trapped in.

We are living in a limited virtual world. I have learned that we are surrounded and governed by inept people. Their lack of vision and fast actions have put us in the place we are now. Some countries like Taiwan, Australia, and New Zealand seem to have done things correctly. They are living a "normal life" without limitations. They are not open to other countries, but they keep going with their everyday lives. They are not trapped in this virtuality we have been forced to live in.

It is the population's fault too. Human beings are selfish by nature. As a collective, we don't respect anything, and governments don't know how to enforce their laws.

THINKING BACK ON YOUR PROJECTS AND EXHIBITIONS THUS FAR, WHICH GAVE YOU THE MOST SATISFACTION? WHICH WAS THE MOST DISAPPOINTING?

Working on this book is the most satisfying project I have done so far. It is a breath of fresh air and a milestone in my career. I am expressing myself in ways I've never done before. This book is like my own confessionary; it's time for me to tell my secrets. It is a way to be transparent with myself and the art I'm creating. I am incredibly thankful for this opportunity and for all the support I have received from my friends Nick and Marcello, my Plan X gallerists. I would also like to thank Skira editore, both of you, Cesare and Jack, for being part of this project. I have had great shows, but this book is a tremendous personal achievement and project.

The most disappointing show I had was in Venice in 2019. The positive side of it was that it helped me grow as a person and artist because I had to face difficult situations and deal with all sorts of people. The pieces I made for the show were among my best and favorite works, but this show did not compensate for the love and effort I put in creating them. It was not a good show.

WHICH ARTIST OF THE PAST OR PRESENT WOULD YOU MOST LIKE TO COLLABORATE WITH?

I am not a fan of collaborations. There has to be chemistry between the other artist and me for a collaboration to happen. I might like someone's work, but that doesn't mean I will work with them. I need some sort of chemistry to make it happen. I need to connect with both the art and the artist. The perfect collaboration would include getting to know the person first and maybe work with them later. If I had to name someone to answer this question, I would say Duchamp,

Warhol, or Bosch. I really enjoy and admire their work. Honestly, choosing one of them would be merely based on their work because I would never have the chance to meet them and explore our chemistry. This is just a superficial answer.

HAVING WORKED AND EXHIBITED IN MANY PARTS OF THE WORLD, WHAT DO YOU SEE AS SOME OF THE MAIN DIFFERENCES IN THE CONTEMPORARY ART SCENE IN THE EU AND US?

In general, the European crowd tends to have higher cultural knowledge, a more extensive understanding of art history. They live in the Old World and are born surrounded by cultural heritage. Europe is smaller than the US and—artistically speaking—this is an advantage. Culture and art travel easily from one country to another. The European audiences are more inclined towards classical art and formality.

On the other hand, the US is massive and has not been greatly influenced by neighboring countries. However, the US is a country built by immigrants; it is a melting pot. The combination of all these factors and an unstoppable accelerated way of living gives them a different vision about things, a faster speed of reaction. To a certain extent, they are more open-minded and embrace all types of art manifestations. Not being greatly affected by art formalisms allows them to accept and embrace contemporary art. There is no urge to understand; they feel art and take it as it is. They have an informal approach to all this mumble-jumble.

YOUR WORK OFTEN EMPLOYS VARIOUS CANONICAL WORKS FROM ART HISTORY. AS A CONTEMPORARY ARTIST, DO YOU FIND IT IMPORTANT TO SEEK CONNECTIONS WITH ART HISTORY?

The past is significant. We cannot live in it, but we need to learn from it and consider it for our present. To build something new and valuable now, it is essential to go back to the past, learn, and remember our valuable lessons.

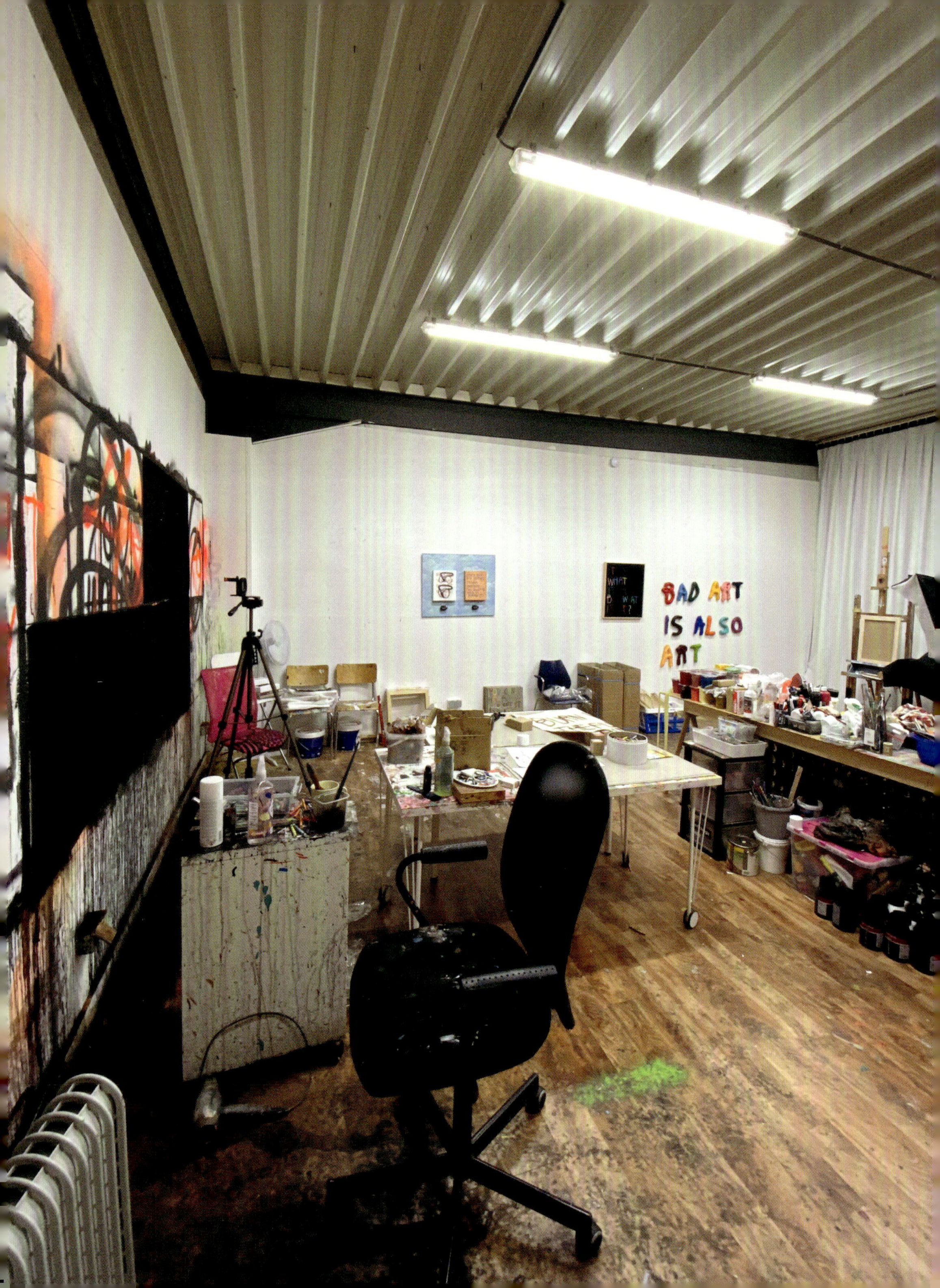
BAD ART
IS ALSO
ART

It is also vital to create your own history. Art is expressing what's
going on. It is good to use techniques and subjects from the past
to compare them to your present reality, to adapt them to our current
situation.

**ALL OF YOUR WORK OFFERS OBSERVATIONS ON THE STATE
OF THE ART WORLD TODAY—WHAT ARE YOUR TOP
CONCERNS WHEN CONSIDERING THE PRESENT SYSTEM OF ART
AND CULTURE?**

Everything in life is about connections. You can be the best artist,
capture things properly, and be the best in what you do, but things
will not work out if you are not with the right people. One of my top
concerns is that everything is in the hands of a small group that
controls everything. The system should be more open and inclusive,
more participatory.

It is about taste. I could like dembow, and somebody else would
probably prefer opera, but that doesn't mean that dembow is not
culture. There are many artists and artworks that are annihilated
even before they start because this "elite" decides that they are not
worthy. This little group should agree to disagree. They don't need
to like certain things but should recognize they exist.

My second concern is this need of having to label everything. What
is more important, the TYPE of art I make or my art itself? I do what
I do; the name it has is not relevant. I wouldn't say I like it when
I'm asked to classify the art I'm creating. I am not a fan of labels;
I refuse to label my work.

Placing my art into a label takes away its meaning. My objective is
to make art, regardless of the style or movement I fit in. Name it as
you wish; just leave me out of it. I don't care about the fucking
label. Obviously, if I have created multiple works with similar
characteristics, subject, and techniques I'll give them a name and
classify them as a new series of work. All the other classifications
can be done by someone else.

The artistic voice has to follow the correct channels to impact society. In my opinion, good art is art that captures the moment and what the artist was feeling when the work was created. If you can do it properly, your audience will react to it. The impact and connection with the audience are always worthy, even if their interpretation and feelings do not coincide with mine as an artist. If I make the audience feel, my job is done. It is crucial to make people think.

HOW DO YOU SEE YOUR OWN PRACTICE FITTING INTO THIS SYSTEM THAT YOU CRITIQUE?

I am a slave of the system—a hypocrite, to a certain extent. We are living contradictions. It is impossible to escape the system. I have gallerists; I have dealers, I am a collector, I buy from the system I sometimes criticize. We are stuck in the system, and it is not something bad, necessarily.
I am forced to fit even if, from time to time, I protest against it. I try to bring changes, and sometimes the only way to succeed in this constant struggle is by realizing what is wrong with the system. Things don't get fixed overnight. The first step to solve a problem is to recognize such problems exist. I am a part of the system, but hopefully, what I do will somehow improve it.

Page 134
Studio shot, 2020

Recycle, 2020
Color pencils on
paper, 27.9 x 21cm

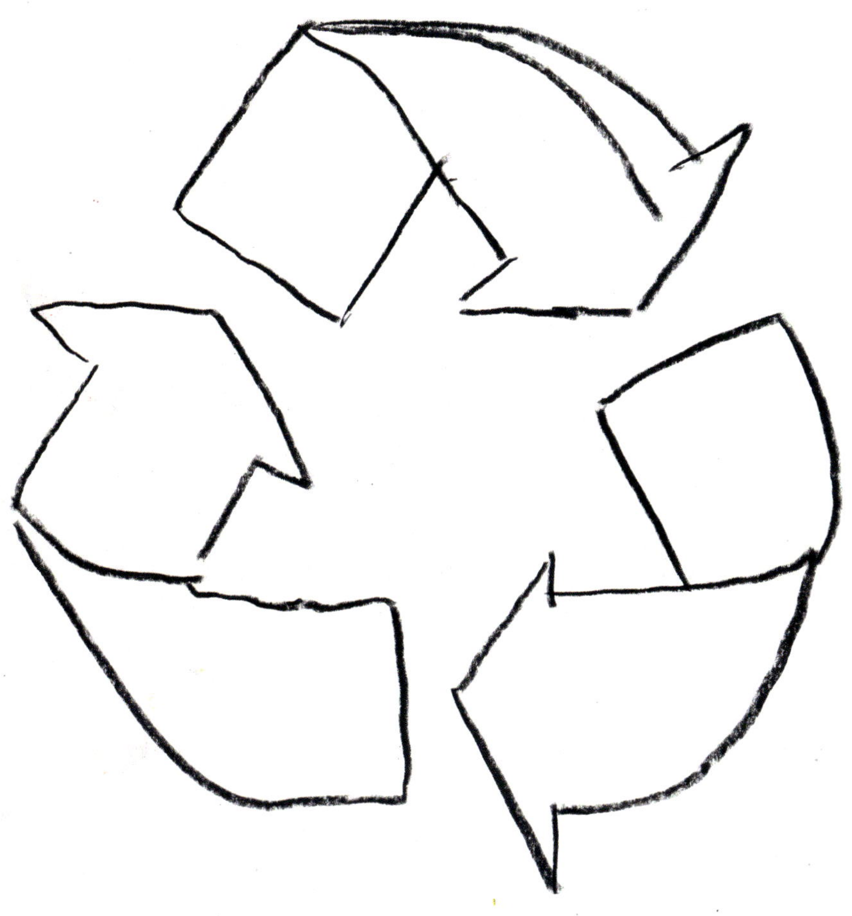

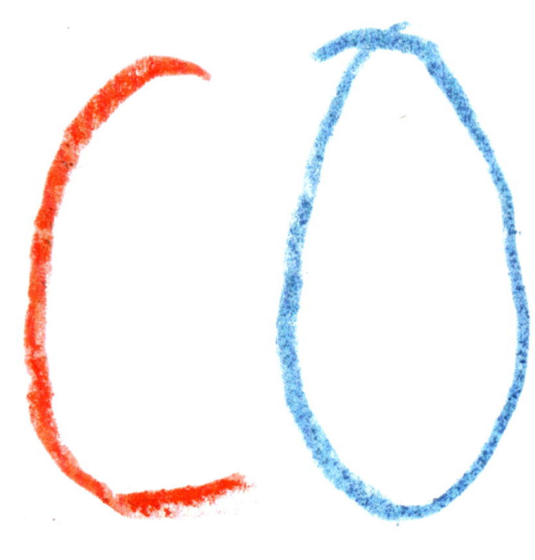

ANY

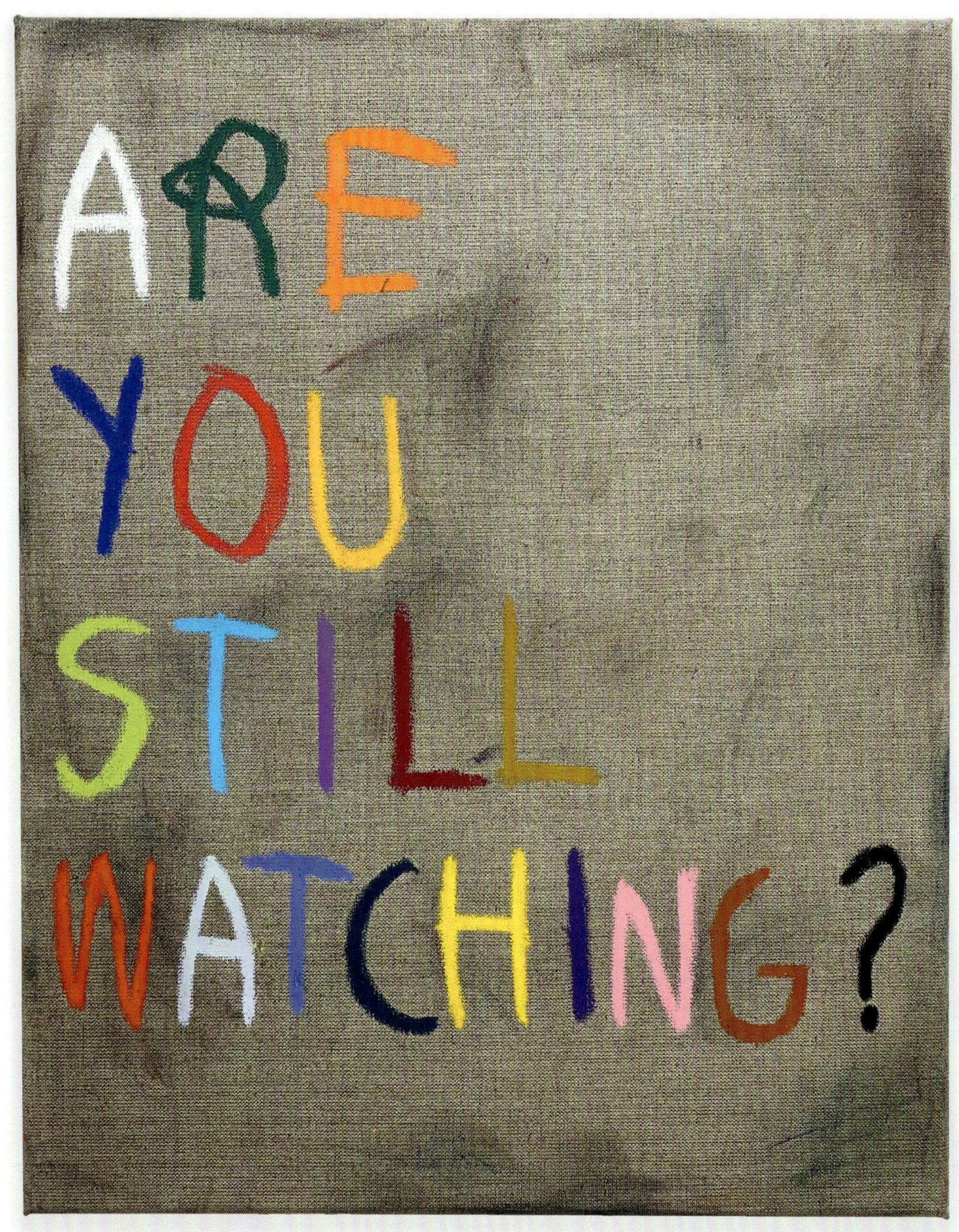

ARE YOU STILL WATCHING?

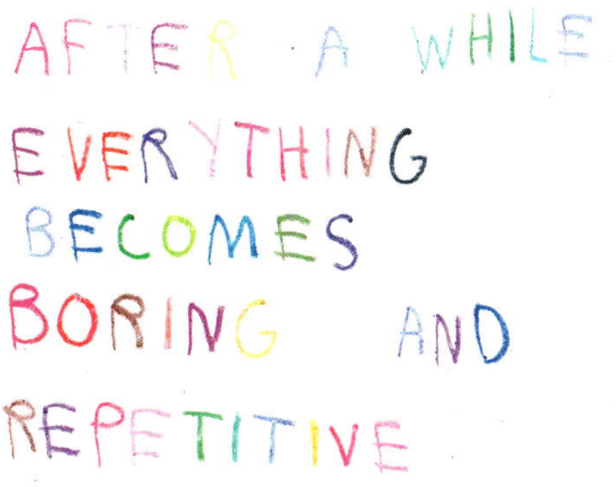

AFTER A WHILE
EVERYTHING
BECOMES
BORING AND
REPETITIVE

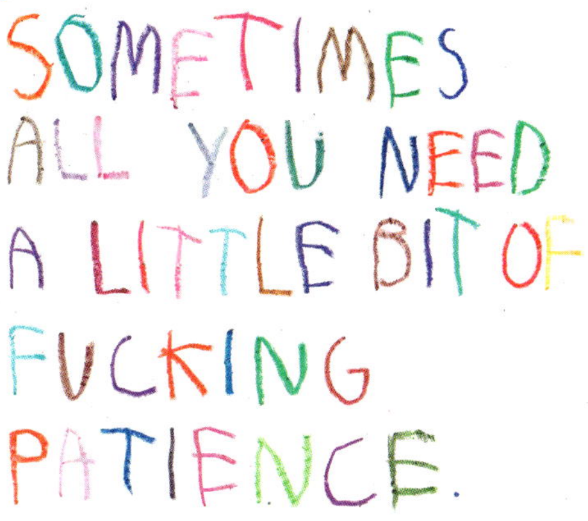

SOMETIMES
ALL YOU NEED
A LITTLE BIT OF
FUCKING
PATIENCE.

*I Have a Limited
Attention Span*, 2020
Wax oil pastels on raw
linen, 50 x 40 cm

Untitled (Study), 2019
Wax crayons on paper,
27.9 x 21cm

Untitled (Study), 2020
Wax crayons on paper,
27.9 x 21cm

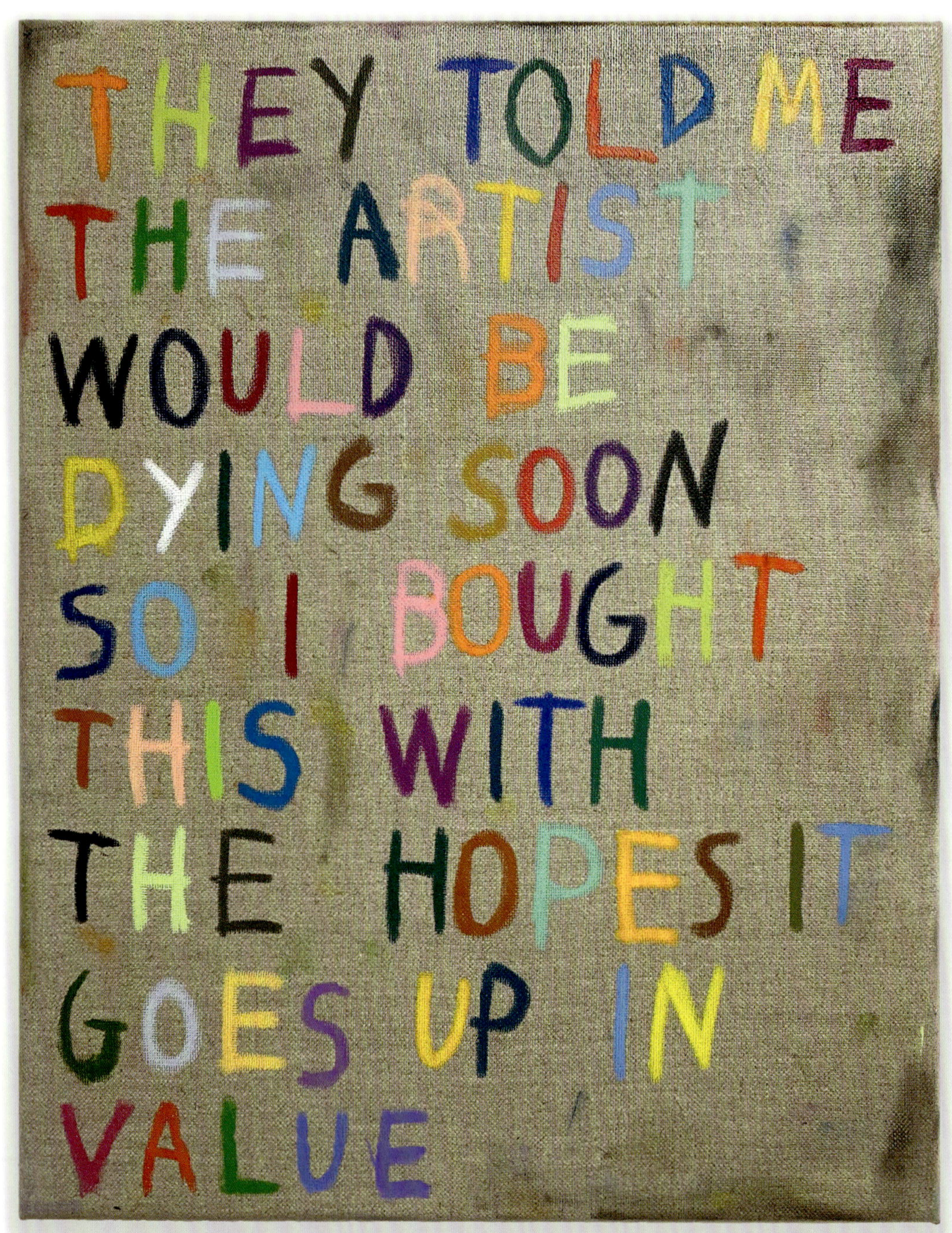

THEY TOLD ME
THE ARTIST
WOULD BE
DYING SOON
SO I BOUGHT
THIS WITH
THE HOPES IT
GOES UP IN
VALUE

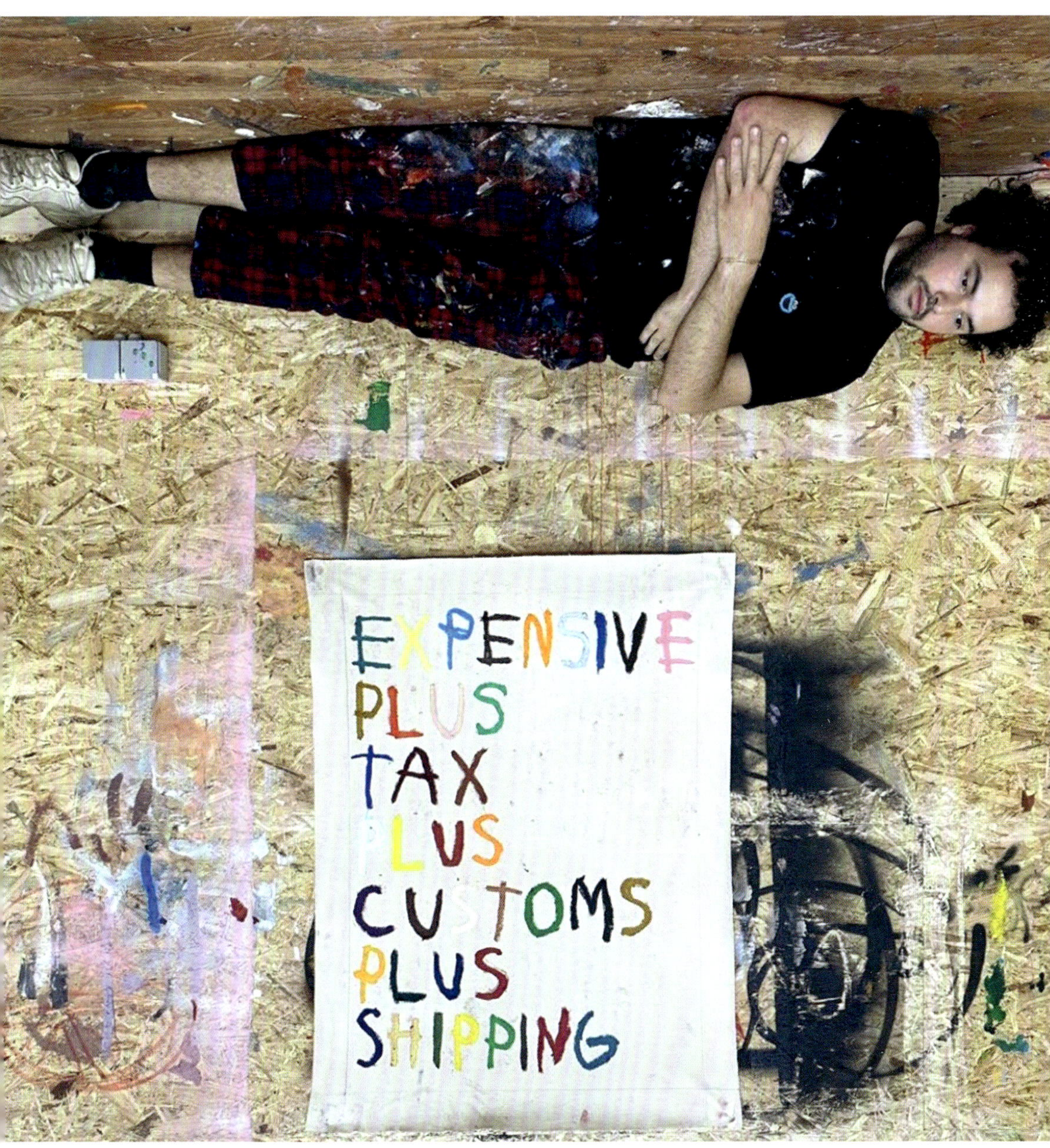

*Can't Wait for the Artist
to Die Soon LOL*, 2020
Wax pastels on raw
linen 50 x 40 cm

Expensive, 2020
Oil bars on raw cotton
canvas primed with
transparent gel medium,
95.4 x 69 cm

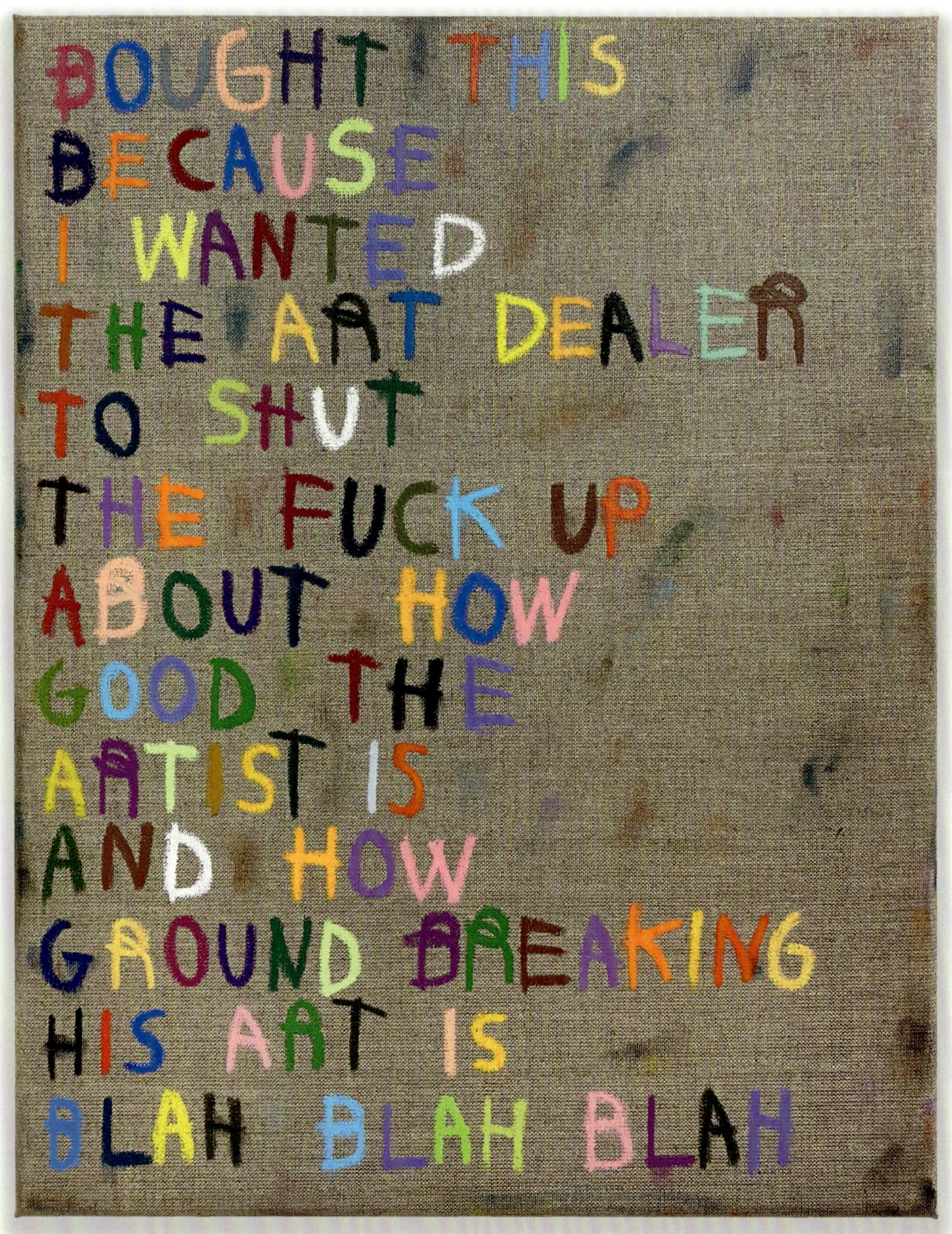

BOUGHT THIS
BECAUSE
I WANTED
THE ART DEALER
TO SHUT
THE FUCK UP
ABOUT HOW
GOOD THE
ARTIST IS
AND HOW
GROUND BREAKING
HIS ART IS
BLAH BLAH BLAH

If I Buy This Will You Leave Me the Fuck Alone?, 2020
Wax pastels on raw linen, 50 x 40 cm

Untitled (This Is to Art What Taco Bell Is to Cuisine), 2020
Markers on paper, 27.9 x 21cm

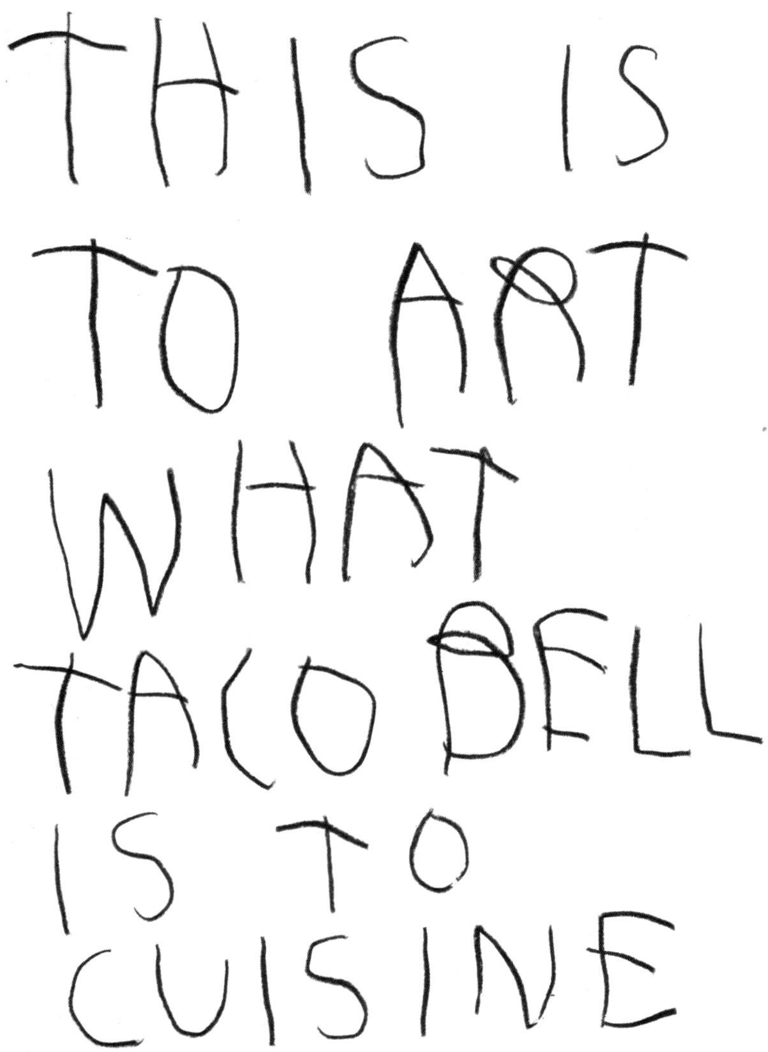

THIS IS
TO ART
WHAT
TACO BELL
IS TO
CUISINE

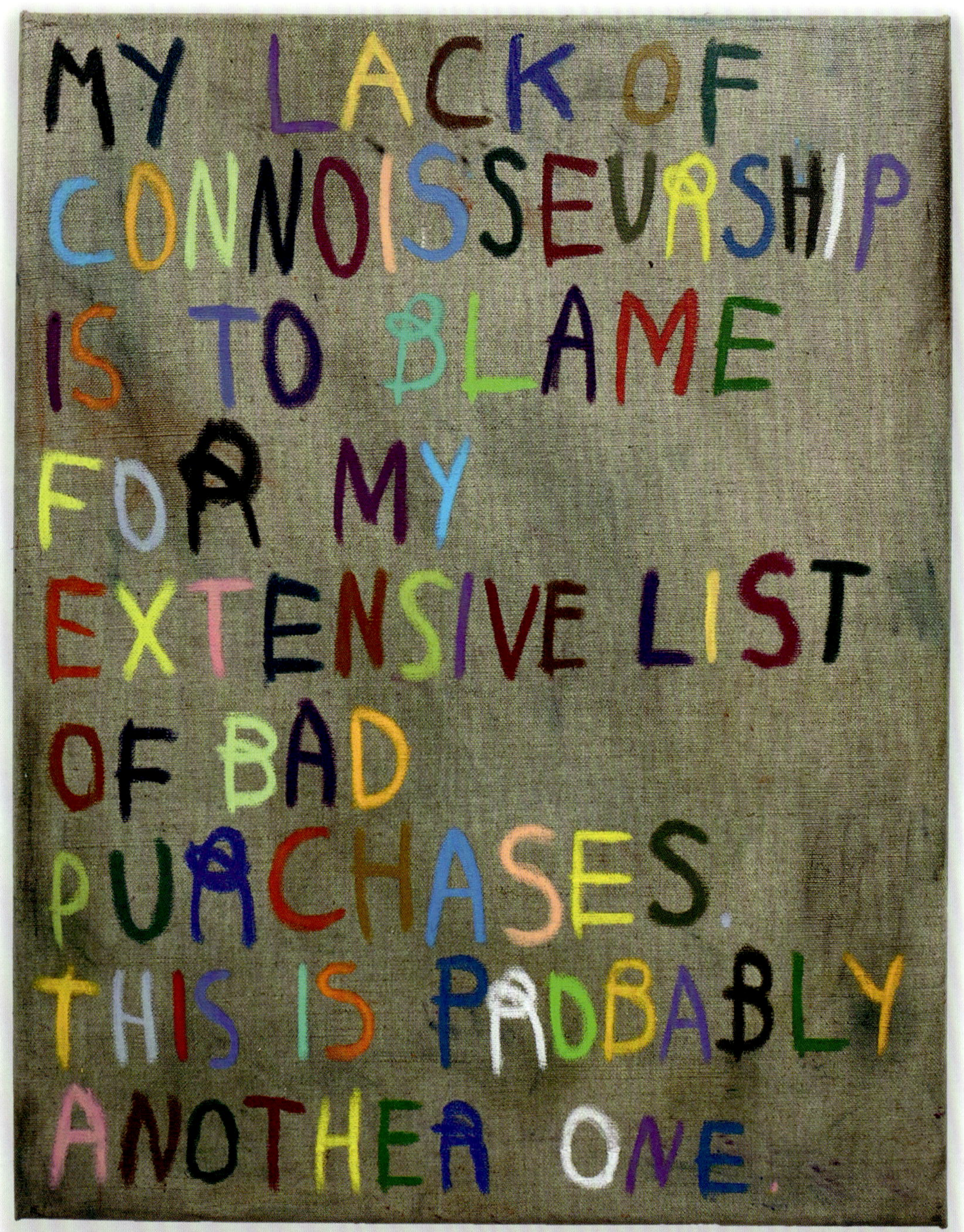
MY LACK OF
CONNOISSEURSHIP
IS TO BLAME
FOR MY
EXTENSIVE LIST
OF BAD
PURCHASES.
THIS IS PROBABLY
ANOTHER ONE.

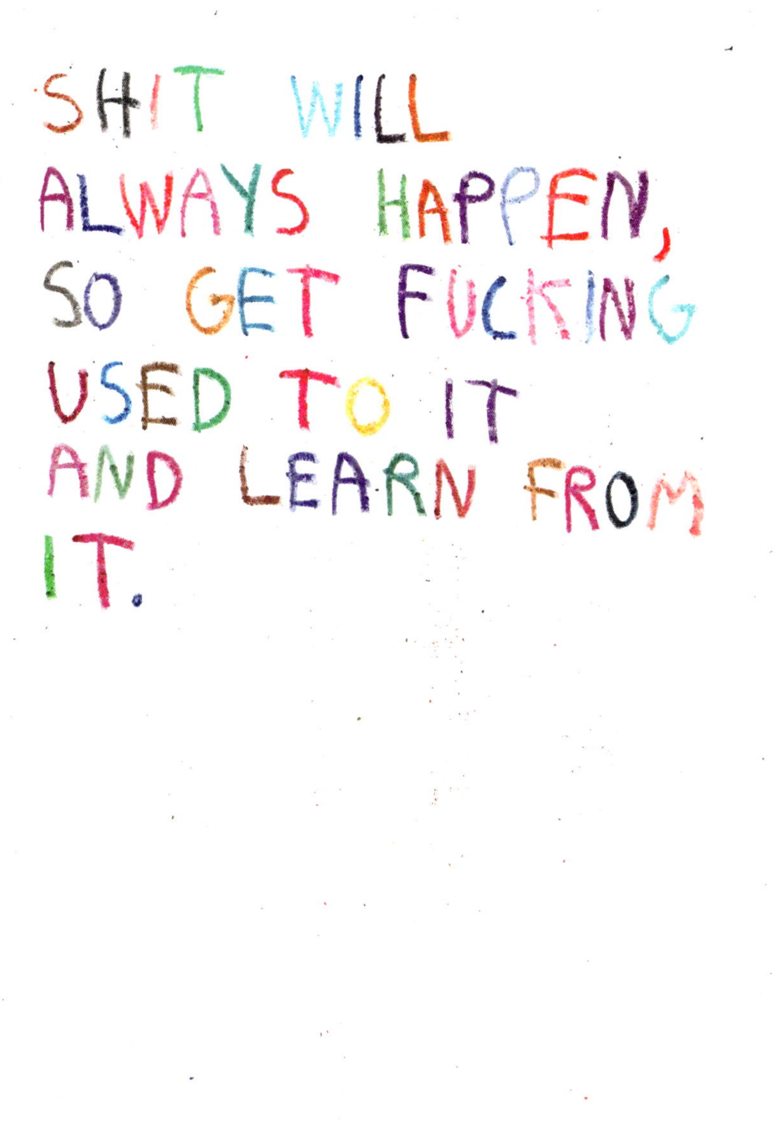

You Can't Imagine All the Shit I've Bought, 2020
Wax pastels on raw linen, 50 x 40 cm

Untitled (Shit Will Always Happen), 2019
Wax crayons on paper, 27.9 x 21cm

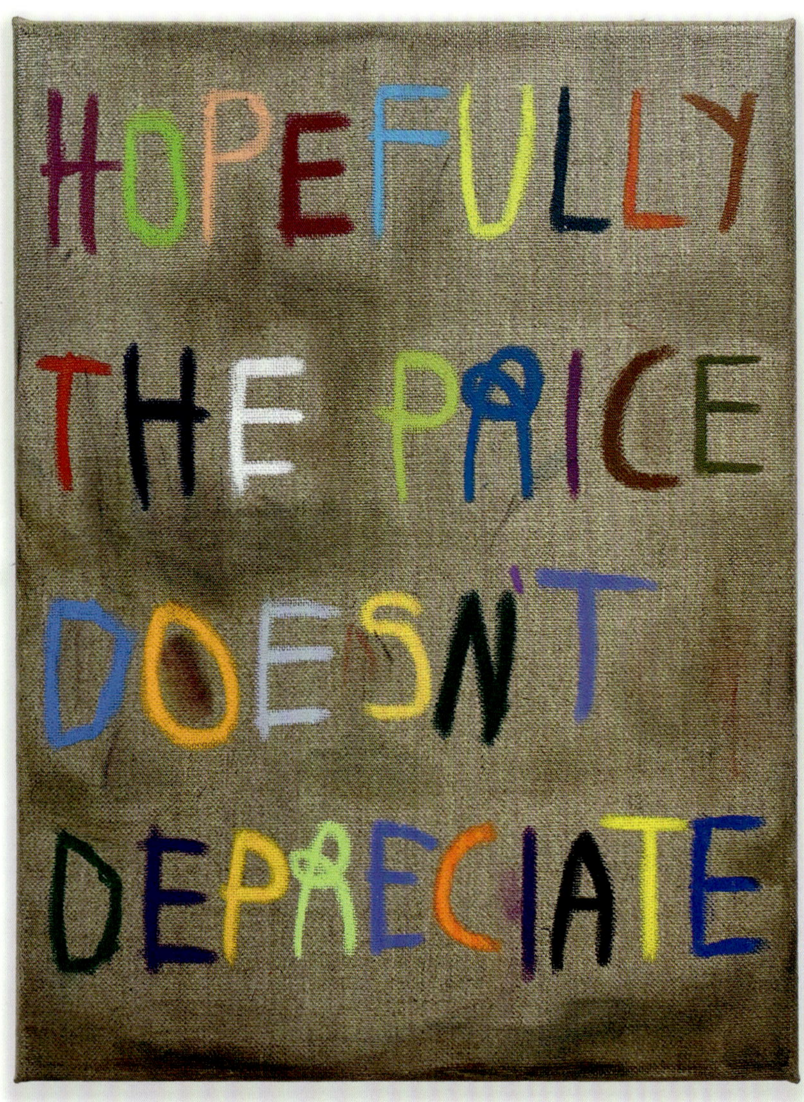

Hopefully It Wasn't Hype and Speculation, 2020
Wax pastels on raw linen, 40 x 30 cm

Hopefully I'll Be Able to Sell It at Auction or in the Secondary Market, 2020
Wax pastels on raw linen, 50 x 40 cm

IT'S ALL A
MATTER OF
TIME UNTIL
I FIND OUT
I GOT
SCAMMED
BUYING
THIS PIECE

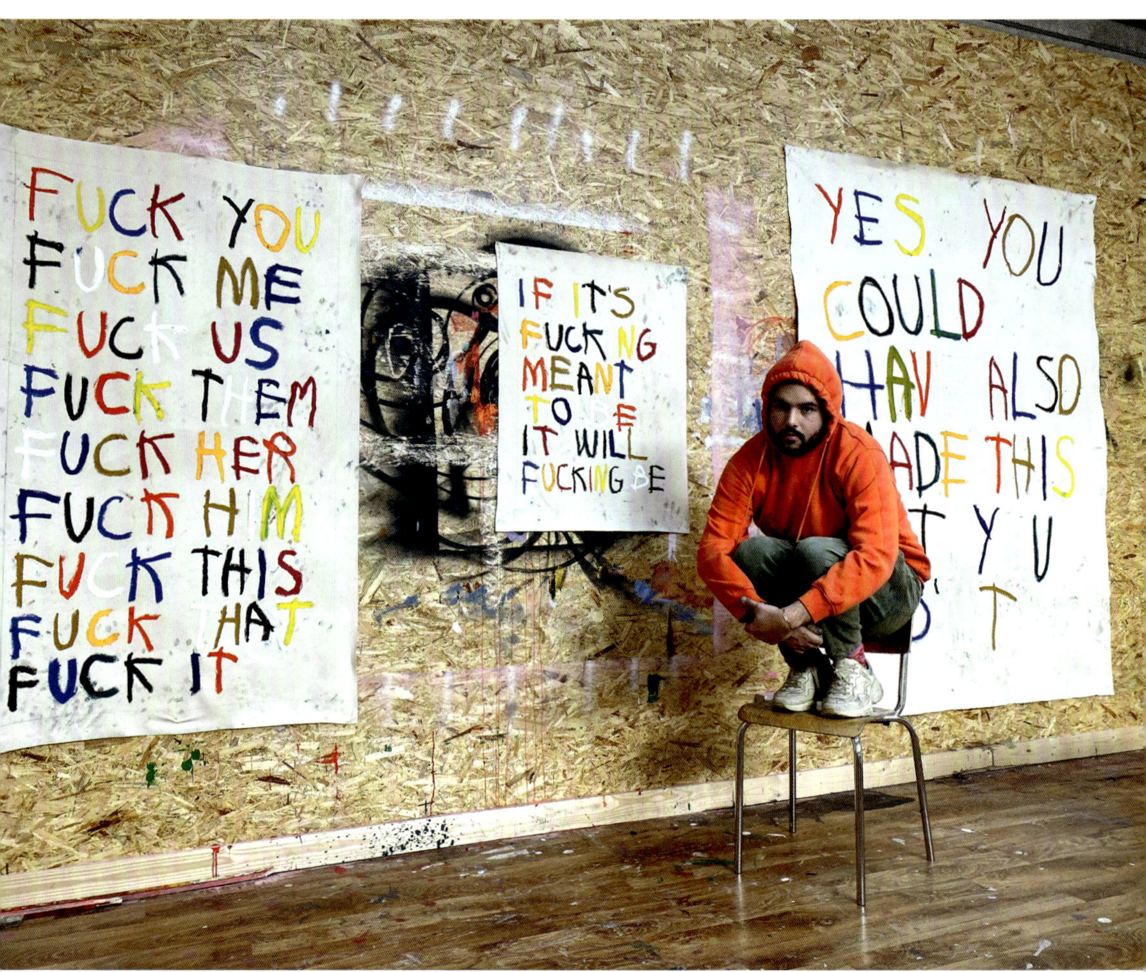

CB in the studio, 2020

Does It Really Fucking Matter?, 2020
Water-soluble oil pastels, oil sticks, mineral water, and acrylic paint on raw cotton canvas, 50 x 40 cm

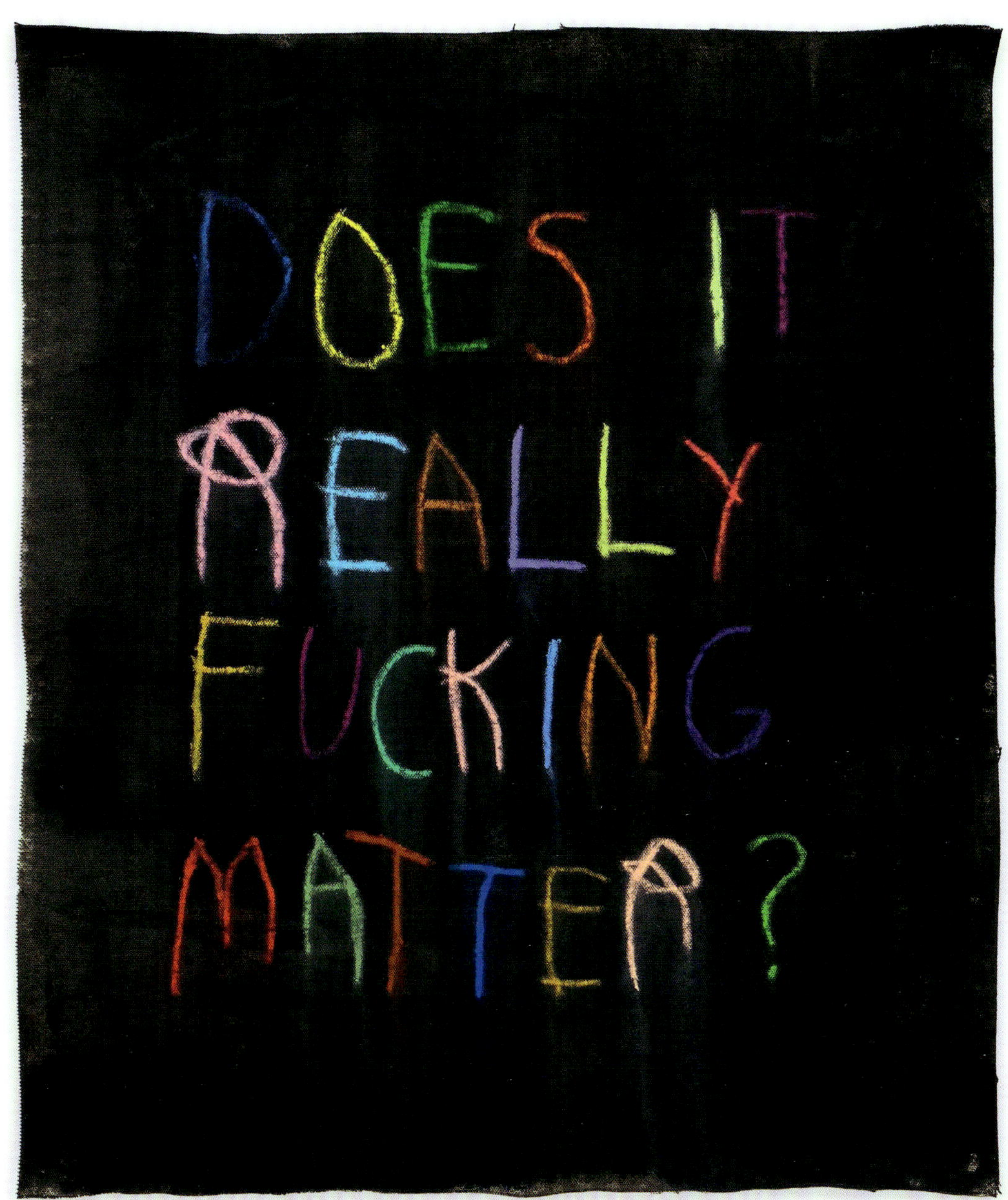

DOES IT
REALLY
FUCKING
MATTER?

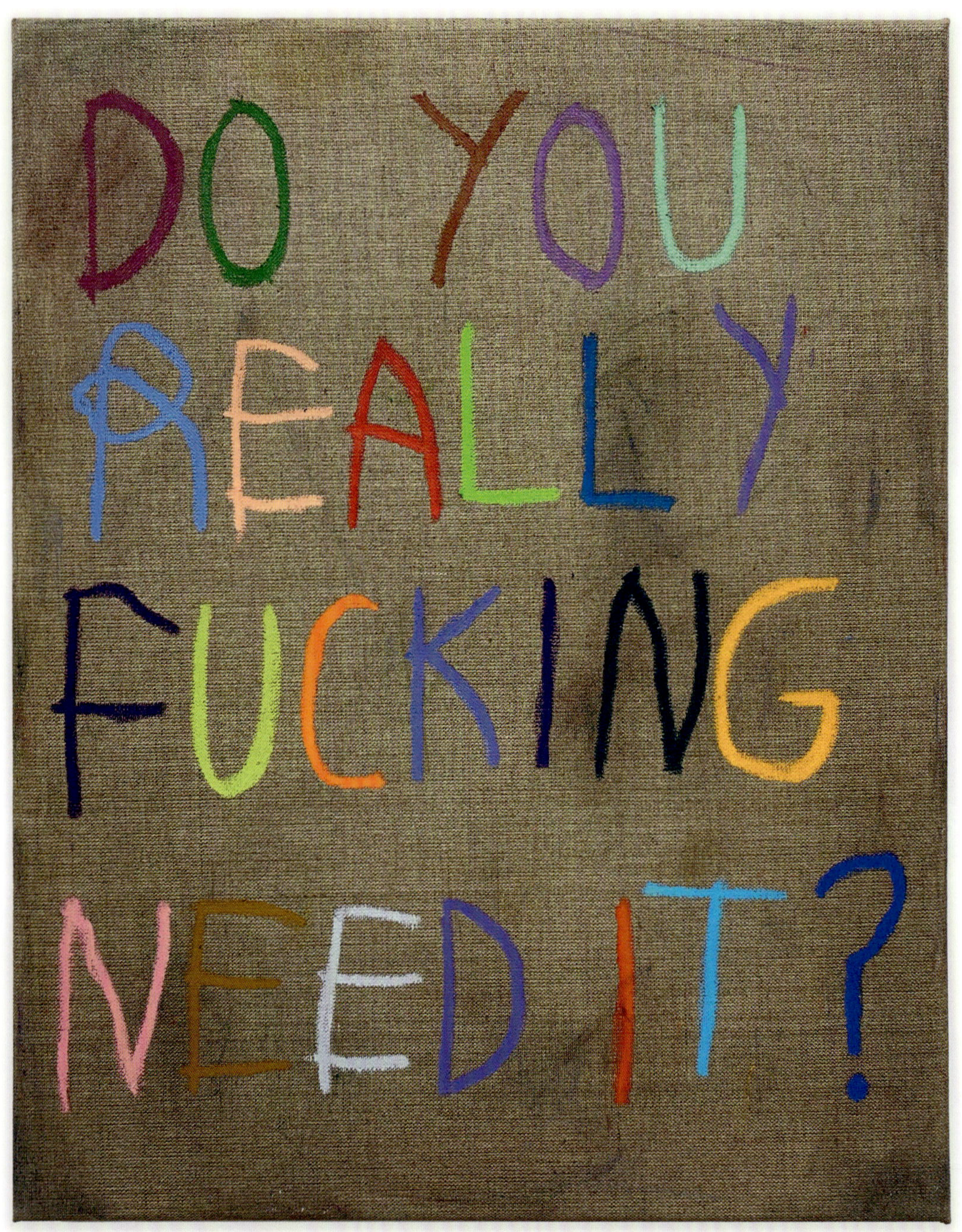

DO YOU
REALLY
FUCKING
NEED IT?

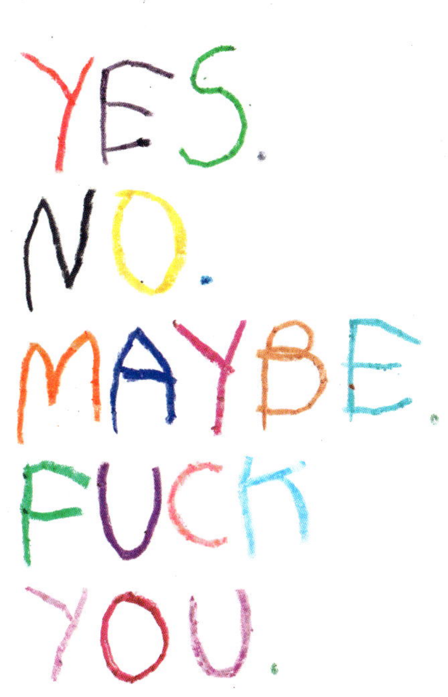

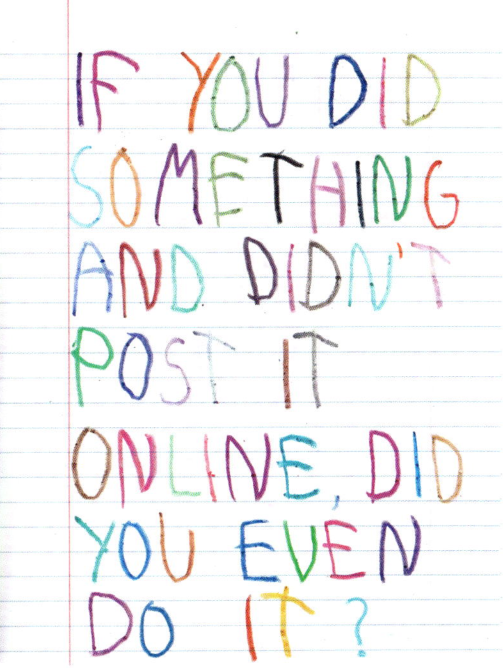

Yes No Maybe, 2020
Wax oil pastels on raw
linen, 50 x 40 cm

*Untitled (Yes No Maybe
Fuck You)*, 2020
Wax crayons on paper,
27.9 x 21cm

*Untitled (Did You Ever
Do It?)*, 2020
Wax crayons on paper,
27.9 x 21cm

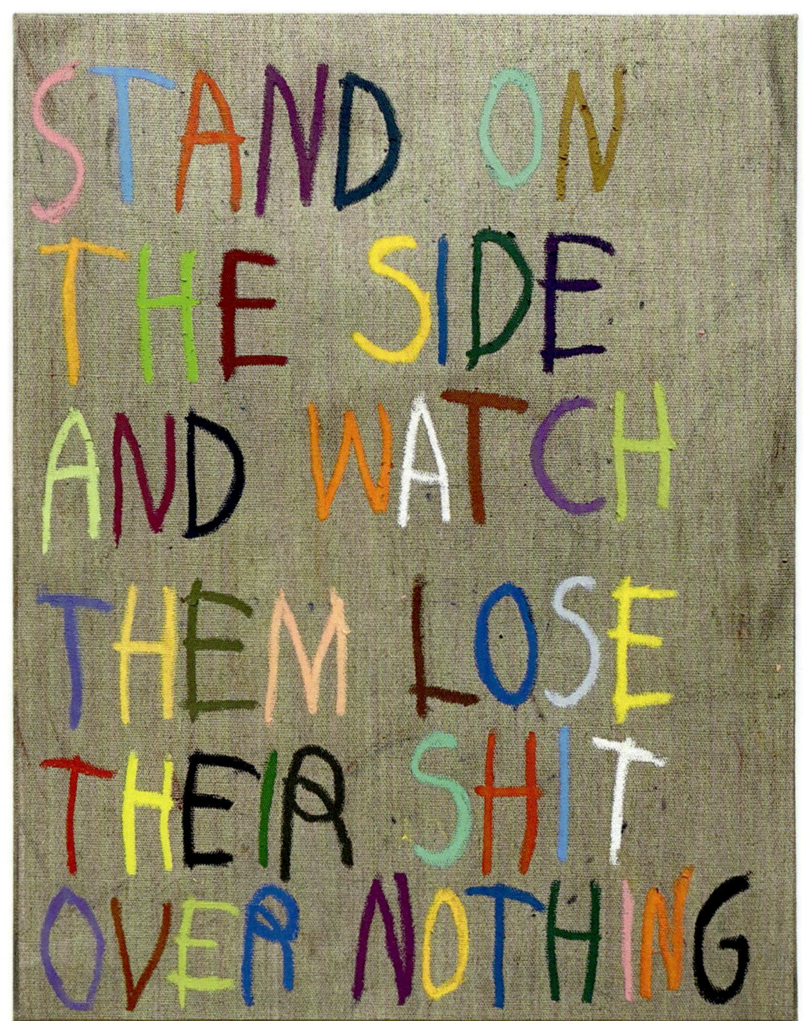

Grab Your Pop Corn, 2020
Wax pastels on raw linen, 50 x 40 cm

Stand in Front, 2020
Oil bars on raw cotton canvas primed with transparent gel medium, 197.5 x 141 cm

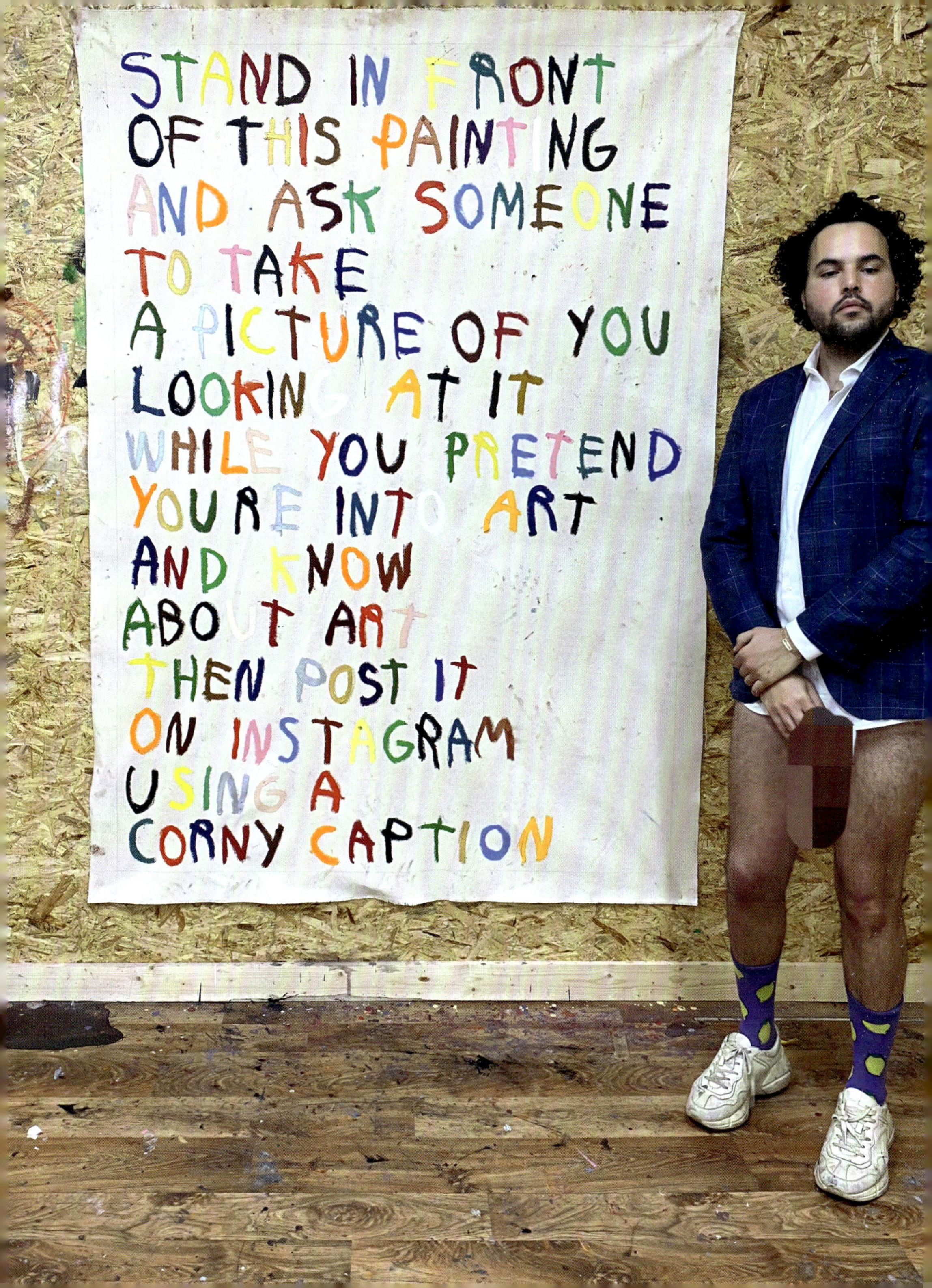

STAND IN FRONT
OF THIS PAINTING
AND ASK SOMEONE
TO TAKE
A PICTURE OF YOU
LOOKING AT IT
WHILE YOU PRETEND
YOU'RE INTO ART
AND KNOW
ABOUT ART
THEN POST IT
ON INSTAGRAM
USING A
CORNY CAPTION

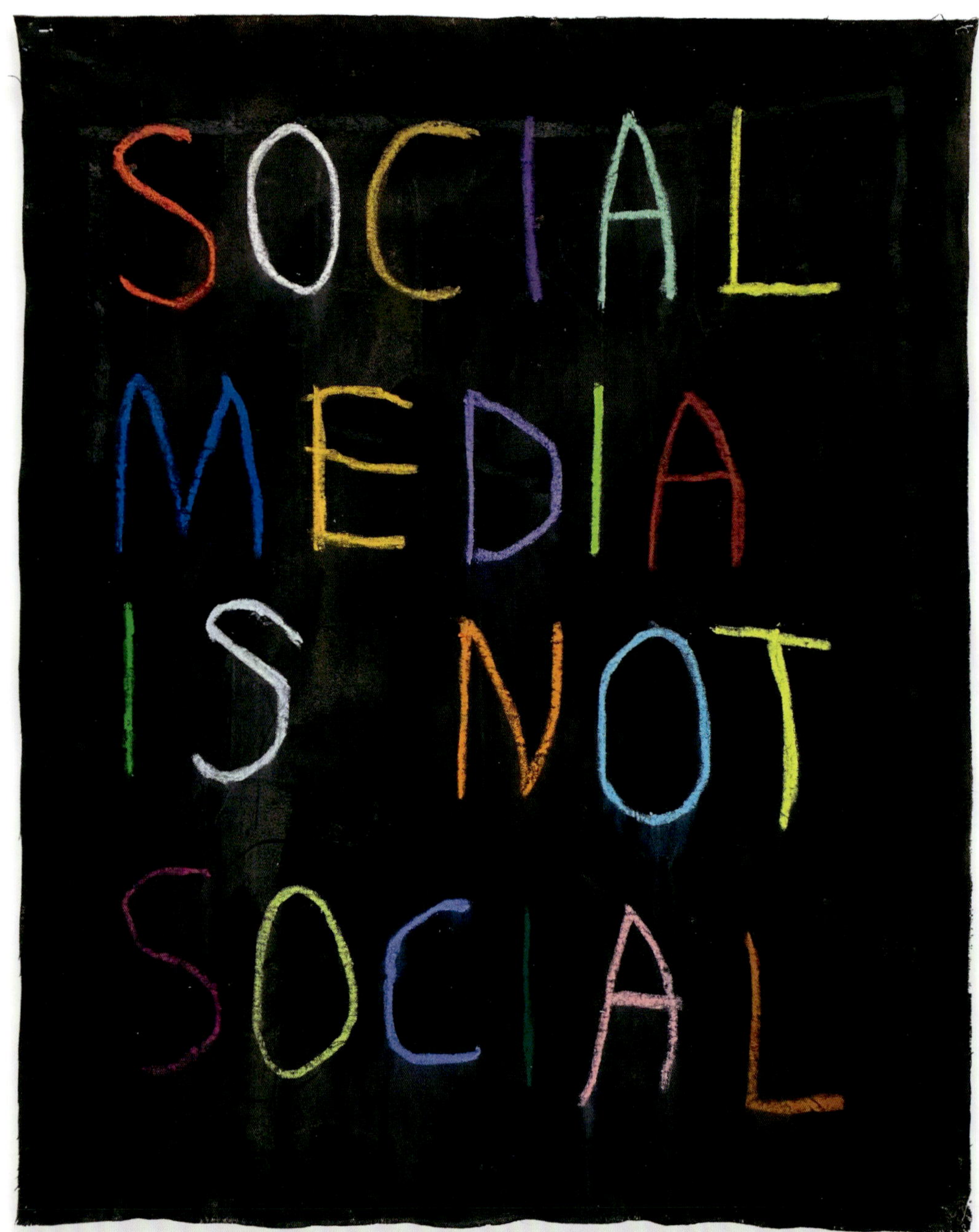

SOCIAL
MEDIA
IS NOT
SOCIAL

Antisocial, 2020
Water-soluble oil
pastels, oil sticks,
mineral water, and
acrylic paint on raw
cotton canvas,
106 x 88 cm

*Untitled (Don't Anyone
Fuck Around with Your
Happiness)*, 2019
Wax crayons on paper,
27.9 x 21cm

Study for *Overthinking*,
2020
Wax crayons on paper,
21 x 27.9 cm

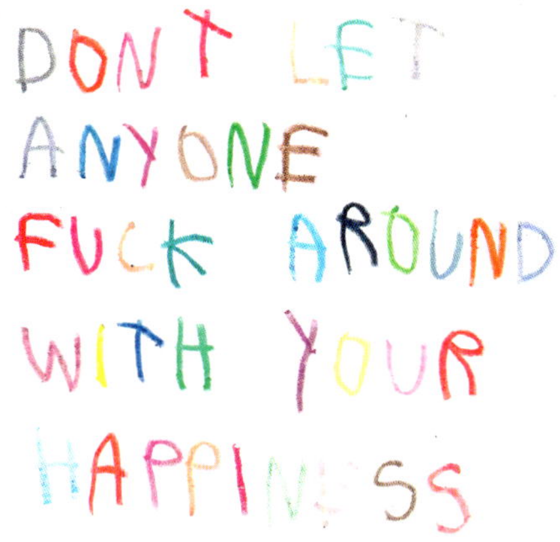

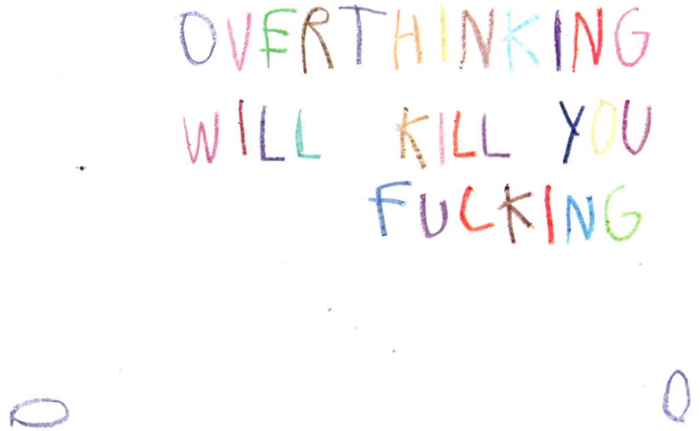

DON'T LET
ANYONE
FUCK AROUND
WITH YOUR
HAPPINESS

OVERTHINKING
WILL KILL YOU
FUCKING

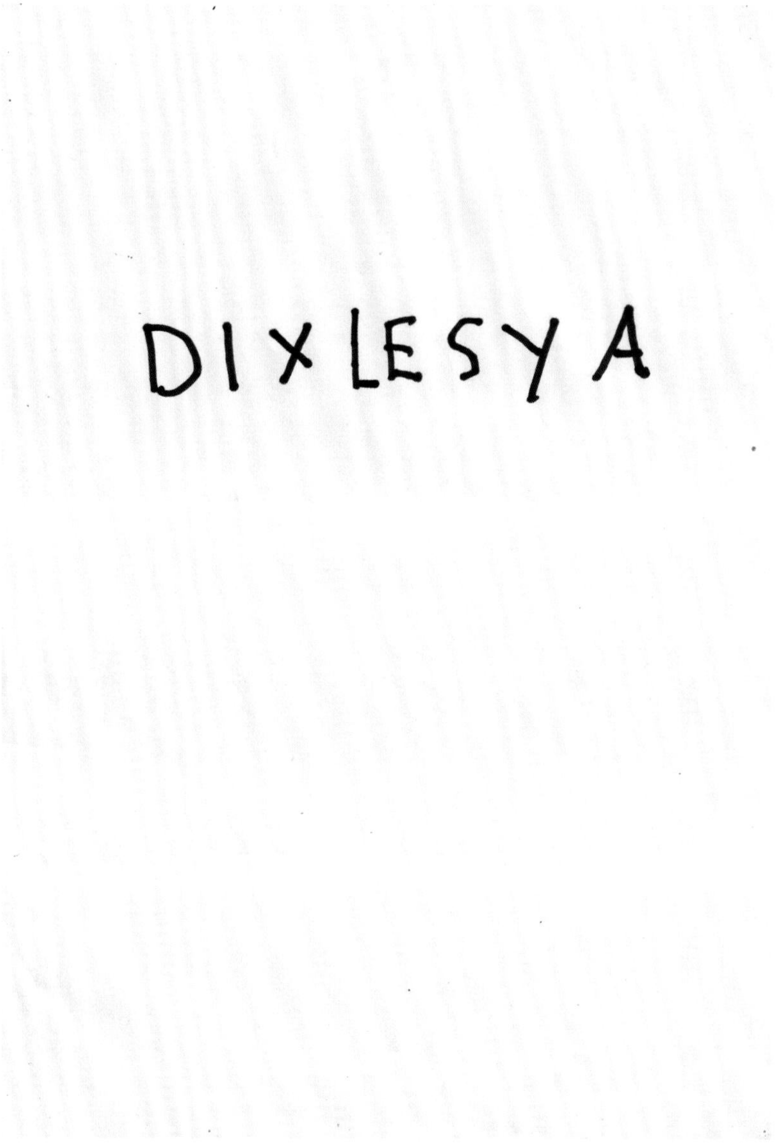

DIXLESYA

Dixlesya, 2017
Markers on paper,
27.9 x 21cm

*Big Ass Canvas & Small
Ass Canvas*, 2020
Oil bars on raw linen,
193 x 150 cm,
18 x 13 cm

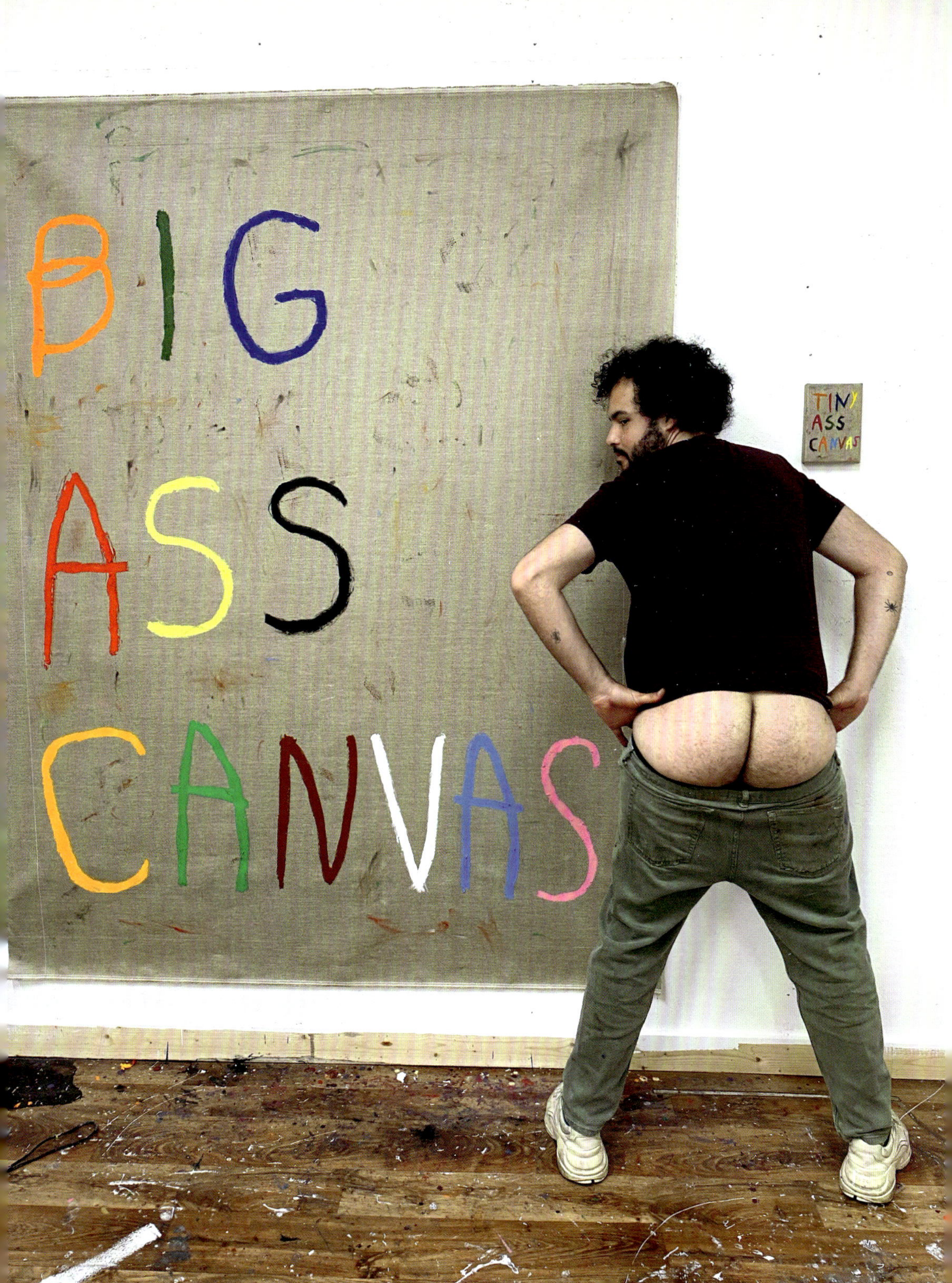

BIG
ASS
CANVAS
TINY
ASS
CANVAS

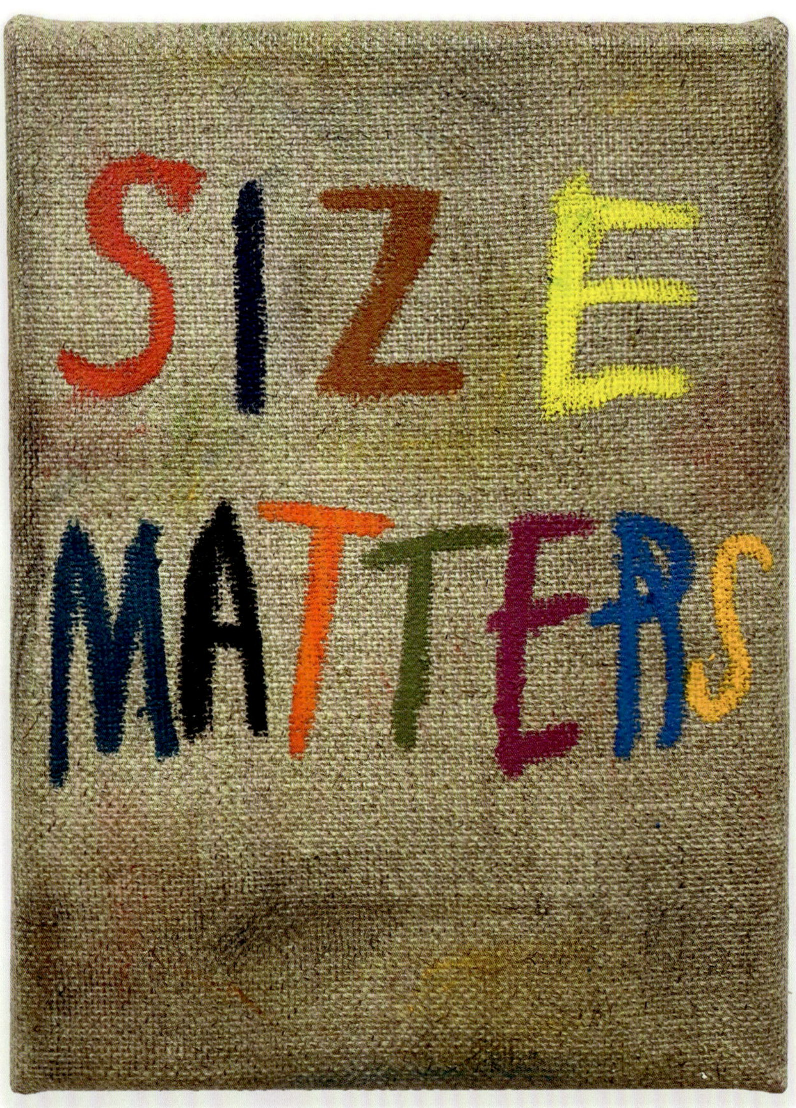

Does It?, 2020
Wax pastels on raw
linen, 18 x 13 cm

*Untitled (It's All Fun
Games Until Life Fucks
You)*, 2020
Wax crayons on paper,
27.9 x 21cm

Pages 162–163
Studio, 2020

IT'S ALL
FUN AND
GAMES
UNTIL LIFE
FUCKS YOU

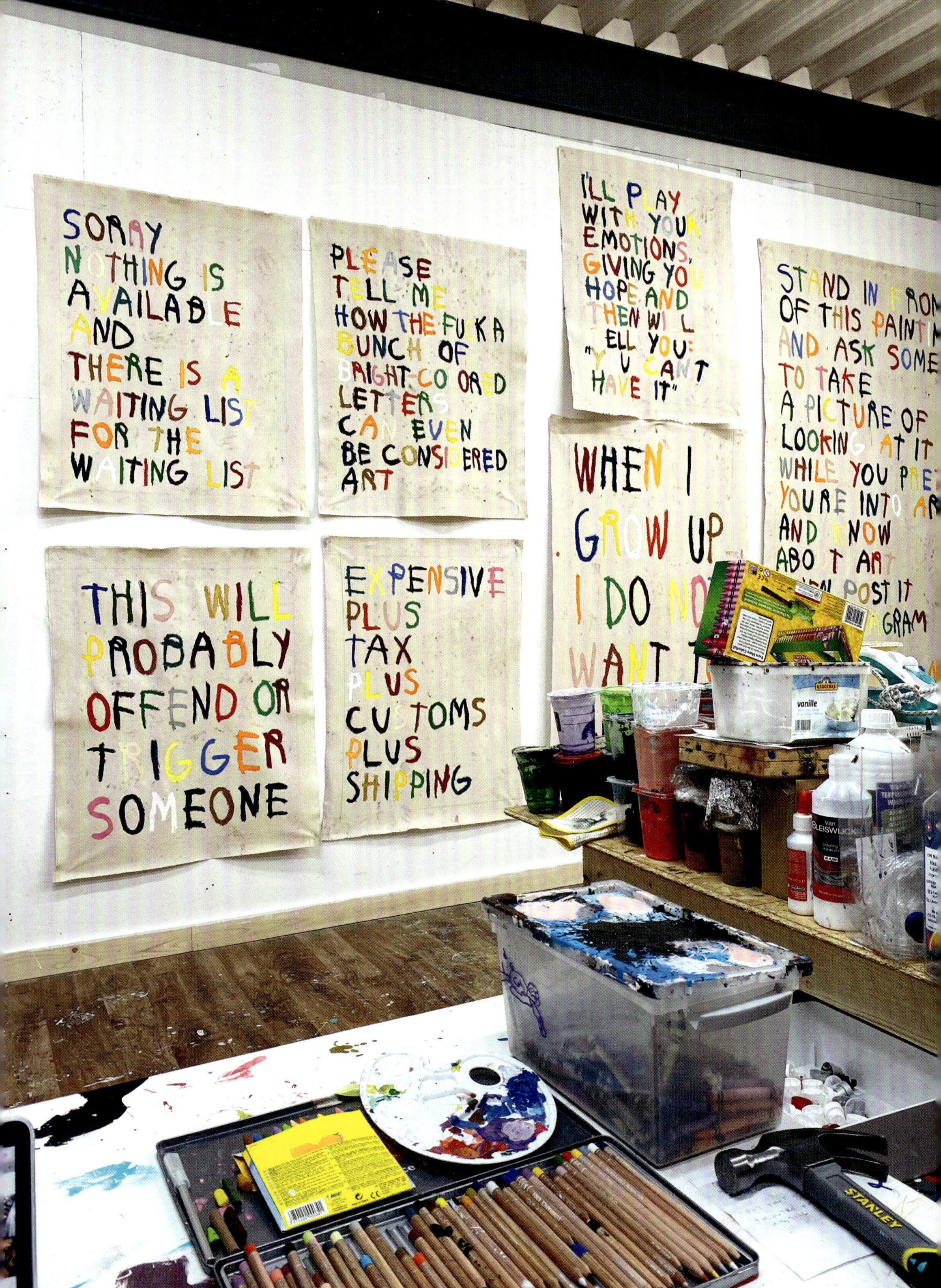

SORRY NOTHING IS AVAILABLE AND THERE IS A WAITING LIST FOR THE WAITING LIST
PLEASE TELL ME HOW THE FU K A BUNCH OF BRIGHT-CO ORED LETTERS CAN EVEN BE CONSIDERED ART
I'LL PLAY WITH YOUR EMOTIONS, GIVING YOU HOPE AND THEN WI L ELL YOU: "Y U CAN'T HAVE IT"
STAND IN FRO OF THIS PAINTI AND ASK SOME TO TAKE A PICTURE OF LOOKING AT IT WHILE YOU PRE YOU'RE INTO AR AND KNOW ABO T ART POST IT GRAM
THIS WILL PROBABLY OFFEND OR TRIGGER SOMEONE
EXPENSIVE PLUS TAX PLUS CUSTOMS PLUS SHIPPING
WHEN I GROW UP I DO NO WANT

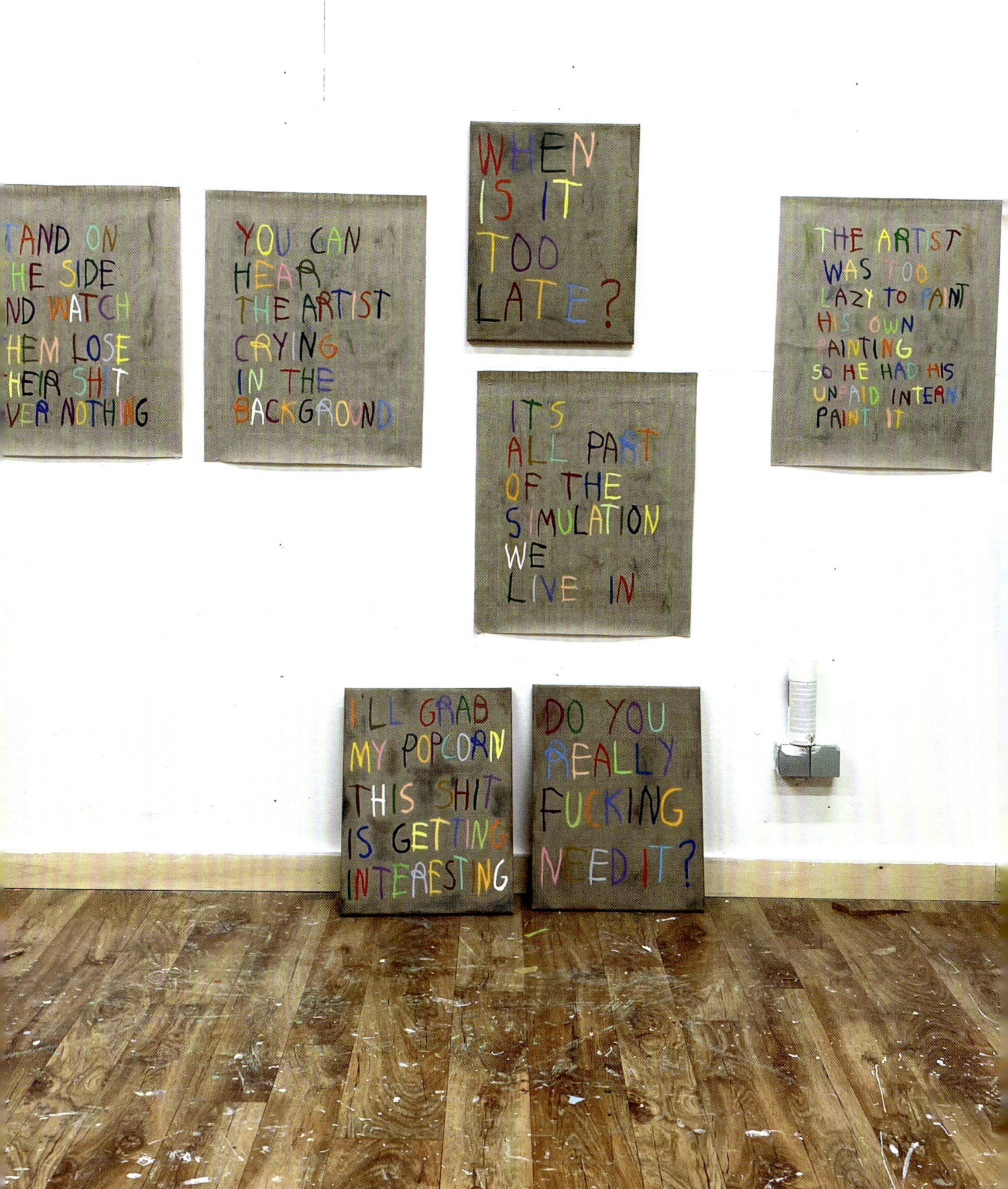

TAND ON THE SIDE ND WATCH HEM LOSE THEIR SHIT VER NOTHING
YOU CAN HEAR THE ARTIST CRYING IN THE BACKGROUND
WHEN IS IT TOO LATE?
THE ARTIST WAS TOO LAZY TO PAINT HIS OWN PAINTING SO HE HAD HIS UNPAID INTERN PAINT IT
IT'S ALL PART OF THE SIMULATION WE LIVE IN
I'LL GRAB MY POPCORN THIS SHIT IS GETTING INTERESTING
DO YOU REALLY FUCKING NEED IT?

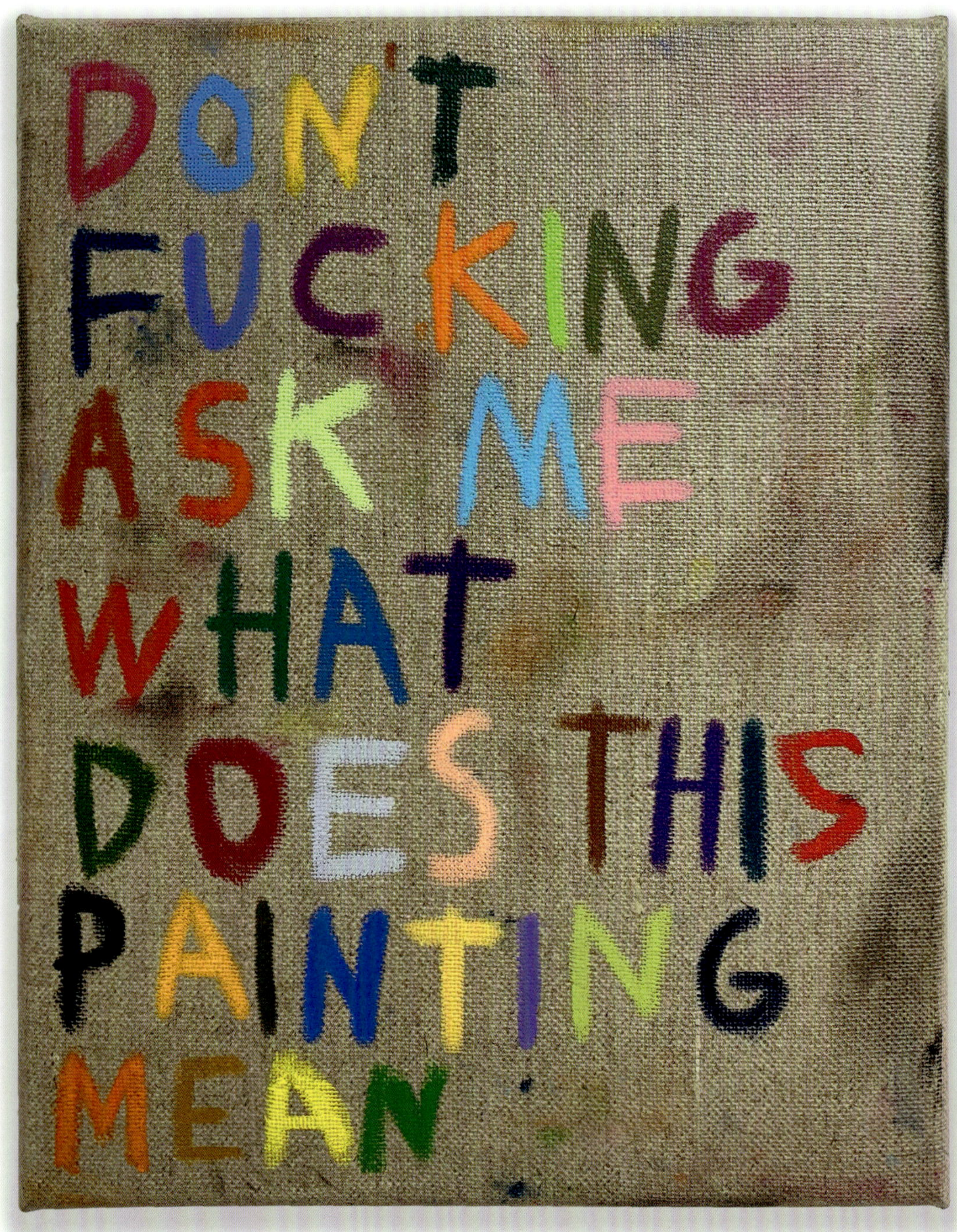
DON'T
FUCKING
ASK ME
WHAT
DOES THIS
PAINTING
MEAN

*I Really Don't Know
What's the Point, Maybe
the Artist Is Trying to
Make a Statement*, 2020
Wax pastels on raw
linen, 30 x 24 cm

Untitled, 2020
Wax crayons, color
pencils, and acrylic on
canvas, 27.9 x 21cm

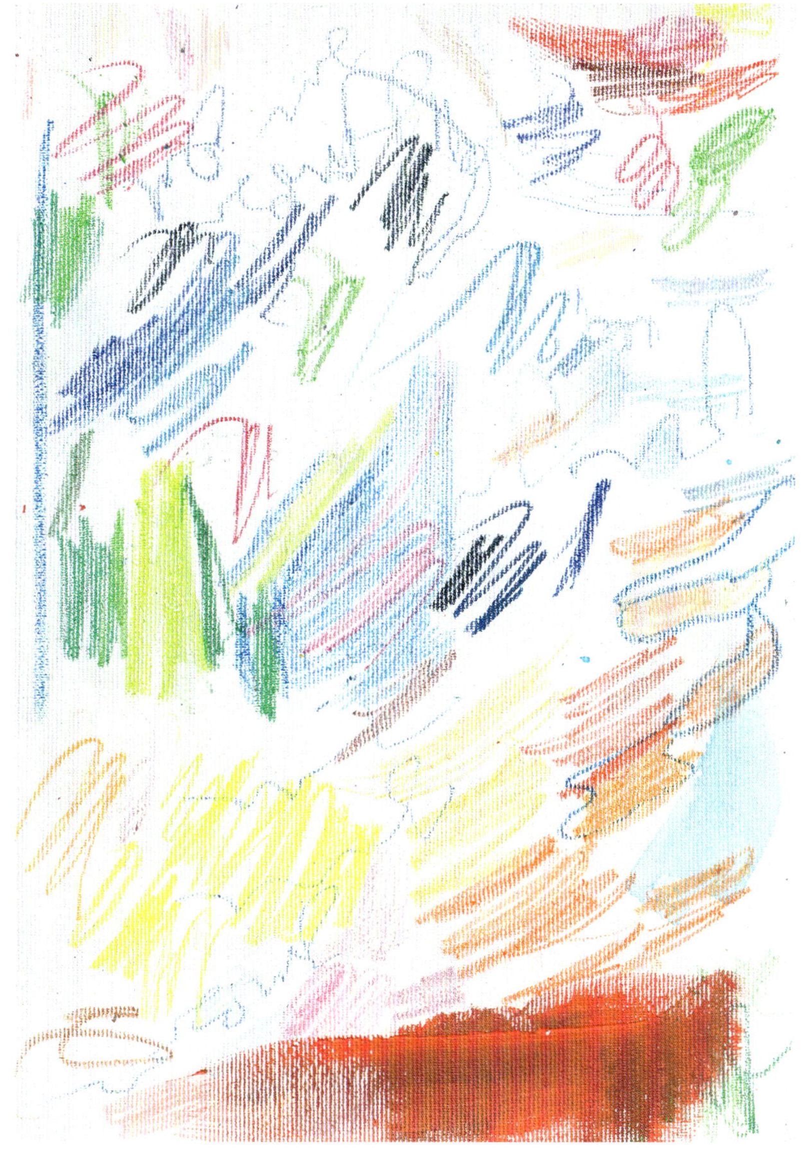

Untitled (Open Your Fucking Eyes), 2020
Wax crayons on paper,
27.9 x 21 cm

Untitled (Nothing Is Permanent), 2019
Wax crayons on paper,
27.9 x 21 cm

A Very Very Very Very Very Thin Line, 2020
Wax pastels on raw linen, 40 x 30 cm

166

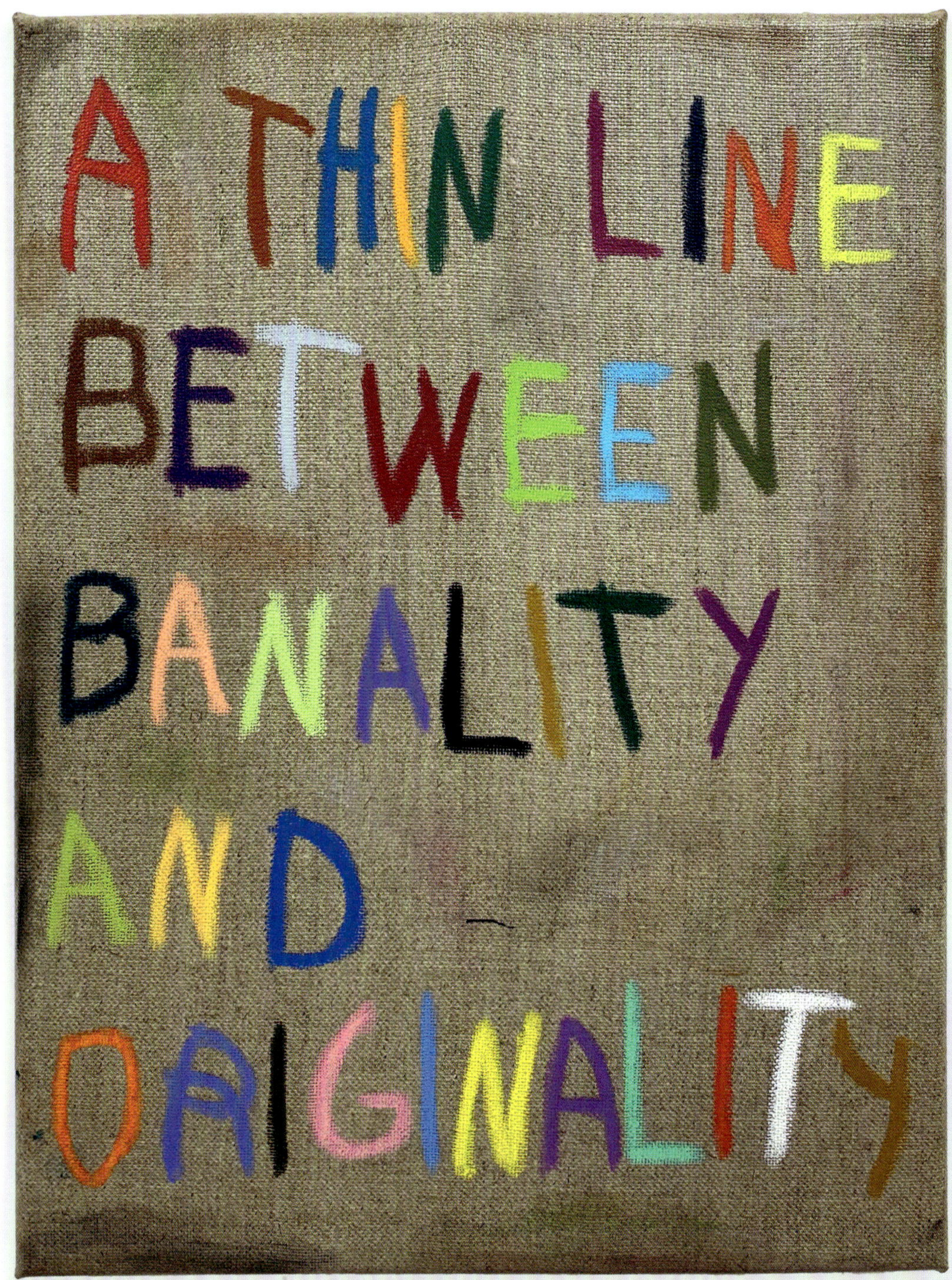

A THIN LINE
BETWEEN
BANALITY
AND
ORIGINALITY

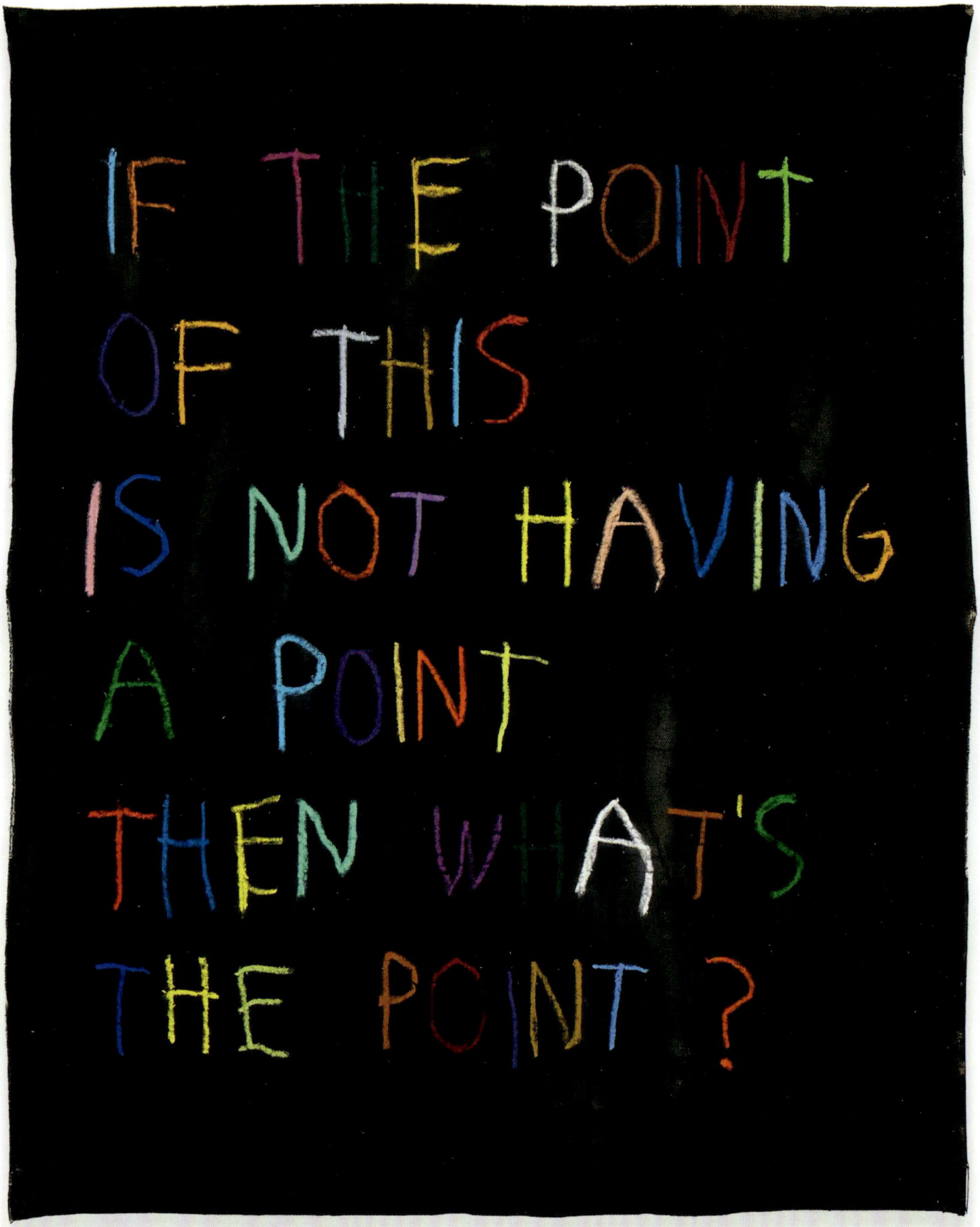

IF THE POINT
OF THIS
IS NOT HAVING
A POINT
THEN WHAT'S
THE POINT ?

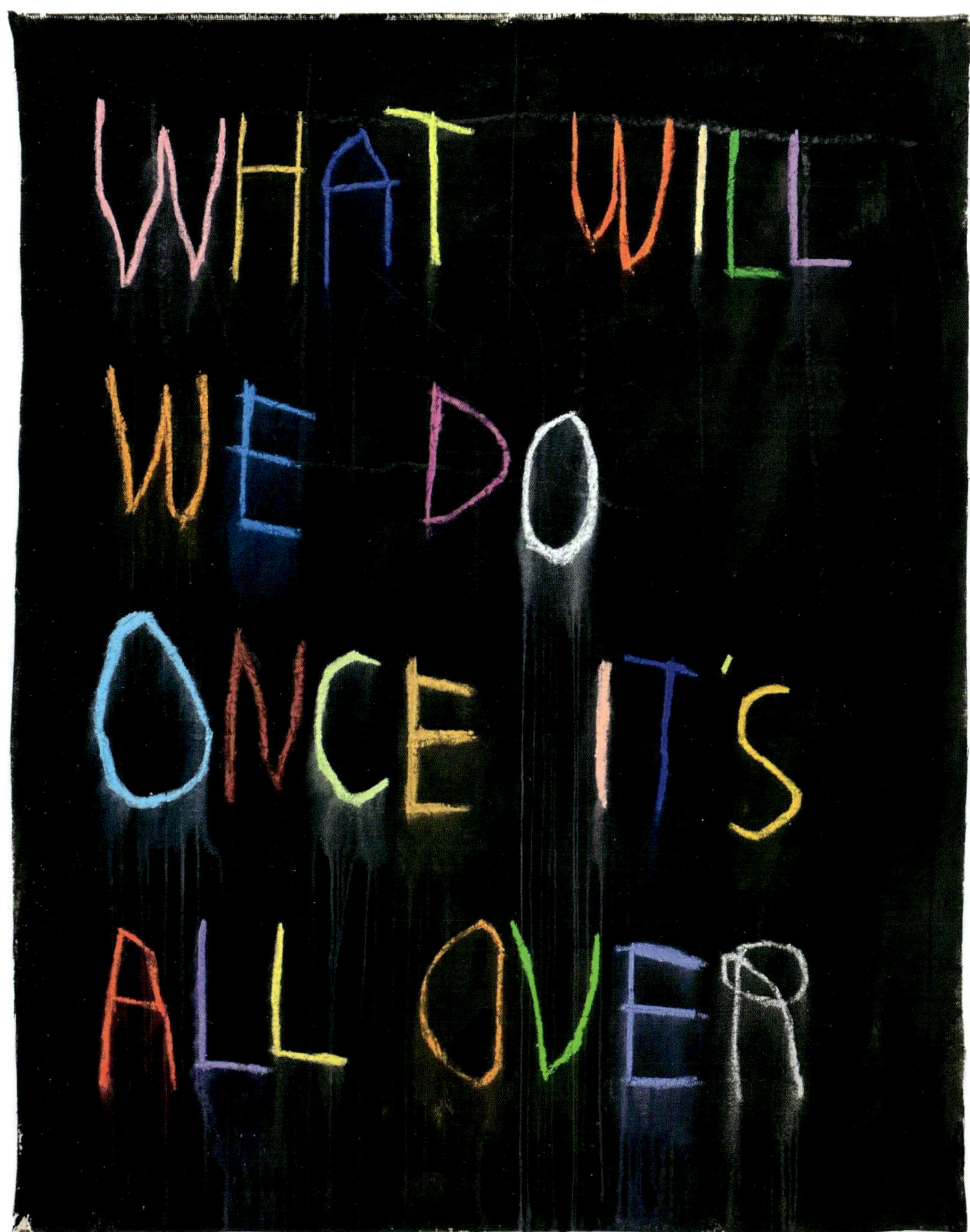

WHAT WILL
WE DO
ONCE IT'S
ALL OVER

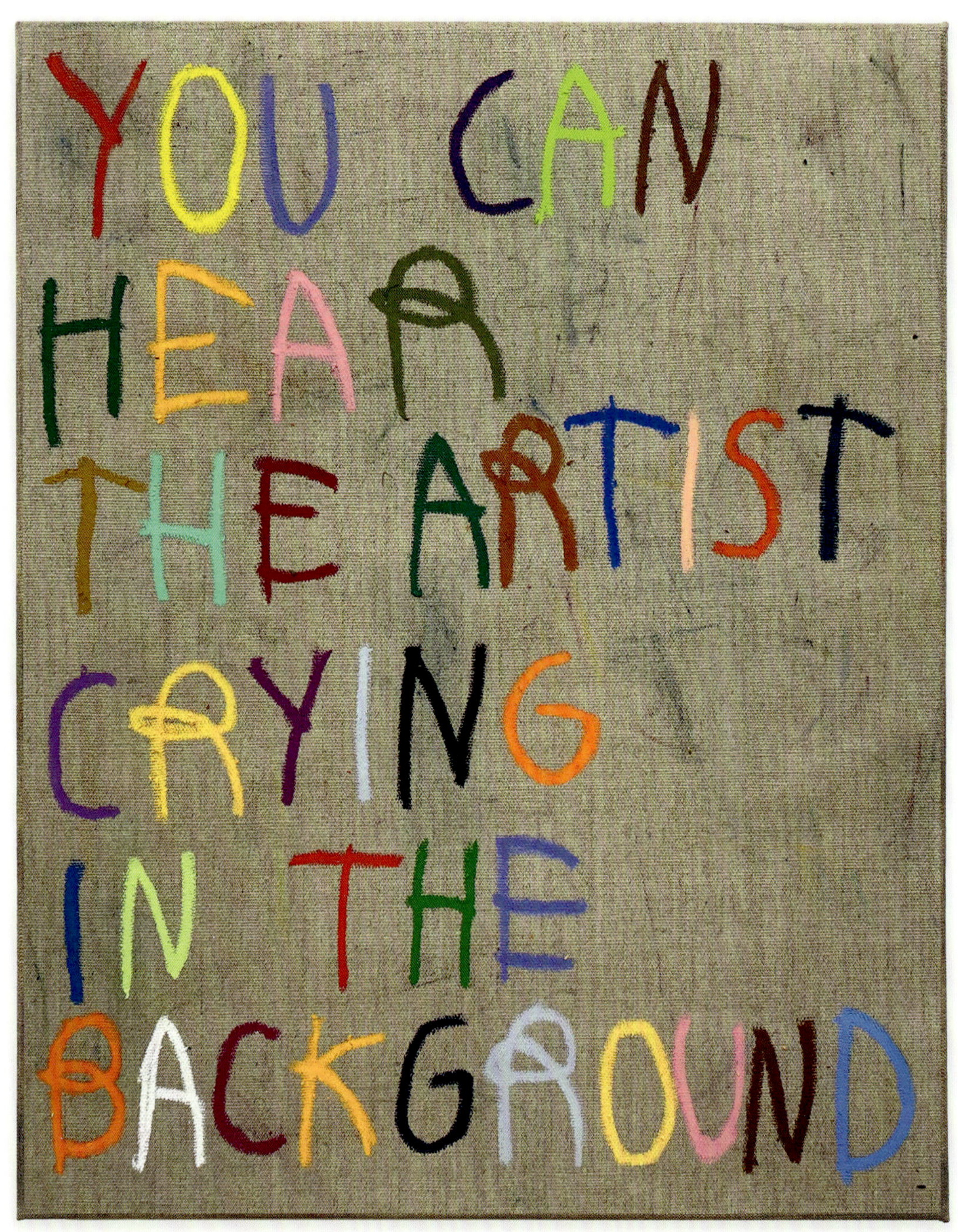

YOU CAN
HEAR THE ARTIST
THE ARTIST
CRYING
IN THE
BACKGROUND

THIS WAS PRIMED WITH THE TEARS OF A FAILED ARTIST

1 WANT TO BE AN
ARTIST BUT,
I CANT REALY
DRAW OR PAINT
THATS WHY
I WRITE RANDOM
SHIT, AND
SELL IT AS
ART.

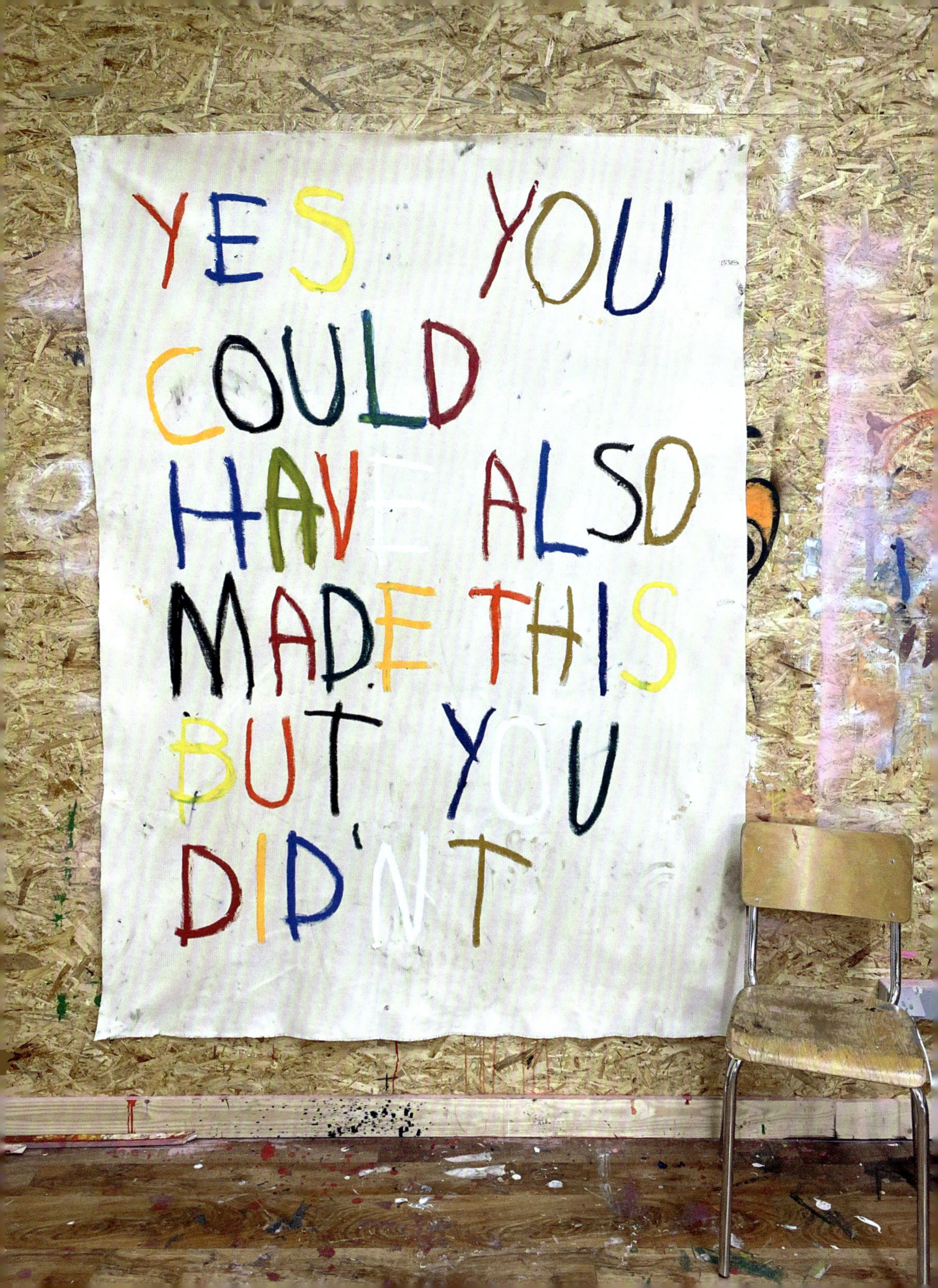

YES YOU
COULD
HAVE ALSO
MADE THIS
BUT YOU
DID'NT

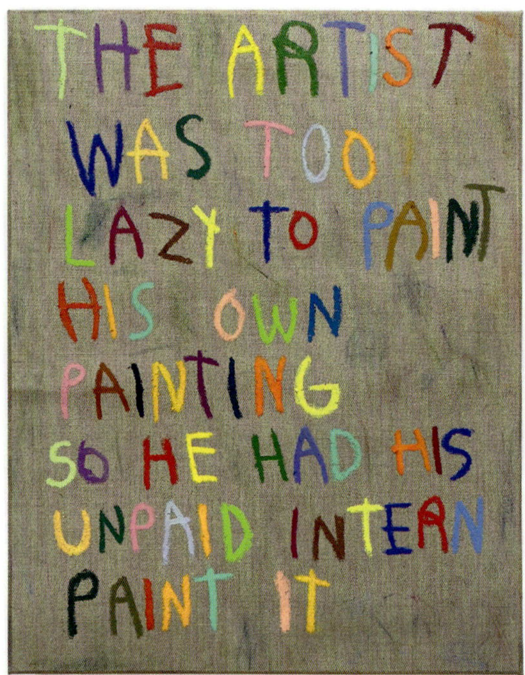

Honestly Nowadays Who the Fuck Makes Their Own Paintings, 2020
Wax pastels on raw linen, 50 x 40 cm

CB's intern making art for him, 2020

Which I Probably Overpaid For, 2020
Wax pastels on raw linen, 30 x 24 cm

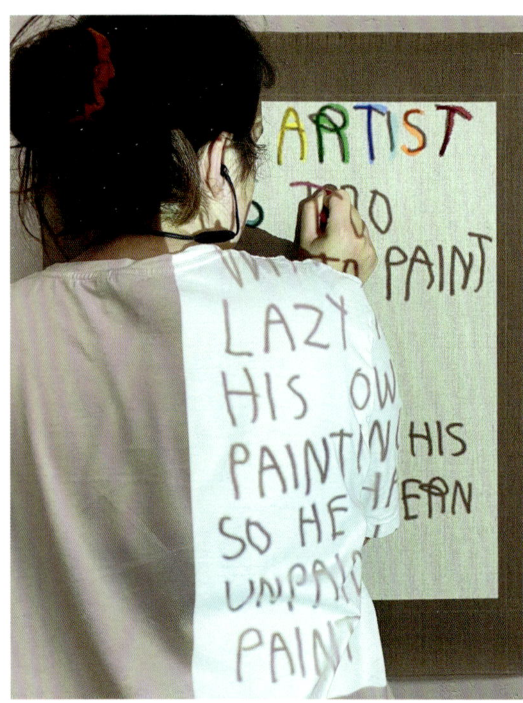

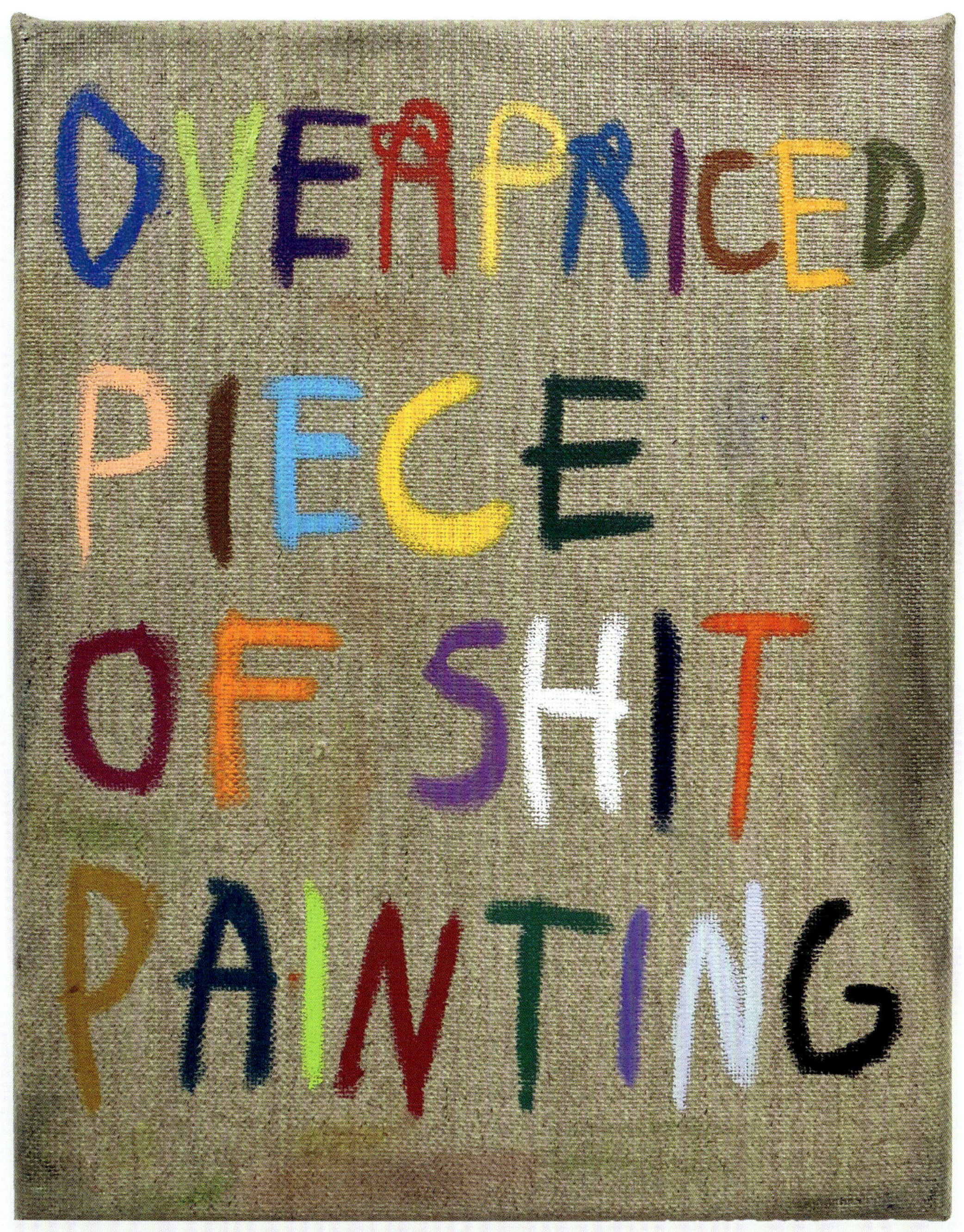

OVERPRICED
PIECE
OF SHIT
PAINTING

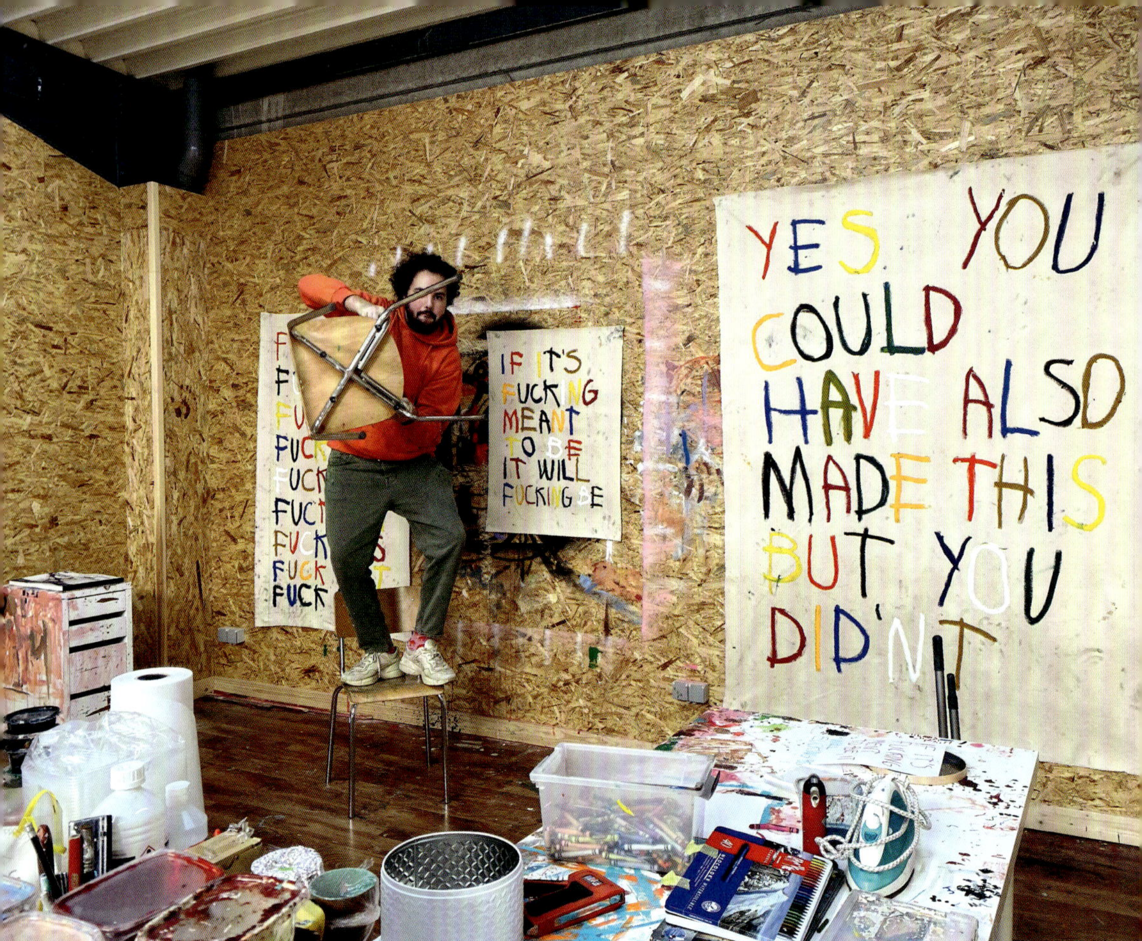

CB in the studio, 2020

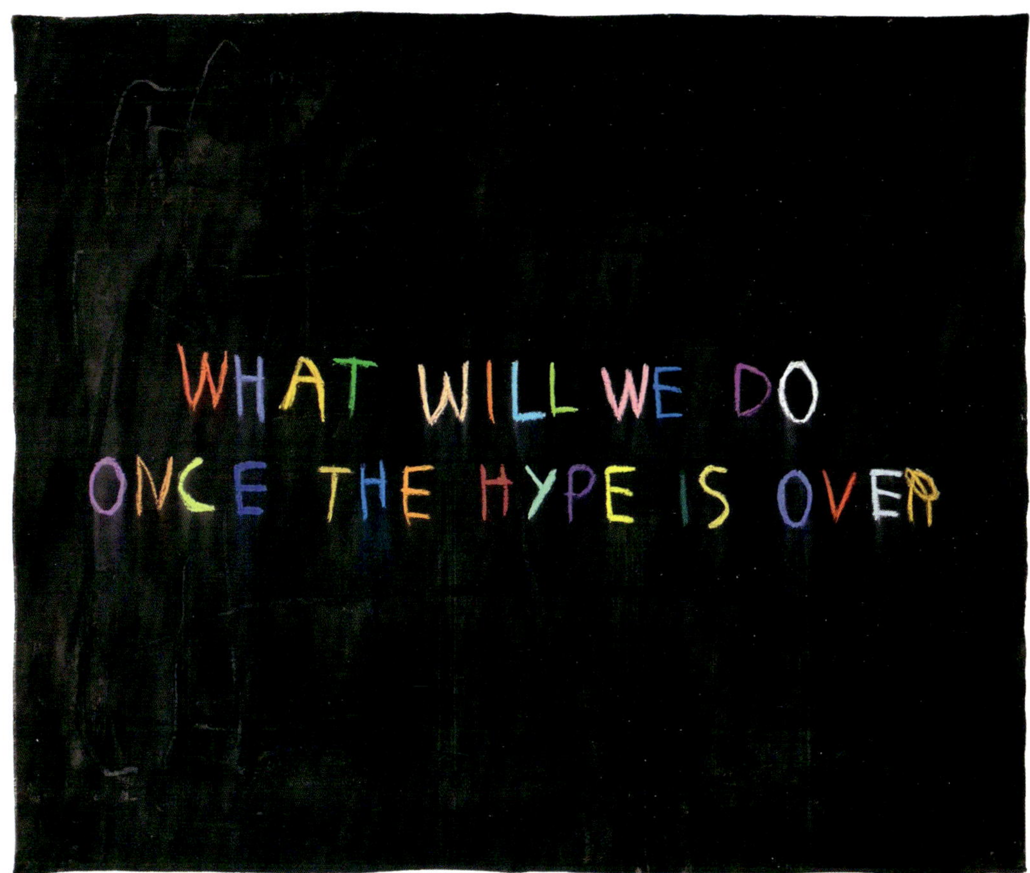

*Once the Hype Is Over
We Will Be Fucked*,
2020
Water-soluble oil pastels,
oil sticks, mineral water,
and acrylic paint on raw
cotton canvas,
175 x 212 cm

EVENTUALLY
YOU'LL
FUCKING
GET OVER IT

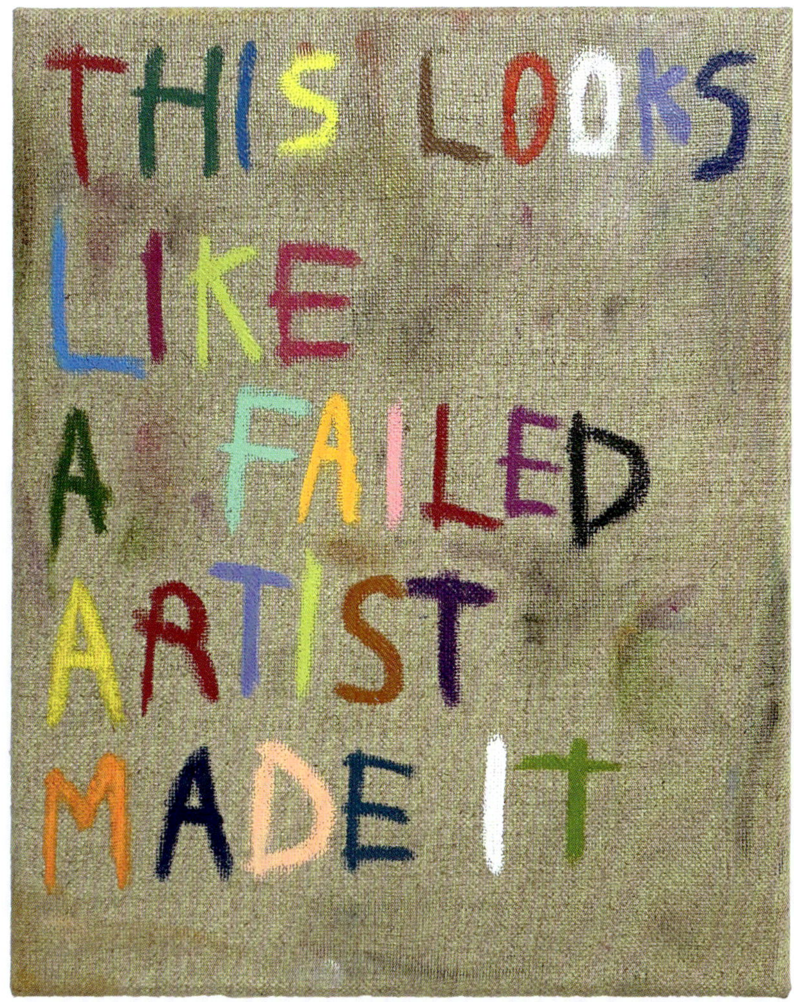

Untitled (You'll Get Over It), 2019
Wax crayons on paper,
27.9 x 21 cm

This Piece Lacks Technical Skills, 2020
Wax pastels on raw
linen, 24 x 30 cm

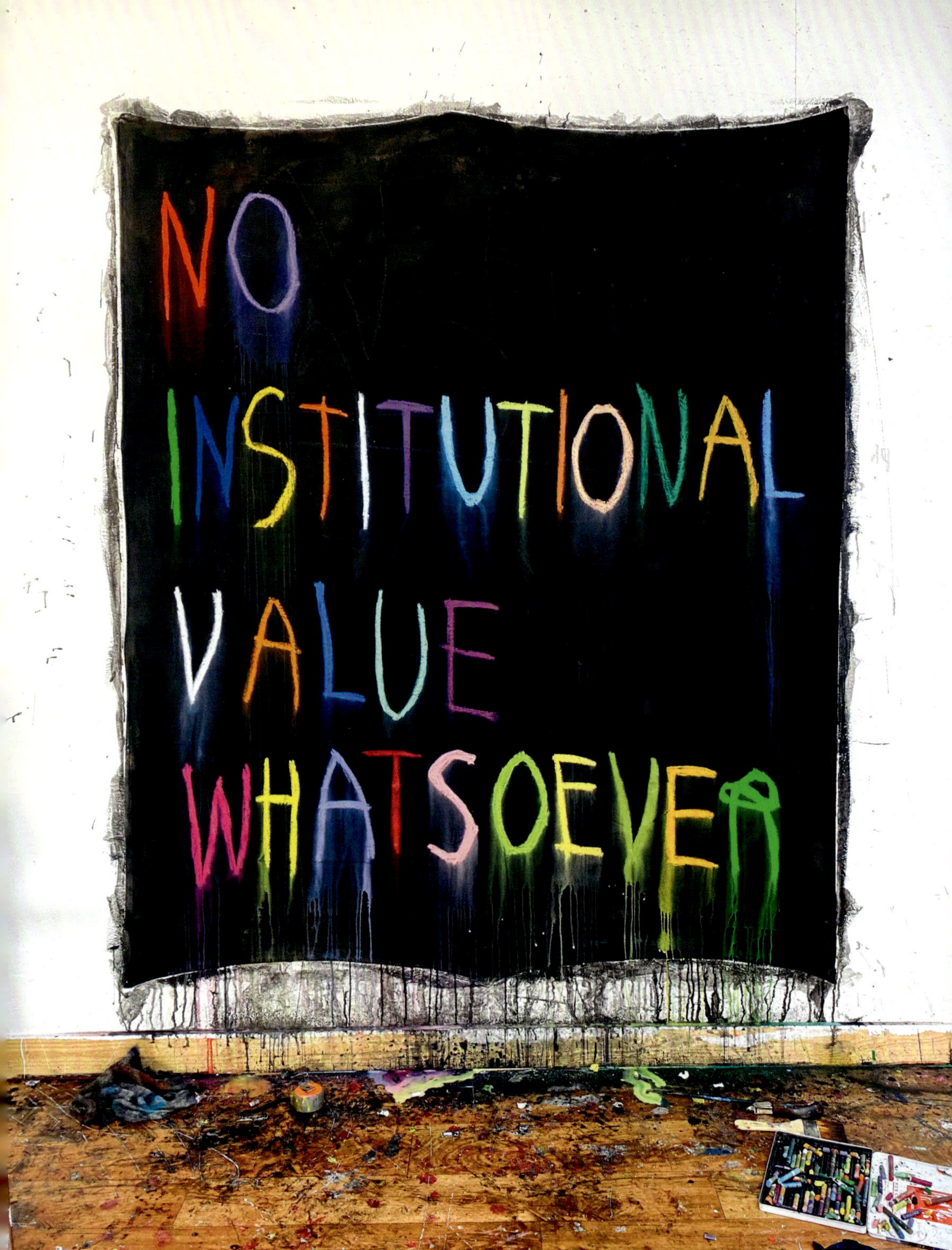

NO
INSTITUTIONAL
VALUE
WHATSOEVER

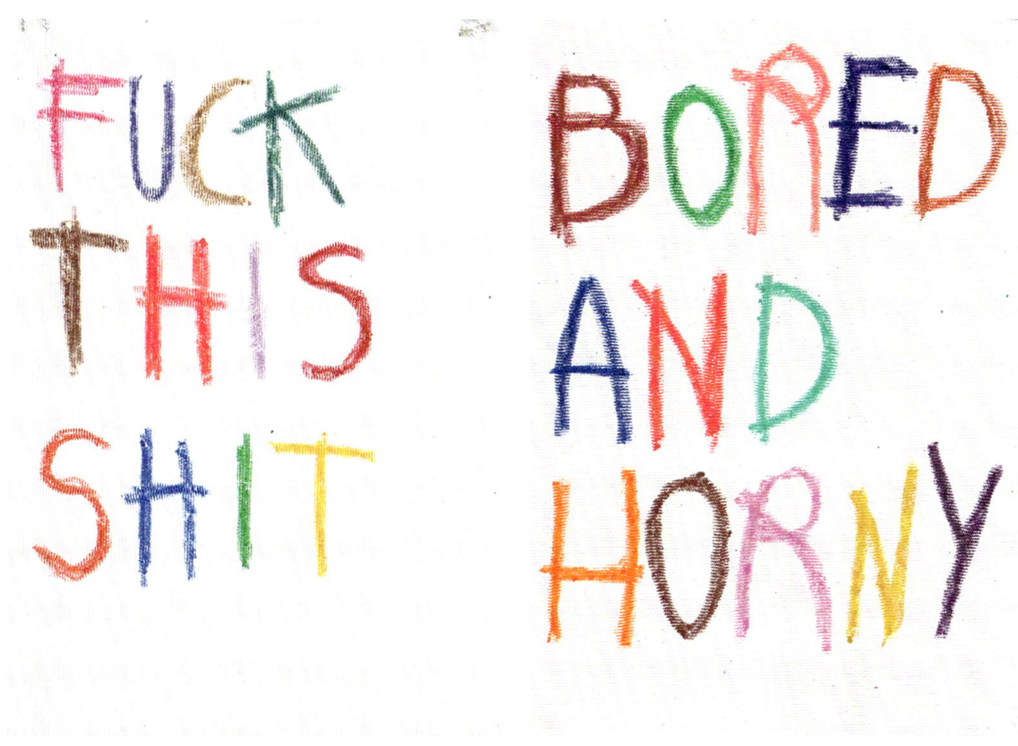

Institutional Value, 2020
Water-soluble oil pastels,
oil sticks, mineral water,
and acrylic paint on raw
cotton canvas,
185.5 x 164 cm

Fuck This Shit, 2020
Wax crayons on canvas,
27.9 x 21 cm

Bored and Horny, 2020
Wax crayons on canvas,
27.9 x 21 cm

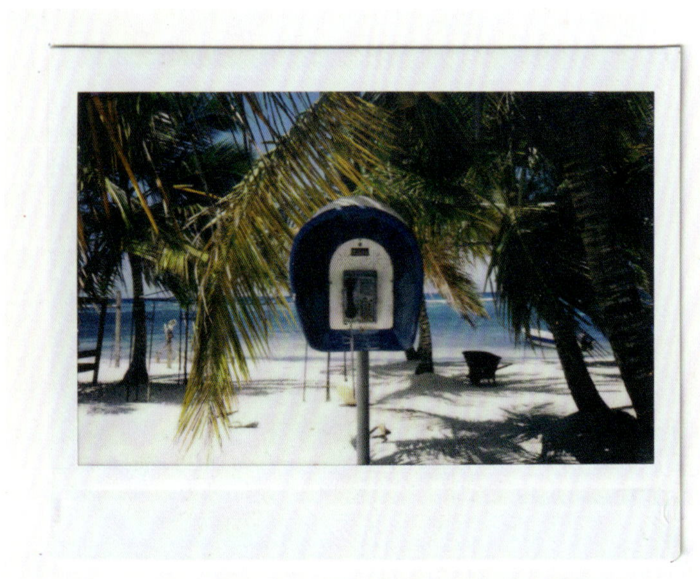

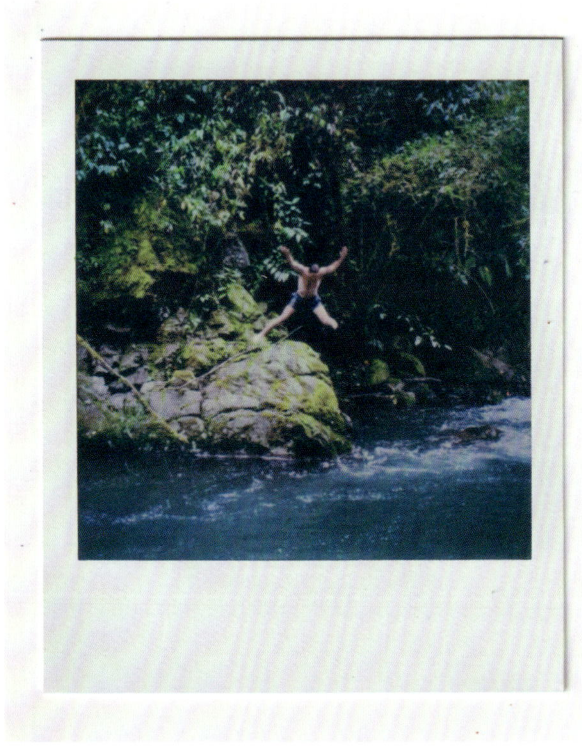

Don't Fucking Call Me,
2019
Fujifilm Instax Colorfilm
Glossy, 8.6 x 10.8 cm

Jump, 2019
Polaroid film,
10.752 x 8.847 cm

Late, 2020
Water-soluble oil pastels,
oil sticks, mineral water,
and acrylic paint on raw
cotton canvas,
106 x 88 cm

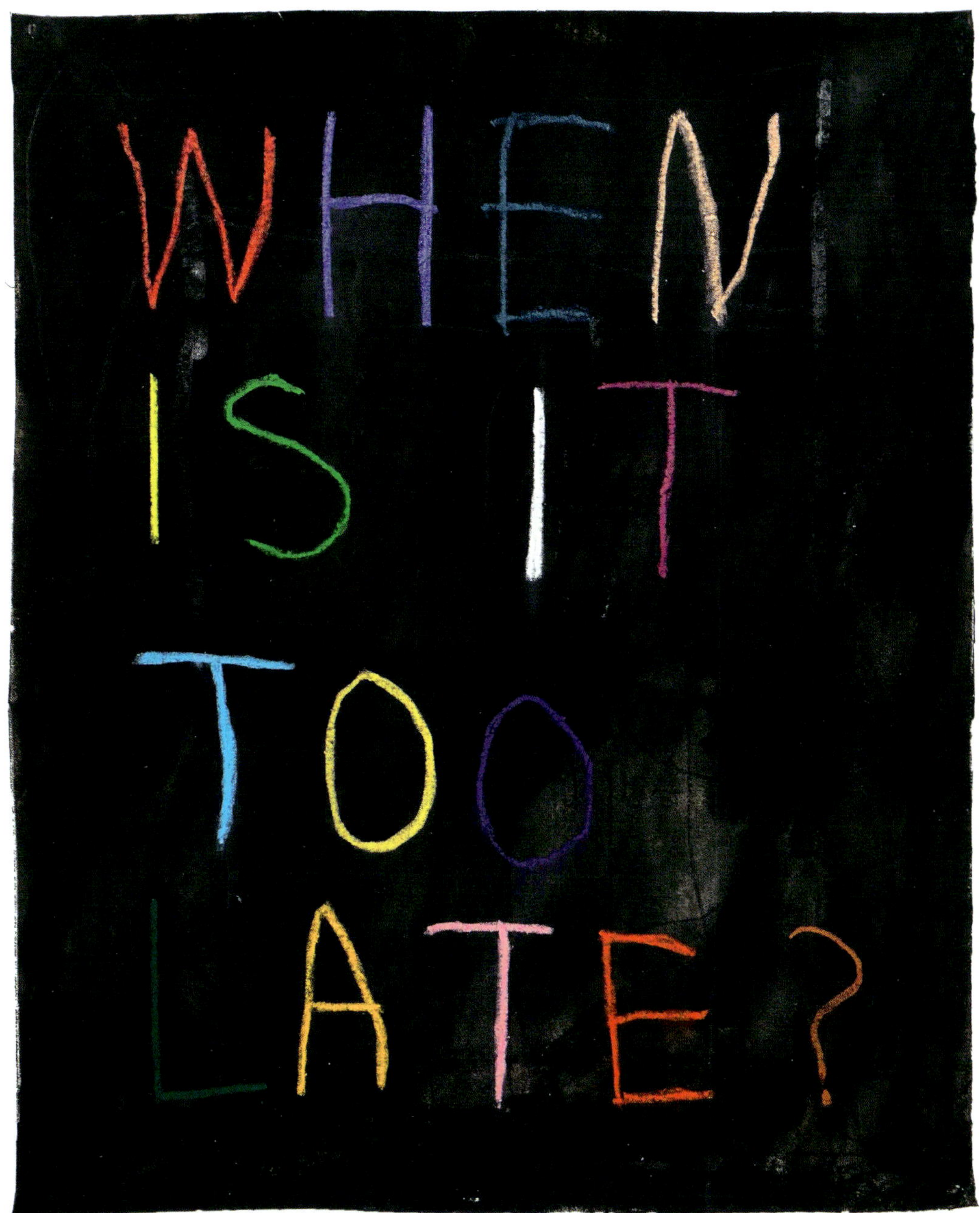

WHEN
IS IT
TOO
LATE?

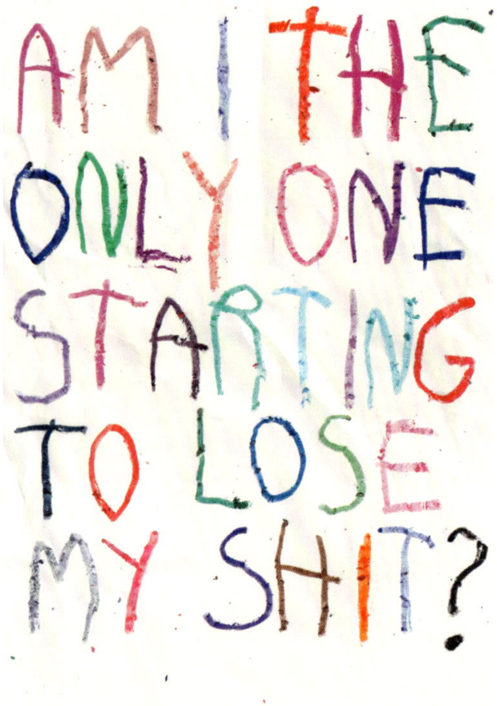

AM I THE ONLY ONE STARTING TO LOSE MY SHIT?

CORNY ART FOR THE MASSES

Losing My Shit, 2020
Wax crayons on paper,
27.9 x 21 cm

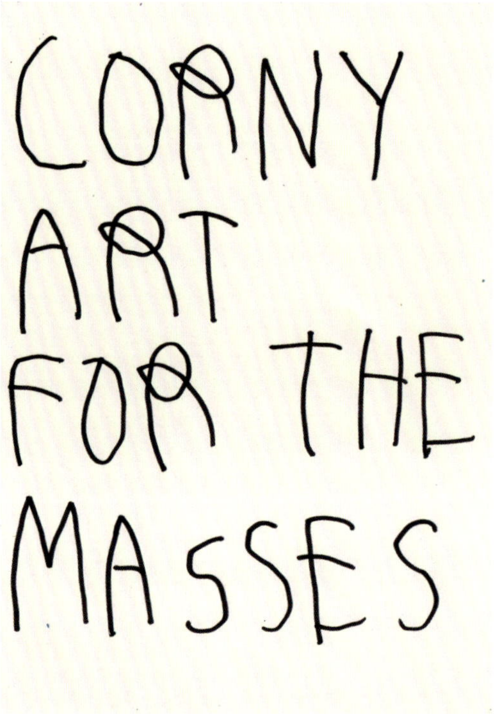

*Untitled (Corny Art for
the Masses)*, 2020
Markers on paper,
27.9 x 21 cm

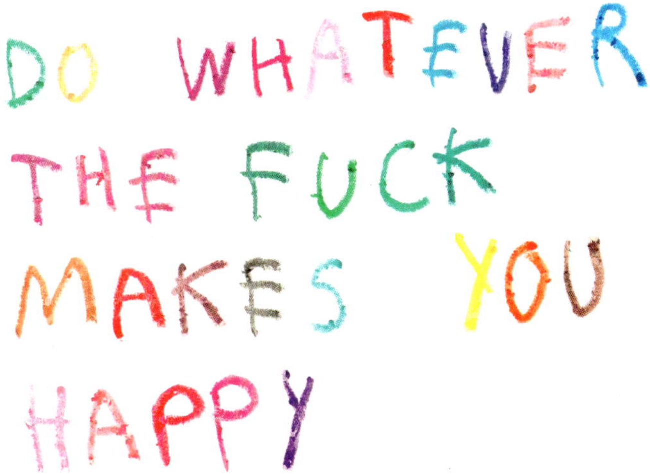

DO WHATEVER
THE FUCK
MAKES YOU
HAPPY

Study for *Do Whatever
the Fuck Makes You
Happy*, 2019
Wax crayons on paper,
21 x 27.9 cm

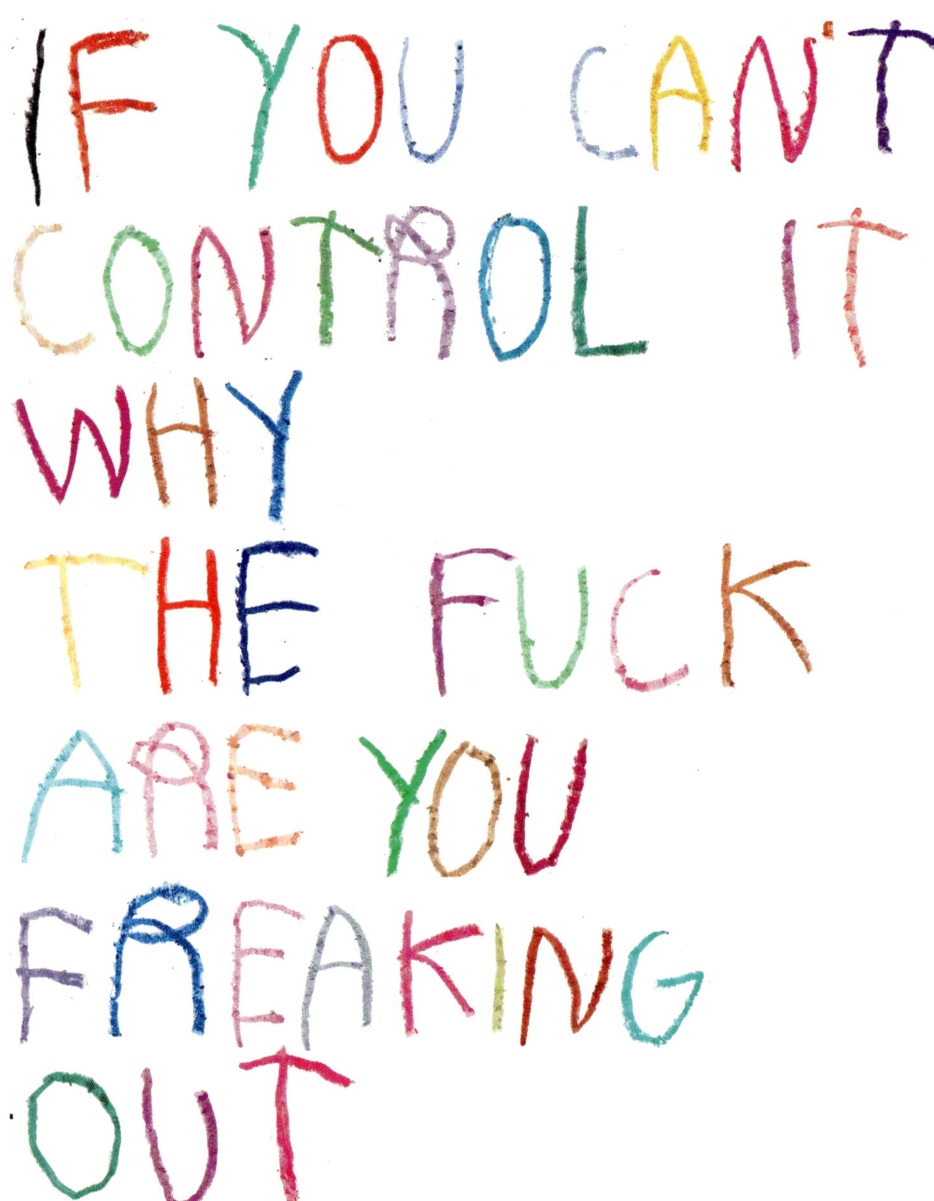

Untitled (If You Can't Control It), 2020
Wax crayons on paper,
27.9 x 21 cm

Untitled (True Colors),
2019
Wax crayons on paper,
27.9 x 21 cm

DON'T BE AFRAID
OF SHOWING
THE WORLD
YOUR TRUE COLORS.
IF SOMEONE
DOESN'T LIKE THEM
THEY CAN GO
FUCK THEMSELVES.

WHEN, YOU TAKE A SHIT, DO YOU KEEP WHAT CAME OUT YOUR ASS? NO, RIGHT, YOU FLUSH IT DOWN THE TOILET. SO FUCKING DO THE SAME WITH THE SHITTY PEOPLE IN YOUR LIFE.

Untitled (Shit), 2019
Wax crayons on paper,
27.9 x 21 cm

Untitled (Disappointing),
2019
Wax crayons on paper,
27.9 x 21 cm

*Untitled (Learn Not to
Give a Fuck)*, 2019
Wax crayons on paper,
27.9 x 21 cm

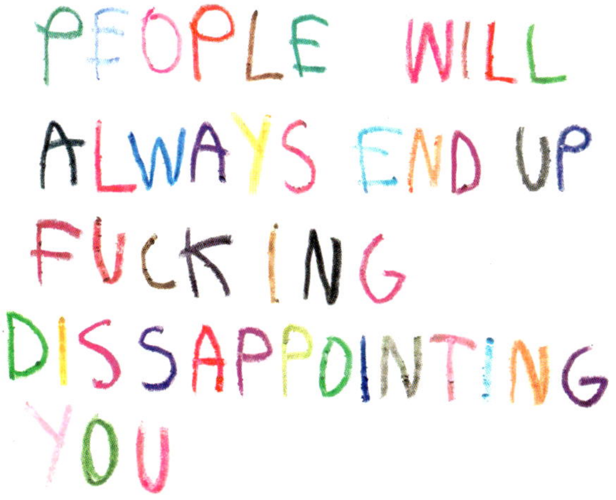

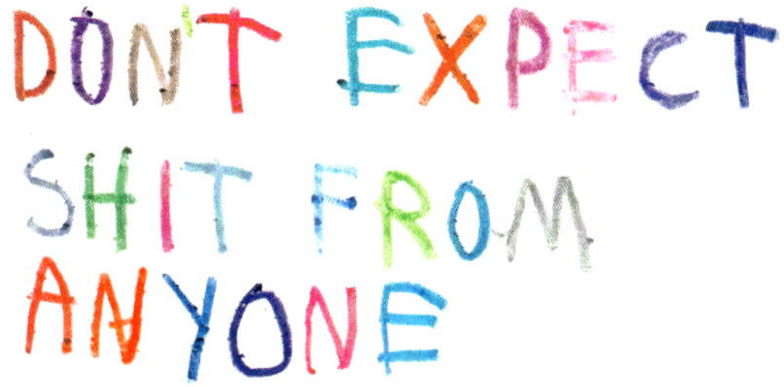

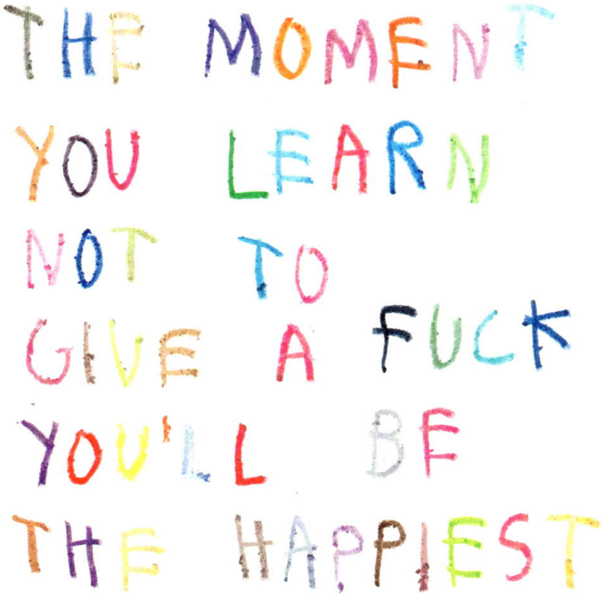

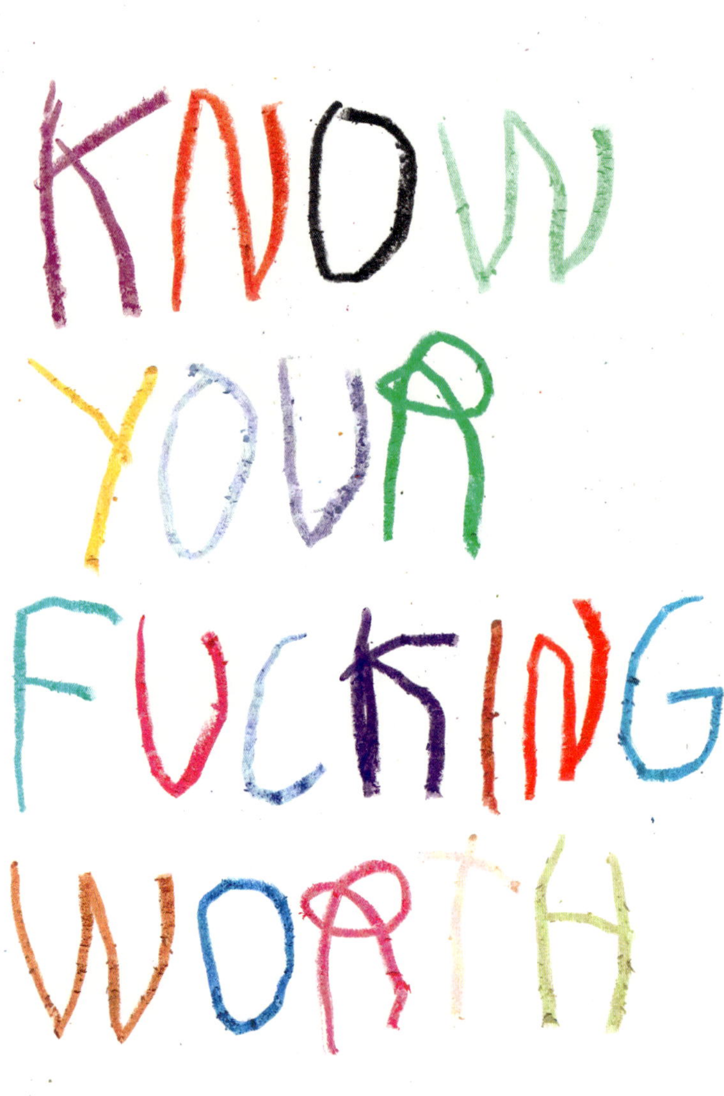

Untitled (Know Your Fucking Worth), 2020
Wax crayons on paper,
27.9 x 21 cm

Untitled (It May Not Be What You Fucking Need), 2020
Wax crayons on paper,
27.9 x 21 cm

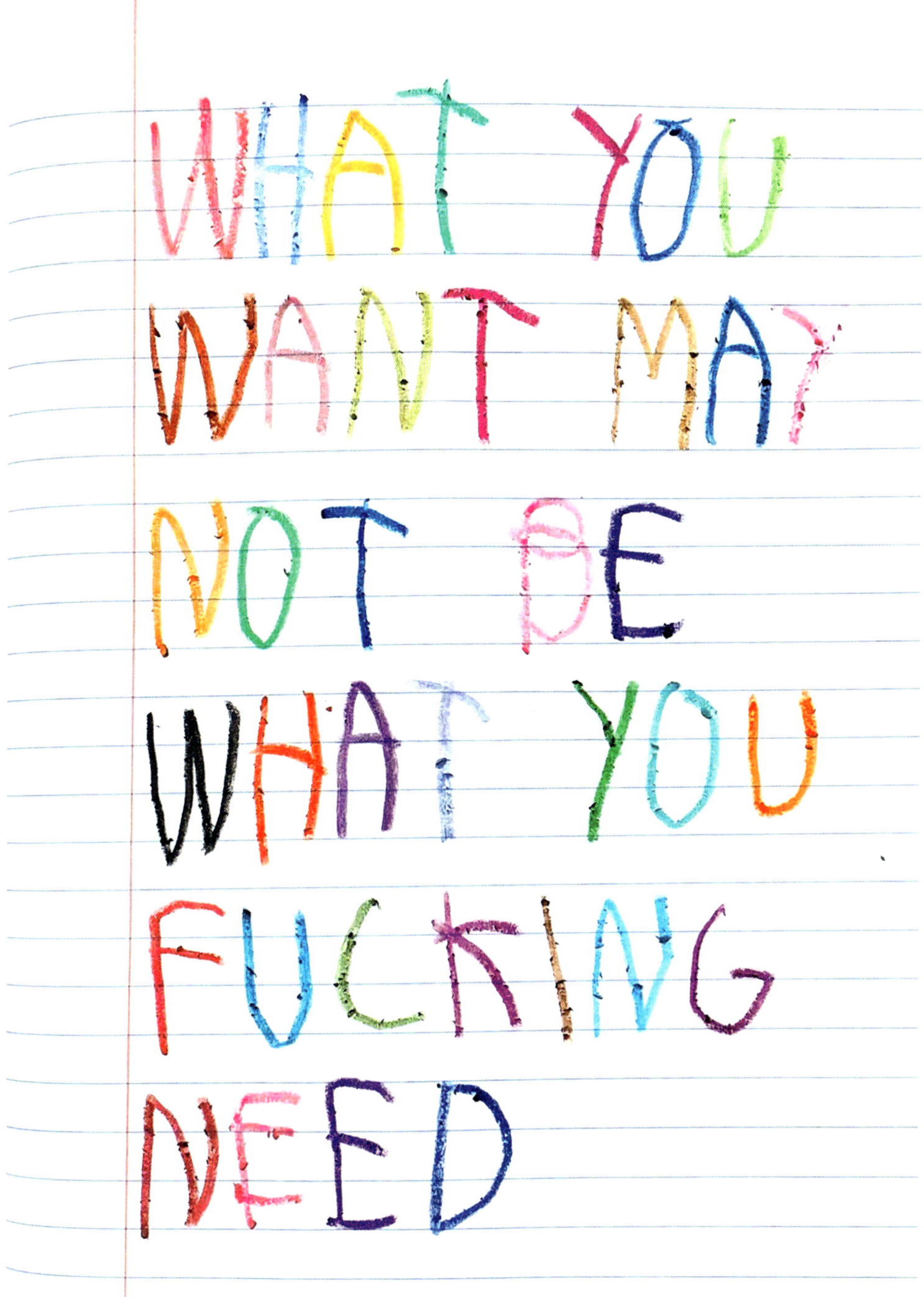

WHAT YOU
WANT MAY
NOT BE
WHAT YOU
FUCKING
NEED

HORNY
ANXIOUS
SAD
BORED
HUNGRY
DEPRESSED
FRUSTRATED
HAPPY
CONFUSED
SCARED

Untitled (Emotions),
2020
Wax crayons on paper,
27.9 x 21 cm

Study for *What Is It?*,
2020
Wax crayons on paper,
27.9 x 21 cm

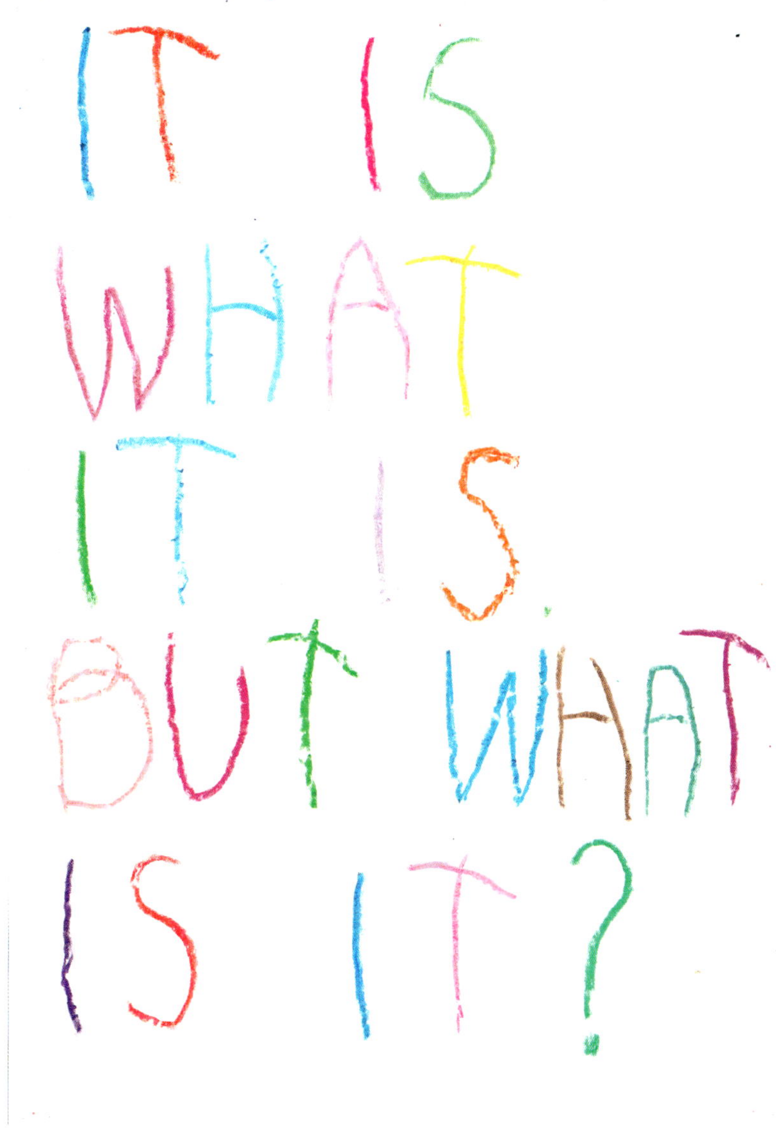

IT IS
WHAT
IT IS
BUT WHAT
IS IT?

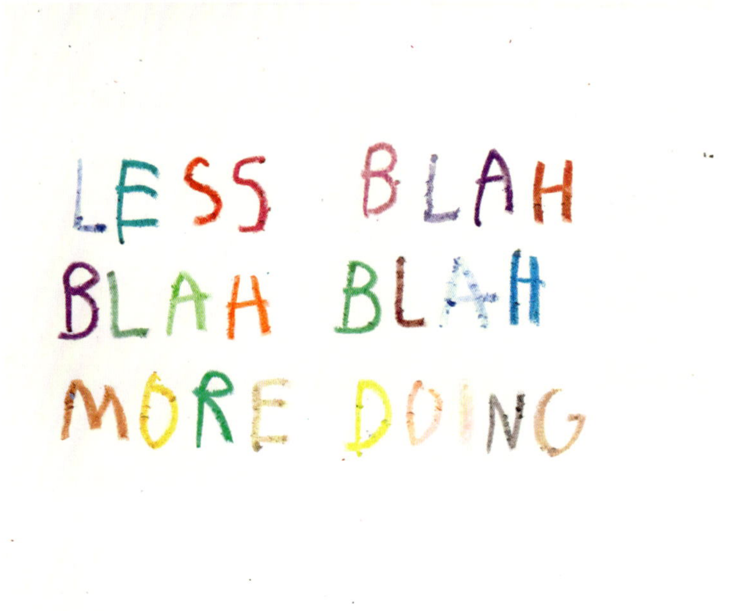

LESS BLAH
BLAH BLAH
MORE DOING

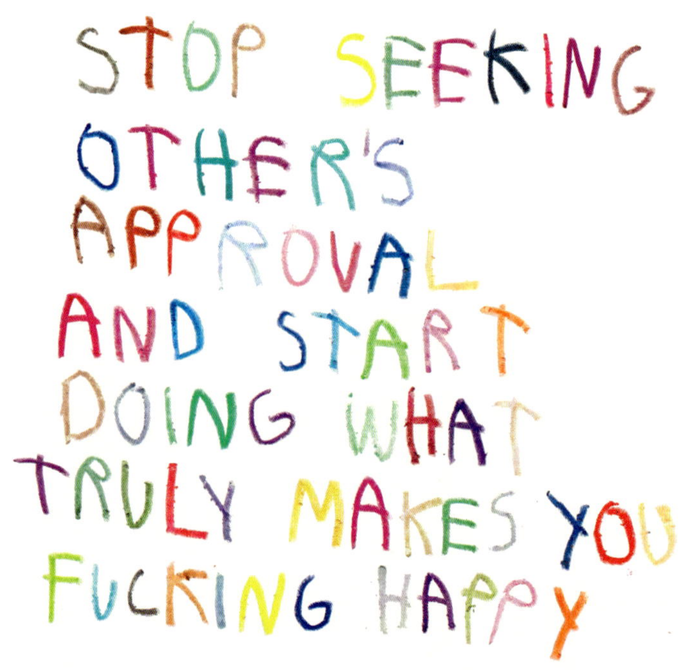

STOP SEEKING
OTHER'S
APPROVAL
AND START
DOING WHAT
TRULY MAKES YOU
FUCKING HAPPY

Study for *Less Blah Blah Blah*, 2019
Wax crayons on paper,
27.9 x 21 cm

Untitled (Stop Seeking Other's Approval), 2019
Wax crayons on paper,
27.9 x 21 cm

Grow Up, 2020
Oil bars on raw cotton canvas primed with transparent gel medium,
135.5 x 89 cm

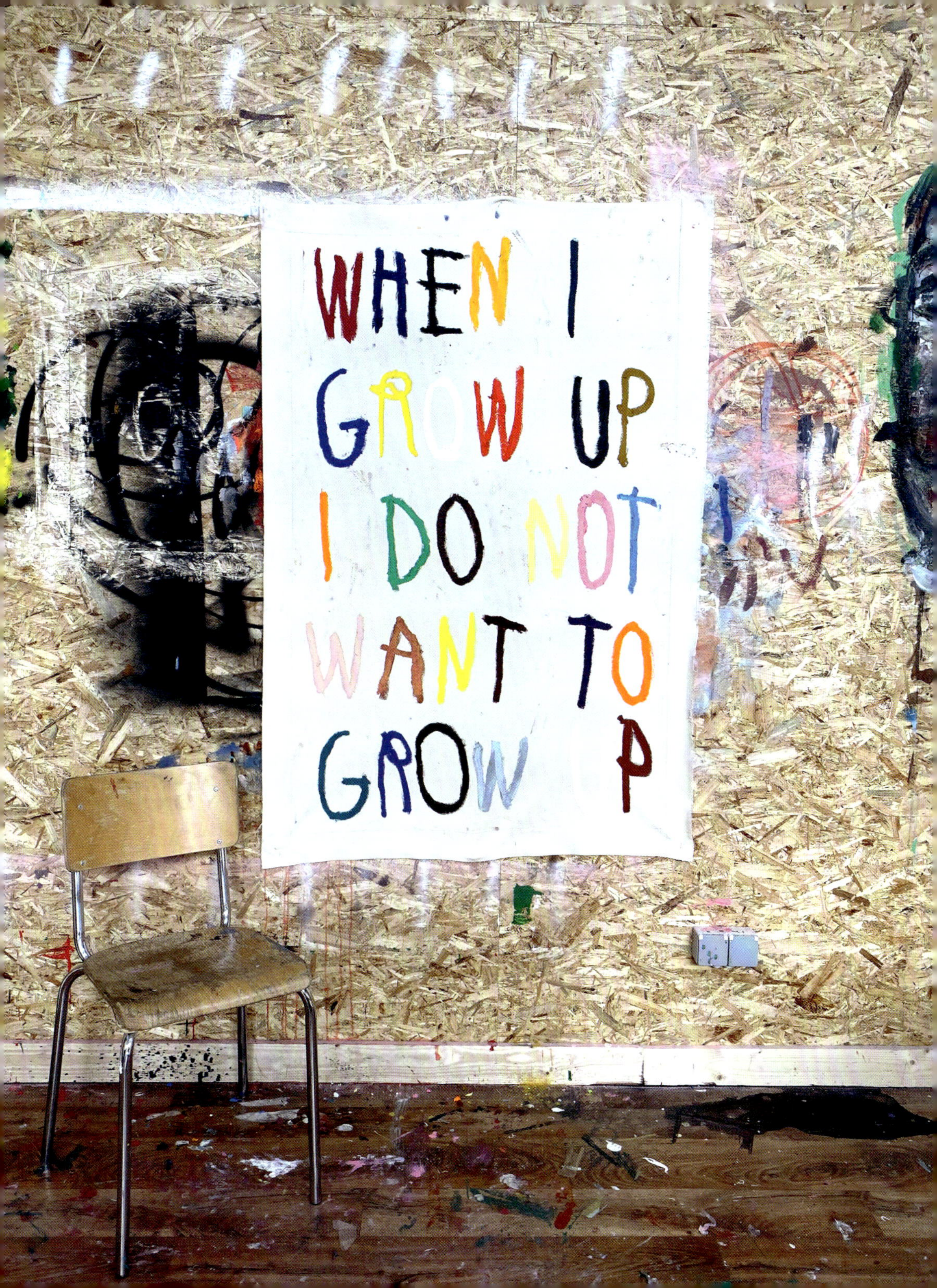

WHEN I
GROW UP
I DO NOT
WANT TO
GROW UP

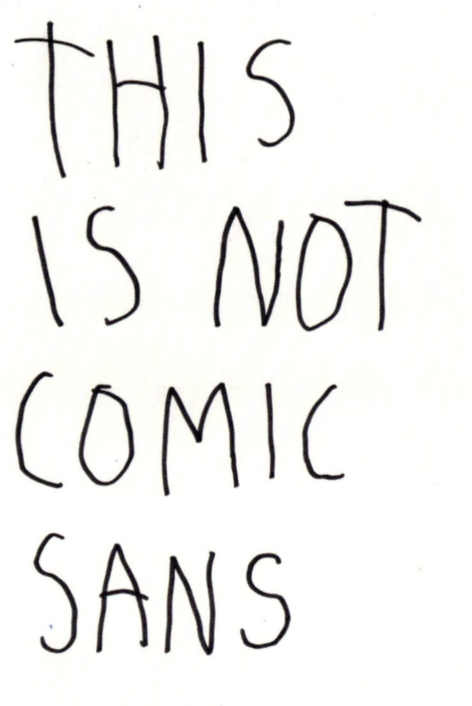

THIS
IS NOT
COMIC
SANS

DO YOU
BELIEVE
IN LOVE?

Untitled (Not Comic Sans), 2020
Markers on paper,
27.9 x 21 cm

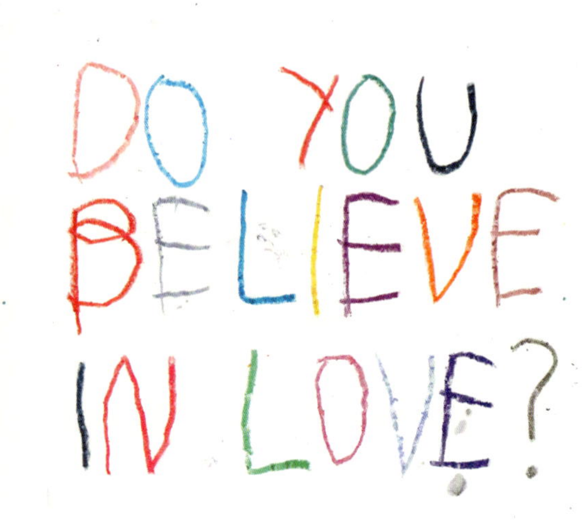

Untitled (Do You Believe in Love?), 2020
Wax crayons on paper,
27.9 x 21 cm

Study for *Fuck It*, 2020
Wax crayons on paper,
27.9 x 21 cm

FUCK YOU
FUCK FUCK ME
FUCK FUCK US
FUCK FUCK THEM
FUCK FUCK HER
FUCK FUCK HIM
FUCK FUCK THIS
FUCK FUCK THAT
FUCK FUCK IT

No, 2020
Water, canvas, wax
crayon, acrylic, wax, oil,
pasted on paper,
15 x 10 cm

Study Fuck You, 2020
Water-soluble oil pastels,
oil sticks, mineral water,
and acrylic paint on raw
cotton canvas,
29.7 x 21 cm

FUCK
YOU

WE ARE
ALL
FUCKED

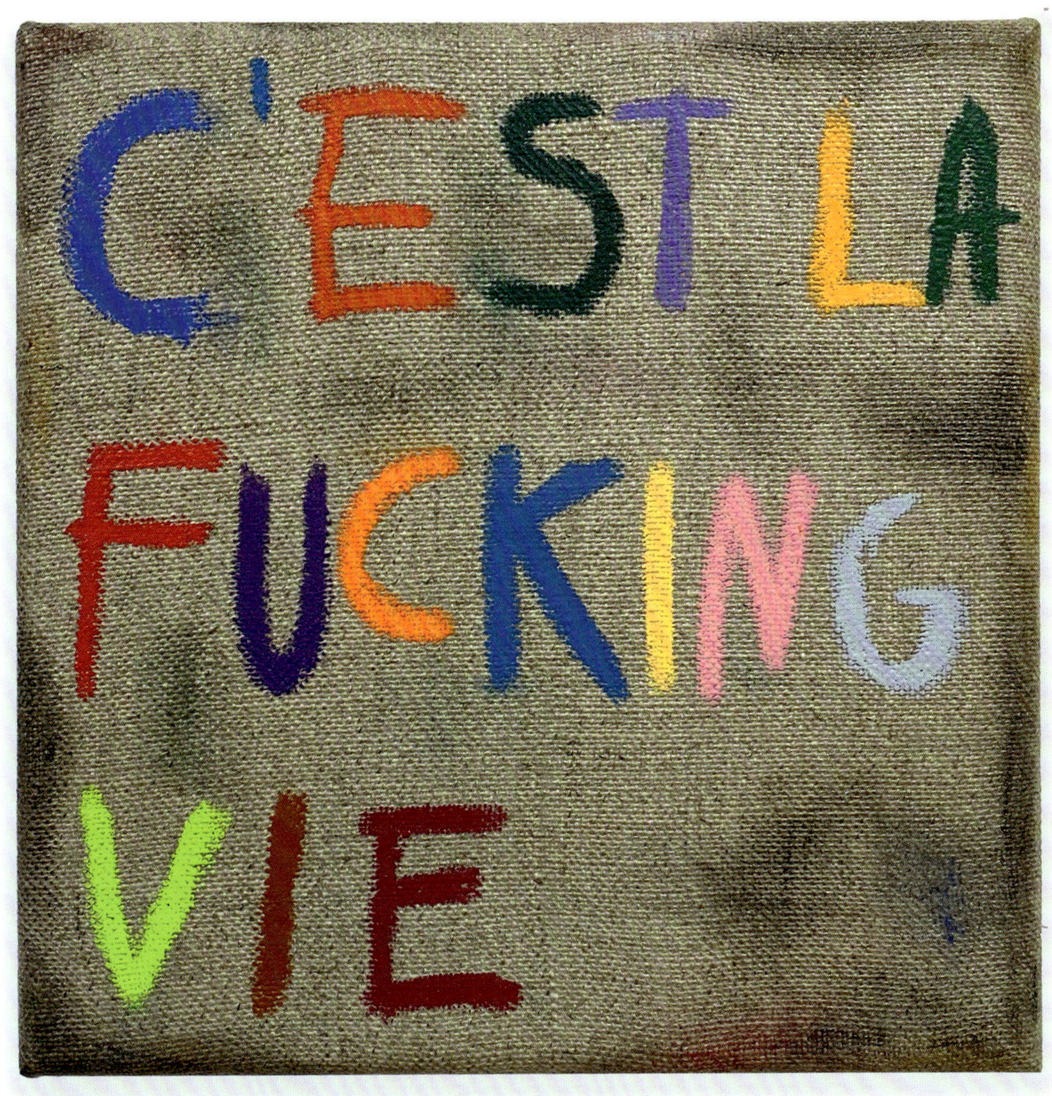

We Are All Fucked,
2020
Wax pastels, mineral
water, and acrylic paint
on raw cotton canvas,
80 x 63 cm

*Life Is an Interesting
Paradox*, 2020
Wax pastels on raw
linen, 20 x 20 cm

Page 202
IS IT?, 2020
Corrugated fiberboard,
isocyanate / polyol
resin, plaster, acrylic
paint, and UV varnish

Page 203
FUCK, 2020
Corrugated fiberboard,
isocyanate / polyol
resin, plaster, acrylic
paint, and UV varnish

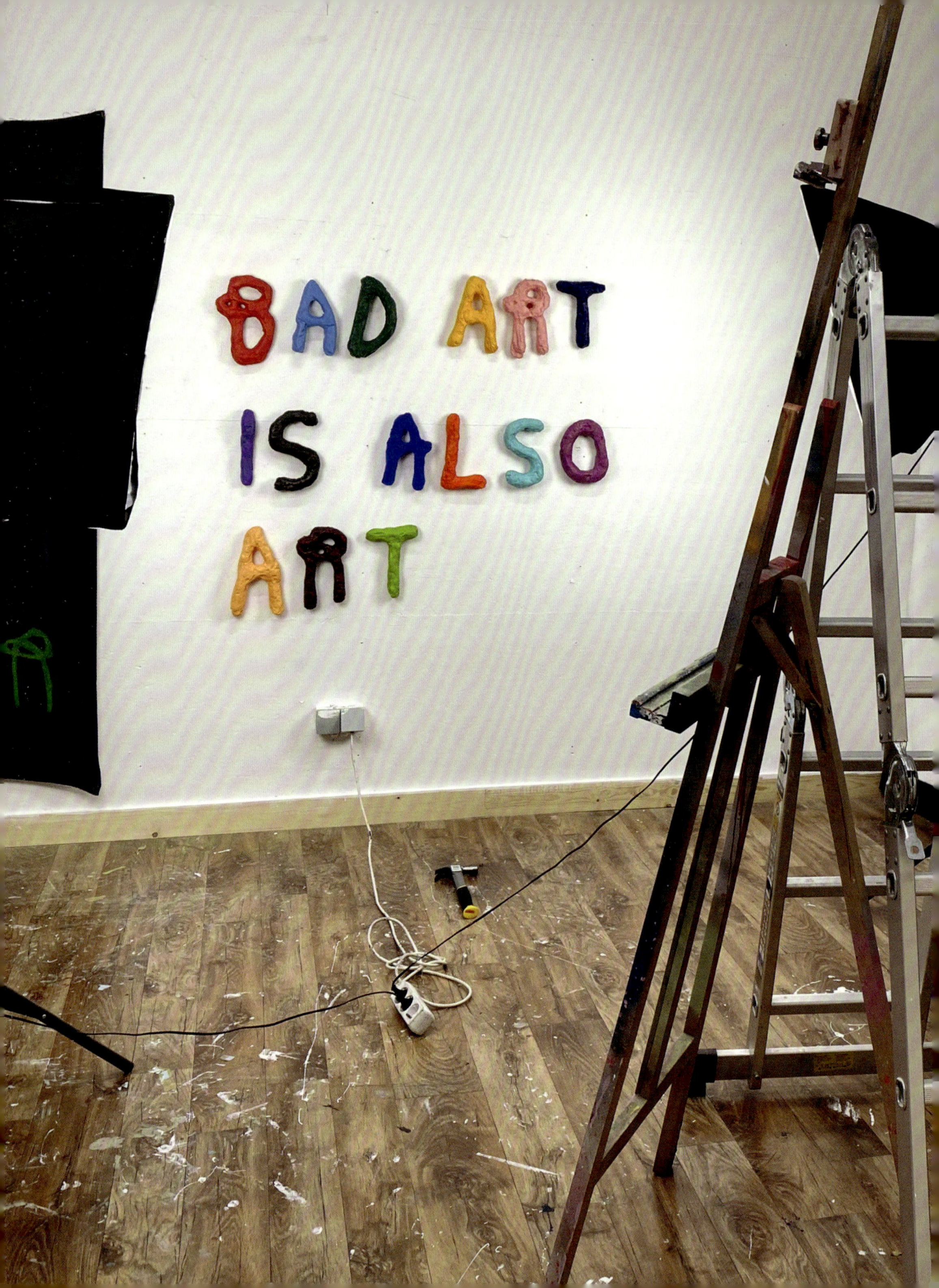

BAD ART
IS ALSO
ART

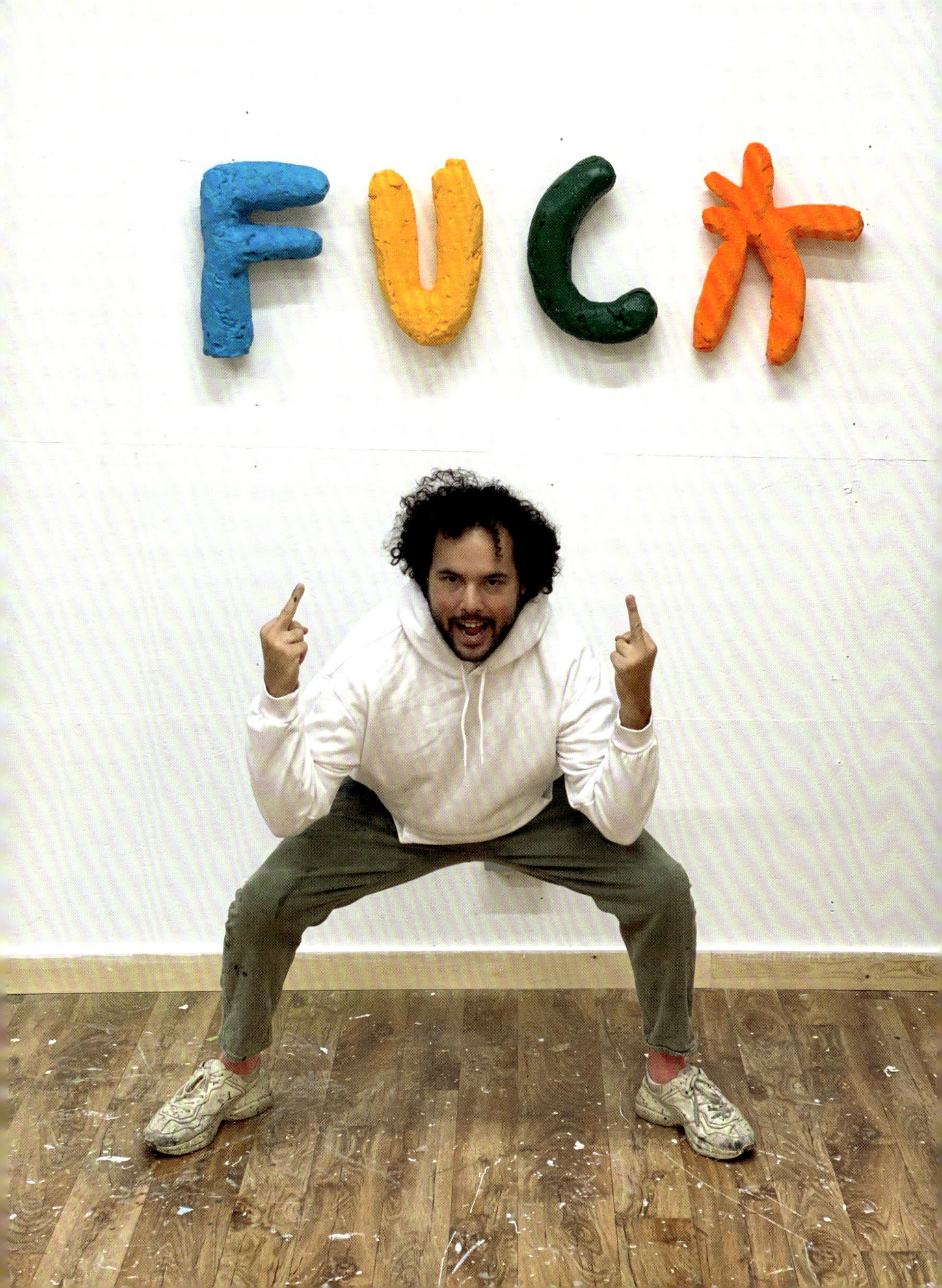

FUCK

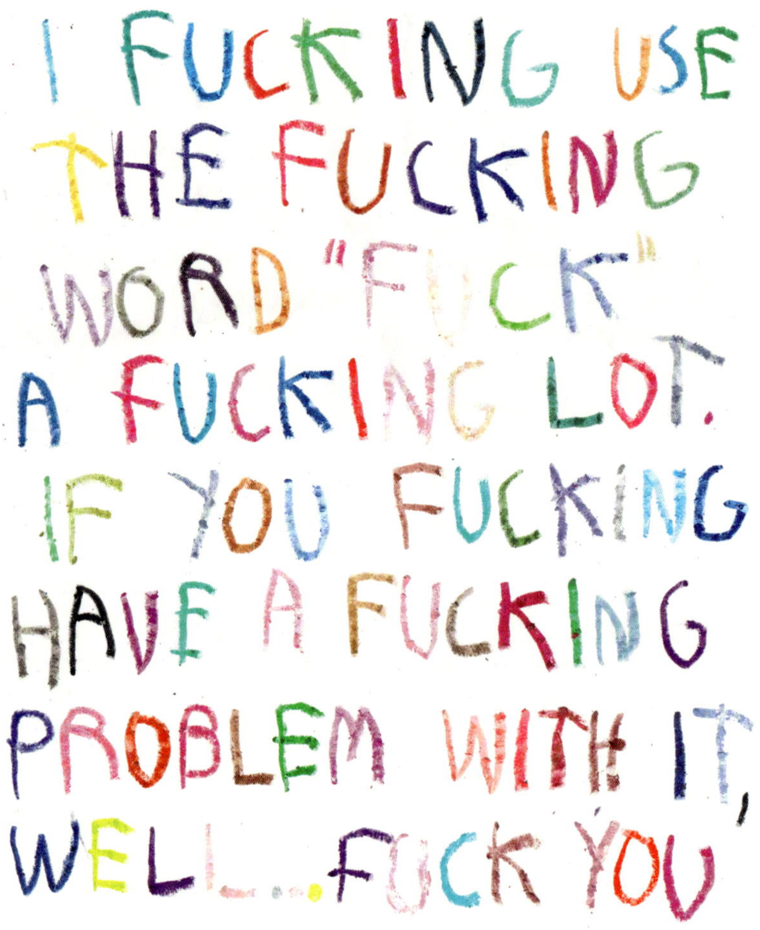

Untitled (I Use the Word Fuck), 2020
Wax crayons on paper,
27.9 x 21 cm

Untitled (Bye), 2020
Wax crayons on paper,
27.9 x 21 cm

BYE

Museum Shows

Dec. 2020, *Ein Museum auf Probe*, Villa Merkel, Esslingen, Germany

Solo Shows

2021, (Forthcoming), Plan X Gallery, Milan, Italy
Jun. 2020, *Fake and Corny*, GR Gallery, New York, NY, USA
Nov. 2019, Two-person solo show *Out of Line* with Giampiero Romanó, Plan X, Milan, Italy
Apr. 2019, *Nothing is Real Nothing is Fake It's all Relative*, Antwerp, Belgium
Sept. 2018, *CB Hoyo, Istanbul Fakeover*, Istanbul, Turkey
Aug. 2018, *Fake in Capri*, Plan X Gallery, Capri, Italy
Jul. 2018, *CB Hoyo, Made in China,* Hong Kong
Feb. 2018, *Keeping It Real: IMITATE MODERN*, London, UK
Jul. 2017, *Fake Rothko: Imitate Modern*, London, UK

Group Shows

Mar. 2020, *Arte San Ramon: The Art of Giving Back*, Dominican Republic
Feb. 2020, *Galeria Impakto: Sobredosis*, Lima, Peru
Oct. 2019, *Galeria Impakto: Leer por el Reverso*, Lima, Peru
2019, *Don't be average, Be Savage*, Plan X Gallery, Milan, Italy
2019, *Emerging to Established*, Krause Gallery, New York, NY, USA
2018–2019, *All The Rage - Urban Art Exhibition*, Taipei, Taiwan
2018, *Fantastic World*, GR Gallery, New York, NY, USA
2018, *Subversion*, Tax Collection x New Street Gallery, Paris, France
2018, *Real Fakes*, Krause Gallery, New York, NY, USA
2018, *Emerging to Established*, Krause Gallery, New York, NY, USA
2018, *Kips Bay Decorator Show House*, Philip Mitchell Design, New York, NY, USA
2018, Summer Edition, Imitate Modern, London, UK
2018, *Down The Rabbit Hole*, Imitate Modern, London, UK
2018, UN/A, *The Art of Giving Back*, Casa de Campo, Dominican Republic
2018, *Bacanal (Fake Reality)*, AREA, Boston, MA, USA
2018, *Papi Chulo*, Krause Gallery, New York, NY, USA
2018, *Emerging to Established*, Krause Gallery, New York, NY, USA
2017–2018, *Mood Swings*, Oliver Cole Gallery, Miami, FL, USA
2017, *Christmas Show: The Return of the Pop*, Imitate Modern, London, UK
2017, *ING Discerning Eye Exhibition*, ING & Discerning Eye, London, UK
2017, *R.APE*, FerArts, London, UK
2017, *Re: Creations*, Imitate Modern, London UK
2017, Summer Edition, Imitate Modern, London UK
2017, *Fake Rothko*, Imitate Modern, London UK
2017, *Emerging to Established*, Krause Gallery, New York, NY, USA

Fairs

Dec. 2019, *Scope Miami*, Imitate Modern Miami, FL, USA
Apr. 2019, *Perú Arte Contemporáneo*, Galeria Impakto, Lima, Peru
Apr. 2019, *Art Lima*, Galeria Impakto, Lima, Peru
Dec. 2018, *Scope Miami*, Imitate Modern Miami, FL, USA
Oct. 2018, *Art Élysées*, Galerie Geraldine Zberro, Paris, France
Jun. 2018, *Scope Basel*, One Arts Club, Basel, Switzerland
Jan. 2018, *Art Palm Beach*, Marcel Katz, Palm Beach, FL, USA
Oct. 2017, *Moniker Art Fair*, Imitate Modern, London, UK

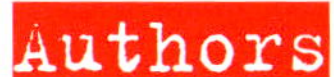

Cesare Biasini Selvaggi
is an independent curator,
art historian, critic and
editor who has worked
internationally since
2000. In January 2017
he became Editor-in-Chief
of *Exibart.com* and *Exibart.
onpaper*, the leading Italian
contemporary art magazine.
He has published over
two hundred art books,
and has written on art for
many leading Italian and
international newspapers
and periodicals. He lives
in Rome and travels
extensively.

Jack Kyle Franklin
is an American
interdisciplinary artist and
writer based between Rome
and Chicago. He received
an MFA from the School
of the Art Institute of
Chicago and previously
studied at Central Saint
Martins in London and
the Columbus College
of Art & Design. He has
published, performed, and
exhibited work throughout
the United States, Canada,
and Europe.

Page 208
Untitled (Bye Bye), 2020
Wax crayons on paper,
27.9 x 21 cm

BYE
BYE